NOW READ ON

NOW READ ON

BERNARD LEVIN

Jonathan Cape
London

First published 1990
© Bernard Levin 1990
Jonathan Cape Ltd, 20 Vauxhall Bridge Road, London SW1V 2SA

Bernard Levin has asserted his right to be
identified as the author of this work

A CIP catalogue record for this book
is available from the British Library

ISBN 0-224-03008-6

Phototypeset by Falcon Graphic Art Ltd
Wallington, Surrey
Printed in Great Britain by
Mackays of Chatham PLC, Chatham, Kent

Contents

Acknowledgements

My indispensable assistant and friend, Catherine Tye, checked a thousand and one things in these items as they appeared week by week in *The Times*, and then checked two thousand and two in their book form; any errors are quite certainly mine. Brian Inglis read the proofs as thoroughly as he has done for eleven books past; I am most grateful to him. C.H. Rolph not only read the proofs but actually asked in advance to be allowed to do so, a gesture probably unique in the annals of publishing. I salute him for his assiduity as well as his generosity.

Once again I have the pleasure of thanking Oula Jones of the Society of Indexers for her meticulous and essential contribution. One of the articles in this book is about a particularly lamentable index; if only its compiler had had the good sense to entrust it to her!

I thank the publishers who have kindly allowed me to quote matter in copyright, as follows: Faber and Faber Ltd, for four lines from 'This Be the Verse' from *High Windows* by Philip Larkin; Nick Hern Books, a division of Walker Books Ltd for an excerpt from *Ghetto* © 1989 by Joshua Sobol and David Lan.

Introduction

THIS IS THE sixth volume of my selected journalism to appear; the first was *Taking Sides*, published in 1979, and there followed *Speaking Up* (1982), *The Way We Live Now* (1984), *In These Times* (1986) and *All Things Considered* (1988). I have never been under any illusion as to the permanence of any of the articles I have included in these anthologies; journalism is by definition an ephemeral trade, dealing as it does with mayfly news and mayfly comment. Of course, the great themes are always with us, and it is these to which I have most often addressed myself in selecting the matter for the next collection – as, indeed, I have done in writing them on the wing, while watching the world turn.

I do not, obviously, pick for inclusion the articles which I think will last longest, if only because it is impossible and absurd to try to make such predictions. For instance, in 1980, I wrote an article about the four greatest Mozart operas, claiming that it is possible to deduce the character of a listener according to which of the four he or she loves most deeply. Thus, those who put *Cosi Fan Tutte* first are those with at least a touch of cynicism, those who nominate *The Magic Flute* have the strongest hope of Heaven, those who choose *Don Giovanni* – men as well as women – are the romantics, and those for whom *The Marriage of Figaro* is supreme (I am of that company myself) believe that love rules the world and will always do so. (Of course, I have greatly simplified the argument I deployed, but that was the gist of it.) I didn't cheat, either – I thought of the categories first, and only then measured my friends against the fourfold test. The article was published in *The Times*, and that, I thought, was that; I did not even include it in the next anthology. Yet I still get letters about it, some giving the details of a dinner-table debate on the subject the writer has taken part in, some arguing with my categories, some saying that they have heard from others about the article, and could they have a copy? (My secretary keeps a pile of photo-copies, and has to replenish it from time to time.)

Now who would have thought that that light-hearted essay, dividing the four categories of Mozart-lovers and telling their fortunes if they would cross the gypsy's palm with silver, would endure in such a fashion? Not I; but it was a warning to me not to make guesses in this world to see if they were correct in the next.

But on one subject I claim, if not immortality, pre-science (which was easy) and confidence (which at times was far from it). 1989 was truly *annus mirabilis*, a year (to be precise, it was seventy-two days near the end of the year) which saw the collapse of one of the mightiest empires the world has ever known. Moreover, it was a collapse nothing like the slow putting out of the candles in the Roman world, or the 'wind of change', as Harold Macmillan called the more or less orderly retreat from Britain's scattered possessions, or the final retreat from the French North African territories, which very nearly destroyed French democracy.

It is worth pausing to look back on those astounding ten weeks that shook the world. It had begun much earlier, of course, with the overnight rise, abrupt fall and gradual resurrection of Solidarity, the Polish grouping which, for those with eyes to see, was the instrument that was to bring the Soviet Empire to the ground. But the leaves began to flutter in the breeze early in the year, when the Polish viceroys realized that without some kind of help from Solidarity Poland would fall apart, if only because its economy had collapsed altogether. They called on Lech Walesa and his closest allies and advisers to help avoid the catastrophe; at first, in the historic meeting on March 2nd, the tottering government thought it could buy Solidarity's support for empty promises of reform. Solidarity had been through that, though, and was not to be caught again, as one of Walesa's advisers at the meeting pointed out. 'You can violate democracy once,' he said, 'but not three times.' Up against the wall, the Polish governors had to concede a second chamber for the Polish 'Parliament', with free elections.

From that moment, though it was several months before the historic consequences worked themselves out, the end of Communism was assured.

'Watchman, what of the night? The watchman saith: the morning cometh.' Hungary, with the replacement of Janos Kadar by Nemeth, and a series of liberating measures, had very cautiously opened the door of freedom and peered round it to see what was outside; what she found in the corridor was an extraordinary incursion from East Germany. The East Germans, tired of oppression multiplied by poverty, were not yet ready to revolt; but they were ready to vote with their feet. Tens of thousands were pouring over the Hungarian border, ostensibly on holiday; their government took fright, and demanded that the Hungarians should close the border and repatriate the refugees. The Hungarian rulers, already set on the road to democracy, refused, and not only refused but opened the Hungarian-Austrian border as well.

Those who understood what was happening held their breath; they had to hold it until the night of October 9th, and as they breathed out, the wind blew up into a colossal hurricane, the greatest storm the marches of Eastern Europe had faced since the armies of Genghiz Khan were on the march. That night, it looked as though before dawn the streets of Leipzig would run with blood, as the people, heartened by the allies they had found in the Hungarians, came out on to the streets to stand face to face, and unarmed, with the security forces. Two days previously a similar crowd had been dispersed with savage violence but without shooting; it was clear that if the government was to keep control now, there would have to be something like a massacre. The crowd knew that, too; what they did not know, but the satraps did, was that Mikhail Gorbachev, who had just left East Germany after a visit to Erich Honecker, had made clear that Honecker and his regime could count on no support from the Soviet Union in any confrontation with the East German people. The Western outpost of the empire was on its own.

Even then, Honecker gave the order to fire; but the cannier ones around him knew the kind of vengeance that they would face if they started the battle and lost it, and they pushed him out, never to see power again.

Roll up that map; it will not be wanted these ten years – no, not these thousand years. One by one, the lights went out in the chancelleries of oppression; on November 9th, Zhivkov of Bulgaria fell, and none so poor to do him reverence. On November 17th, the crowds of Prague crammed Wenceslas Square, where only a few days before – the pattern was exactly the same as the German one – the people were dispersed with even greater violence, and with one fatality, a student battered to death by the police. Again, the Czechoslovak people, like the East German people, were ready to face death. The troops were withdrawn, the crowd left in peace, and exactly a week later, the government fell. Prague, too, had been told by Gorbachev that the game was up.

Now there was only one coconut in the shy: Romania, and its unspeakably cruel and corrupt dictator Ceausescu. Here, for a moment, the gale dropped. Warnings from Gorbachev had no force in Bucharest; Ceausescu had virtually broken with the Soviet Union years before (when the 'Czech Spring' was crushed in 1968 Romania sent no troops – the only country in the Warsaw Pact that refused to take part). The unwritten pact laid down that Romania would not be coerced back into colonial status if its leader made sure there was not the slightest relaxation of communist control; Ceausescu needed no instruction in tyranny, his rule being the most brutal in all Eastern Europe.

The experts and wiseacres declared that Romania would survive the storm; Ceausescu had long lived without Soviet backing, and he would go on doing so indefinitely. He fell on December 21st, and great was the fall thereof. The Seventy Days, days the like of which the world had never seen before, and could hardly believe it was seeing now, were over.

I dwell on these momentous hours for more than one reason. Even in the darkest times of the post-Stalin Soviet empire, I never wavered in my certainty that it would fall one day, and that I should live to see that day. I based my conviction not just on hope but on much more solid ground. First, it had long been clear that it was impossible to seal a nation from ideas coming from abroad, however meticulous were those charged with the sealing and however complete the *cordon sanitaire* of surrounding colonies. It could be said, indeed, that when Khrushchev threw Stalin out of the mausoleum in Red Square he had sealed the fate of communism – not just because of the demotion of the tyrant, but because from the day of the 'Secret Speech' it was clear that the extermination of millions in Stalin's mode was the only way to keep total control, and that neither he nor any other Soviet leader could go back to such methods without destroying the country.

Second, and perhaps more practical, the Soviet economy had been ruined irretrievably; however many the guns available to keep down dissent, enough hunger and misery will embolden a nation to face them. To avoid such a confrontation, reform was essential. Even Brezhnev, whose stupidity was not mitigated by any touch of instinct, shrewdness or peasant wisdom, understood that, though he certainly did not know what to do about it.

Third, a house builded upon sand cannot stand. That is not just a Biblical cracker-motto, but a profound truth, which can be tested by the most rigorous modern instruments. The Soviet system was a lie, right through, and in the end a lie is inadequate to hold up an entire national house. Even if nothing worse than apathy assails such a hollowed-out, worm-eaten, termite-beset structure, it will fall in time; and its progress to destruction is greatly accelerated by the corruption which is inevitable and endemic in such a system.

Fourth, I have repeatedly drawn attention to an even more remarkable phenomenon. Within the Soviet Union, and the same must be true of every tyranny that seeks to extirpate all independent thought inside its borders, men and women have grown up without access – literary, familial, educational – to any scrap of the truth that might confound the lies fed to them every hour by the rulers, yet they have arrived at the truth none the less. If that truth did not come to them from outside – as plainly it did not – it came from inside them.

The question of how it got there can be debated elsewhere; suffice it to say for the moment that it did, and that the fact that it did reinforced my certainty that the Soviet Union was dying, and that I would live to dance at its funeral. In 'From Spark to Furnace' p.68, I have set out, step by step, my path to such certainty. But I have to say now that, surveying the two years of writing from which I have culled the articles in this book, there is very little else for me to be certain about, and an ominous amount, as far as I can see, for a wide and singularly unpleasant variety of people determined to impose their own self-righteous certainty on others.

Those who have read my previous anthologies, or who read me *seriatim* in *The Times*, will know of my unchanging enmity to the Nanny State, a term which I believe I coined. There is an obvious irony in our world following the decline of the Soviet Empire; the newly liberated nations are busy throwing down walls, tearing up restrictions, searching every cellar and hole and crack in the brickwork to find, brush down and put into service every scrap of freedom that has survived the long night. Meanwhile, in countries like ours, a very different kind of search, instigated by a very different kind of searcher, goes on.

I have written repeatedly about those who are not content to point out the dangers of tobacco, of an excessive consumption of alcohol, of eating foods considered inimical to health, but are adamant that they must and will impose their beliefs on others, eventually putting them on a statutory basis, so that smoking, drinking and eating potato crisps will be illegal except, perhaps, in specially designated premises set aside for the purpose, and under the most rigorous conditions. I do not propose to go over that ground again – though see 'Playing silly burgers' (p. 108) for a different kind of Nannying – but a new element has entered into the argument. There is rising hysteria on the subject of drinking too much for safety; the Nannies, egged on by the police (always keen to extend their powers), have been persecuting – the word is not too strong – not just those who drive when they are over the legal limit, which few would not condemn, and which can lead, very properly, to severe punishment, but those who drink anything at all before driving, even if it is far below the limit which the law specifies as dangerous. More, and worse, the demand for random testing of motorists by the police has been feverishly, and to a scandalous extent dishonestly, promoted; the most recent attempt to give the police what they long for was turned down by the government, but the police in some areas have announced that they were anyway going to do what Parliament forbids, and the Home Secretary has urged them on in their intention.

But that is not what worries me. There will always be people hungry for splinters of power with which to jab and prick and torment others. Much more serious is the likelihood – the evidence is not yet entirely clear – that a great majority of the population applauds the idea of random testing. Can it be true (the evidence, incidentally, is that random testing is wholly inefficacious in the discovery and apprehension of those who drink more than the limit while driving) that the slave does, after all, love his chains? I have spent my life denying that terrible proposition; am I to accept it now, when real slaves have just been released from their captivity?

Over the years, as I have watched the captive nations of the East writhing in their bonds, I have remarked again and again on the apparent indifference with which the shrinking of our own liberties has been met. I thought that the revolution in Eastern Europe would stir us to defend every sliver of liberty stolen from us, not because we seriously fear totalitarian control, but because we can now see, in the mirror held up by the peoples of East Germany, Hungary, Bulgaria, Poland, Czechoslovakia and Romania, how precious and irreplaceable is even the tiniest scrap of freedom. It is too early to be sure, but I can see no great new demand for less restriction, fired in us by those who have had no freedom at all for more than four decades. I write this in the early spring of 1990, but I am sure that by the time it is published Yugoslavia and Albania will have been added to the list of liberated nations. Where shall *we* be? Not in prison-camps, to be sure, but certainly weighed down with new restrictions. For it is not only a matter of restriction; there is also the freedom to know.

Read 'Camouflaging the dead' (p.89), if you want to know how our liberties are further reduced by the limits imposed on free speech; for there is no real free speech if we are denied access to the information that enables us to speak. In the two years of this book's compiling, a measure was brought in and passed into law which further restricts and diminishes not just our right to know, but our ability to find out without breaking the law. The Act in question was promoted as a charter of freedom; so, come to think of it, was the Stalin Constitution.

Along with the indifference to liberty I have discussed there goes a rejection of responsibility which is, if you look at it carefully, the other side of it. If you reject responsibility for yourself and those dependent upon you it is hardly likely that you will thereupon join the struggle for freedom. 'The baby's bottle' (p.235) describes an exceptionally extreme form of the unwillingness to shoulder a responsibility that would once have been automatically accepted in any society, but its appalling nature should not conceal from us the fact that less lurid examples can be found all around us. Only a few days before I wrote these words, I read of a man who had been prosecuted for violent behaviour of a not very serious kind. In court, he argued that he was unemployed; not necessarily a *non sequitur*. The magistrate, clearly a kindly man, drew his attention to a page of advertising in the local newspaper, where scores, if not hundreds, of jobs, demanding no great qualifications, were on offer. He scorned them: 'That's no good,' he said, 'I want a proper career.'

Meanwhile, 'The halt and the blind' (p.18) draws attention to another of the devil's victories. There has always been crime, always been violent crime; I dare say there always will be. Yet surely a new and infinitely disgusting element has been added, if such things can be. Let us make a dramatic, perhaps too dramatic, comparison; let us think of the two groups described in that article and then think of the Nazis. The Nazis devised, and put into practice, abominations such as the world had never seen before, and I trust (I wouldn't bet my life on it) will never see again. Yet even they had a logic to what they did, however evil and depraved that logic. If you are told long and often enough that Jews are not human beings but *bacilli*, you are quite likely to believe it, in which case no degree of ruthlessness can be too great for the cause of cleansing the pure Aryan blood. But where is the meaning, let alone the logic, in what I have recorded in that dreadful chapter? And we can find worse than that, if we put our mind to it. Not long ago, a woman in New York was sentenced to life imprisonment. And what had she done to attract so terrible a sentence? She was a drug-addict, hooked on 'crack'; seeking a 'fix', she happened upon a drug-dealer, who was, she knew, a convicted rapist. She offered him her 13-year-old daughter, he duly raped the child, and he handed over the drug. I tell you, mere anarchy *is* loosed upon the world.

Mind you, there are somewhat lesser shocks, which are no less indicative of the way the world is going. Try, for instance, 'Heads you lose' (p. 1). Would you have believed that such a trade could be carried on, not in the back streets of the seedier areas of the more exceptionally run-down townships of Idi Amin's Uganda, but on the premises of an old-established and respectable London auctioneers? I wouldn't; but it seems I shall now have to. I draw attention in that article to something I have repeatedly discussed; the failure of imagination. Imagination is, I believe, something far more important than the comparatively shallow use that is made of it to, say, watch a play. It is the currency with which human beings exchange their humanity for the prof-it of mutual enlightenment; to understand with empathy in what way another soul is like yours, and in what way it dif-fers. There are things – in particular the thing at the centre of that article – which I believe cannot be done, except perhaps by the truly deranged, unless imagination has been stifled or, worse, died out. Another such tendency to bypass imagina-tion can be found in 'In a pig's eye' (p. 172), which should surely revolt (but plainly does not) anybody who reads it. For that matter, even where nothing more than distaste is required, as in 'And a smutty New Year' (p. 136), it seems to me hopeless to try to get into the mind and feelings of people who can do such things, because I cannot think of any way of stirring my imagination into encompassing their action.

You will have noticed that I have said virtually noth-ing about politics in this Introduction; more surprising, to those who have read me regularly in book or newspaper form, there is very little in the entire volume. It is true that I have always selected, for more lasting form, comparatively few of the articles I write on politics, simply because it is political comment which disappears, unlamented, more quickly than any other. Still, no one can maintain that politics doesn't matter, if only because political decisions affect us, sometimes (no, usually) to our detriment. And it is true that I have written less about politics these last two or three years. Mid-term politics is inevitably less interesting than the early days, when promises are ten-a-penny, and the late days, when election fever is mounting. But I have eschewed heavy reliance on politics largely because it has become, on both sides, so shabby, so exclusively aimed at getting or keeping power, so lacking in any kind of principle; above all, so stale. And since the choice of subjects for my articles is entirely mine, and no areas are out of bounds, and since my self-made rule is *never* to write about anything that does not interest me, however important it may be (on the grounds that if it doesn't interest me, I am hardly likely to make it interesting to the readers), I can leave politics alone with a light heart, conscious that those who yearn for more of the subject can be amply accommodated elsewhere.

With which I withdraw and leave the reader to browse among the flowers I have planted since my last anthology. Reading through this Introduction myself, I am inevitably struck, as my readers will be, by a largely pessimistic tone. I am not by nature a pessimist, and I wish I could be more cheerful. I am, actually, in many places in this collection: if you would read 'Unsocial climber' (p. 55), or 'Rude forefathers' (p. 211), or 'Crack pots, not heads' (p. 168), or 'At full stretch' (p. 197), or 'Epic proportions' (p. 225), you will find some more hopeful items, though I have to admit that they are mostly from the arts. Still, I comfort myself with the thought that if I have spent the last two years largely chronicling the darker doings of the world, I cannot be the only one to have noticed that there is a good deal of darkness in the world, though brilliantly illuminated at the very end of the period by the fall of the Soviet Empire. So if you pick up this book in the spirit in which I – item by item –

wrote it, we shall probably find much for agreement, and can boast that we are abreast of the *Zeitgeist*. I don't know about you, dear readers, but I have always longed to be abreast of the *Zeitgeist*, and this seems the best opportunity both of us will ever have.

January 1990   B. L.

Imagination 1:
Heads you lose

THERE SEEMS NO doubt that anything which is possible for a human being to do will sooner or later be done; at the very least it will be seriously contemplated. No less stark a rule could cover the episode of the Maori head. For those who have not been following the story, I offer a brief summary.

A woman in this country had in her possession – acquired when or how I do not know, though lawfully – a preserved human head. It was the tattooed head of a Maori warrior, and experts assigned it to the early nineteenth century; presumably, it was the custom to make such trophies of war, though whether it was the victorious side who treated their enemies thus, or the losing side who mourned in this fashion their fallen comrades, is not clear.

Anyway, the woman in our story apparently saw no difference between a human head and an inlaid escritoire, and sent the object to Bonham's, the auctioneers, to sell for her. Bonham's, for their part, made no demur, and prepared to offer one human head, in good condition, with tattoo, to the highest bidder at a forthcoming sale. Now read on.

Autres temps, autres mœurs; many a ritual once thought perfectly normal has come to seem abhorrent, from cannibalism to burning witches. The Maoris today are peaceful people, and their grievances, which I believe are real, are pleaded in Parliament, newspapers and courts of law, rather than on the battlefield; nor have I heard that even homicide among them is followed by any such ancient and macabre ritual.

And yet there is in England a woman and a firm of

auctioneers who between them are unable to see that they might be doing anything odd by trading in human heads. Moreover, when the story broke, it transpired that these relics are widely admired collector's pieces, and good specimens can fetch large sums; the one under discussion was likely to go for something like £6,000. Indeed, another firm of auctioneers have expressed genuine indignation at the fact that the fuss has obliged them to postpone a sale including a substantial collection of these heads.

For the moment, everything is on hold; legal action from New Zealand has frozen bids until a decision on the ultimate ownership can be come to. On the legal proceedings I naturally make no comment; it is the moral questions involved that interest me. Maori leaders have called the impending sale a 'degrading and deeply offensive desecration', and that strikes me as scoring very high marks for both succinctness and strict accuracy.

Let me ask the seller and the auctioneer (and those who were thinking of making a bid) a question so offensive that it might penetrate even hides which at present seem thick enough to resist a direct hit by a heatseeking nuclear missile.

Among the horrors of Nazism and the Final Solution, there are authenticated instances of flayed Jewish skin being made into lampshades. Now suppose such a thing had come, without any law being broken, into the seller's possession, and she, quite within her rights, asked Bonham's to sell it for what it would fetch, would the parties to the transaction (seller, auctioneer, buyer) feel a sense of unease, attributable after much investigation to the realization that what they were doing was *wrong*?

Obviously, if the answer is 'no', I have nothing more to say to them, which would cut this interesting discussion short; so let us assume that it is 'yes'. The next question, then, must be obvious: what's the difference?

Is it that the Maori died longer ago than the Jew? That cannot be the answer; profaning the dead has no statute of limitations, and if it is wrong to treat as commerce a body violently killed in this century, it can hardly be right to take the opposite view of one done to death in the last.

Can the differing nature of the two deaths establish a defence, so that a body found on a battlefield is less worthy of respect than one found in a gas chamber? I can't see why. Both were, after all, human beings cut off before their time, and in any case it is not how they died that poses the hard question, but what is to be done with what remains; as far as I am concerned, the principle is the same if the dead man died of measles, or even old age.

Or is it that the Maori died in an unfathomable tribal quarrel on the other side of the world, but the Jew was killed in civilized Europe? But since when did morality depend on geography? (I had better stop this catechism before somebody announces that I am quite right, that there is indeed no difference between the two dreadful souvenirs, and that it is therefore equally as acceptable to buy or sell the lampshade as the head.)

We live in a strange and portentous time; I sometimes suspect that those who assert that the world is coming to an end know more than we think, and certainly there is evidence to support such a view. Violence has always been endemic in human societies, but certain kinds of it, wholly independent of gain or any other rational motive, now seem more prevalent than ever. The sniffing of cocaine is, in some circles, considered not just enjoyable, let alone dangerous, but smart, amusing, elegant. Tradition is a joke, the very past a junkyard. As Chesterton sang, 'They twisted even decent sin to shapes not to be named.'

Well, they have given it an extra twist now. Let us examine the nature of it more closely. If a human head is to you a toy, an ornament or another acquisition for your *cabinet de voyeur*, it does not mean that you are wicked, but it does mean that there is something missing in your make-up. I think I know what the missing element is, and there is a curiously recondite yet useful test for defining it.

The touchstone will be found in the twenty-second and twenty-fourth books of the *Iliad*. Achilles, having refused to take any further part in the war, is roused to fury and to battle by the death of his friend Patroclus at the hands of Hector. Achilles goes forth to face the victorious Trojan, and kills him. Up to that point there is nothing special for a reader to feel; this is a war, after all, and people get killed in wars. But mark the sequel. Achilles ties the body of Hector, by the heels, to his chariot, and drags the noble corpse round the walls of Troy.

There is your test. If you can read the passage without feeling a profound pity and revulsion, you could buy or sell a tattooed Maori warrior's head; if not, you couldn't. Go on to the sequel, in which Priam begs the mangled body of his son, so that he can bury it with dignity and the proper rites; if, the boon granted and the obsequies held, you feel a deep sense of fitness and resolution in the story (though Hector, after all, is still dead, and his father still heartbroken), then you have in you that precious element which those who feel nothing as Hector is laid in earth do not have.

Imagination is the missing ingredient. That Maori head once spoke; in a strange tongue, no doubt, but spoke. It kissed its wife; it cursed its enemies; it got wet in the rain; it died, and was severed from its shoulders. The body below the head was just as real; take its hand and feel the warmth of a living being. Imagination stirs, does it not?

It stirs enough to ask questions: did he go fearfully into battle, that warrior, or did he scorn such feelings? Was he killed attacking, or defending? Was he a seasoned veteran, or a raw recruit? You think these questions are pointless and childish? Then you are probably an auctioneer at Bonham's, or the owner of the controversial lot. Homer knew better.

It is imagination that is dying out of the world; the people in those categories I listed a few paragraphs back are devoid of it, and the solipsism they practise is their epitaph. But the danger is that it might be ours, too. For imagination informs every culture; it is the blood of art, the mark of maturity, the guide-dog of ethics, the cornerstone of religion. (For the thousandth time: I am not a Christian. But I would regard myself as much less than fully human if I were not moved to the innermost chambers of my heart by the thought of the Eucharist, and it is imagination that provokes the thought.) If imagination dies, it will make the world a desert. But if it comes riding back in arms to claim its rightful kingdom, we shall hear no more of the selling and buying of human heads.★

The Times June 6th, 1988

★ When last heard of, the head had been withdrawn from the sale, and negotiations with New Zealand seemed likely to result in its return.

Two legs better

MR STANLEY WOOD, a palaeontologist by trade, has discovered a fossilized scorpion's head, which he claims is 340 million years old. Well, it could be 680 million for all I care. But he added that the head was two feet wide, from which he deduced that the whole thing would have been 10 feet long.

I have to say, with the very greatest emphasis, that I do not wish to know that. I am one of those unfortunate people who suffer from a phobia; my particular terror is of all varieties of creepy-crawly, though the disorder is at its most intense when the eight-legged kind comes scuttling towards me. And when I learn that in the Carboniferous era, scorpions more than three yards long abounded, I tend to get into bed and pull all the bedclothes over my head, though not before pushing the chest of drawers against the door and making sure that the cyanide pill is at hand.

Moreover, this is not the first time Mr Wood, may he be found as a fossil 340 million years hence, has caused me to climb half way up the chimney and stay there. He is greatly given to the practice of finding horrors from bygone ages and describing them in a manner well calculated to turn my sleep to screaming nightmare. He seems to find most of his beasties at East Kirkton, in Scotland, and so far, in addition to the 10 feet stinging Thing, he has produced giant millipedes (as any insectophobe will tell you, the more legs the greater the horror), harvestman spiders (whatever they may be, and I fear the worst) and *millions* of the scorpions.

Then it gets worse. It seems that the received belief about

the Carboniferous period has hitherto been that it was ruled by the giant amphibians, who spent their time snoozing from morning to night in the Carboniferous warmth. But no, says Wood; the giant scorpions would have done them in in no time: 'Amphibians', he insists, 'couldn't afford to lie about sunning themselves with these carnivores scurrying around.' I suppose not; just listen to Wood as he warms to his work:

> They would capture their prey and drag it under cover. Then they injected their digestive juices into their prey, and waited until it had become a soup. Then they sucked it up.

Well, it takes all sorts . . . There really is a man who thinks nothing of finding the traces of 10-feet scorpions, together with millipedes that would stretch from *here* to right over *there*, and boasting about his finds – boasting, I may say, to such good purpose that his fellow palaeontologists have taken to calling him 'Stan' and agreeing with him that at East Kirkton at least, the scorpions once ruled the earth. There is some argument about whether his friends were aquatic giant scorpions or terrestrial giant scorpions, but I refuse to take sides; the horrible things might have been *flying* giant scorpions for all the comfort it would bring me.

Do you remember a film called *Them*? The things of the title were a family of giant ants, at least as big as Stan's scorpions, and the female of the species, towards the end of the film, was gravid with millions upon millions of itty-bitty ants, all of which, when they were born, were going to grow up as giant ones, which in a few ant generations would have overrun the entire earth. (I suppose the giant scorpions might have been induced to deal with them, but I wouldn't have bet on it.) Just in time, the hero shot the monster, and the ant larvae perished in their mother's womb.

It will not surprise you to learn that I did not go to see that film; all I know of it was from reading the reviews, and that was quite bad enough. (I did look at the pictures outside the cinema where it was showing, but I did not do so twice.) I took comfort, though, from a faraway memory, so far away, indeed, that it came from my schooldays. The giant ants in the film had, of course, the same shape and proportions as real ones. But I remembered, or I thought I did, that if the length and breadth of a solid object are multiplied by x, its mass is thereby multiplied by x squared. (Or is it cubed?) The giant ants, therefore, could not have existed. Score one for peace of mind.

That, though, was fiction; according to Stan, Stan, the scorpion man, his 10-feet stingers were as real as – well, as his giant millipedes. (The scorpions were, so to speak, made to measure, so the reassurance from the mathematical formula did not apply to them.) And remember that I have not even started to discuss the harvestman spider, largely because I fear that if I did so, I would find Stan insisting that the thing was five yards across – when there would be nothing for it but a spoonful of honey to help the cyanide pill go down.

The Thing doesn't have to be a prehistoric one. Staying in the country, always a dangerous custom for the arachniphobe, not long ago, I found One of Them in my bathroom; it was about the size of a fully-grown octopus, and I flew down the stairs gibbering, in the hope of finding someone still about – other than Stan, of course – to take an interest in my plight. Fortunately, my hostess had not gone to bed, and the brave girl picked it up with a tissue and sent it on its way. (The real phobic, like me, screams as loudly at seeing some normal person dealing with the enemy as he would if he met it alone.)

I suppose we can argue that we are still top creature; we are here, after all, and where are the giant scorpions, the mile-long millipedes, even the basking amphibians which the scorpions turned into soup and then so horridly slurped up? Order after order of almost incredible creatures once ruled the earth, and went their way, none knows whither (well, apart from the ones that fetched up at East Kirkton). But why are we so sure that the same fate is not lurking somewhere to account for us? After all, the number of theories purporting to explain why and how the dinosaurs died out are as numerous as the stars above us.

The truth of the matter is that the universe, whoever is in charge of it, moves in a mysterious way its wonders to perform. But I do feel that it need not have paused in its performance to create 10-feet scorpions and similarly proportioned millipedes, to say nothing of the giant harvestman spider, or for that matter the common or garden one, *Tegenaria domestica.*

I forgot to say that Stan's other discoveries have included the remotest ancestors of frogs. I have no fear of frogs; indeed I rather like the little fellows. But I recognize that one man's smile is another man's cold sweat, and I send greetings and sympathy to all the batrachophobics who are reading this. Mind you, frogs eat spiders. But who will serve up Stan as soup for his scorpions?

The Times February 22nd, 1990

Very white elephant

SOME YEARS AGO I read of a really splendid wheeze. President Houphouet-Boigny, big chief of the Ivory Coast since 1960, announced that he was going to build a basilica much bigger than St Paul's and somewhat bigger than St Peter's, in a little village called Yamoussoukro, distinguished (only, as far as I can see) by the fact that the Pres had been born there, eighty odd years back.

Scepticism at once tugged at my sleeve; the average *annual* income of the citizens of the Ivory Coast is the equivalent of £75 (I take the figure from Charles Humana's indispensable and meticulous *World Human Rights Guide*), and basilicas don't come cheap, particularly if they are 489 feet high and 632 feet long, as this one we were promised would be.

While silently commending old Houph for the fecundity of his imagination, I felt obliged to classify his wheeze along with Idi Amin's projected space programme, of which the only evidence was a number of prospective astronauts rolling down the Ugandan hills in barrels, presumably to familiarize them with the strange forms of motion they would encounter on their way to Mars. So convinced was I that Houph had been at the palm wine that I never bothered to follow up the story, and in due course forgot all about it.

Imagine, then, my stupefaction when the other day I saw in the *Daily Telegraph* (and the entire staff of that organ could hardly have been at the palm wine simultaneously) a *picture* of the thing; it appears to be almost completed apart from the dome, which is still encased in scaffolding. What is more, the specifications have been kept to – it *is* higher and longer than St Peter's, air-conditioned, and on a good day can hold 100,000 of the pious. Plainly modelled on St Peter's, it is called Our Lady of Peace, though seven will get you five that, by unanimous acclaim of the entire population, it will be colloquially known as Our President of the Ivory Coast.

It is said that Houph, to forestall criticism from the rest of the world (he's a dab hand at forestalling it from his own people, I can tell you), is paying for the entire caboodle out of his own funds, but since the project is costing a couple of hundred million quid (well, 700,000 tons of travertine marble doesn't grow on bushes) it is worth speculating on how Houph came by such sums in the first place. (When I say it is worth speculating, I mean it is worth speculating if you aren't one of his subjects: if you are, you would be well advised to speculate on something else, such as the goodness and holiness of the President.)

Three possible avenues to such presidential wealth open before us. First, his auntie left it all to him in her will. Second, it fell off the back of a lorry. Third, he has been, as we old Africa hands call it, 'doing a Mobutu' – that is, removing the national income to a safe place (Liechtenstein, possibly), in case of fire.

It is no use getting all indignant, let alone murmuring proverbs about beggars on horseback. Nor is it any use pointing out that the basilica will have rotted away within five years of Houph's death (not far off, it seems); Africa is very skilled and very experienced in eating away the works of man's hand, and the bigger and more costly they are, the more joyfully the termites feast upon them.

All the same, in the history of folly this will loom large. Roman Catholicism is not the state religion of the Ivory Coast, and indeed Catholics are only a small proportion of the population. Moreover, the country is of considerable size – some 130,000 square miles – and the population, apart from the capital, which holds about a fifth, is widely scattered. Certainly Yamoussoukro is no giant metropolis, and I have not heard that the Ivory Coast enjoys a huge, intricate and nationwide network of speedy trains, which is to say that after the thing is opened, and after the novelty has worn off, it is unlikely that more than a few hundred worshippers will ever be in it at one time.

'What need the bridge much broader than the flood?' If you think of the basilica of Our Wise and Kindly Provider as a place for Catholics to worship, the question is unanswerable. But of course it was not built as a place for Catholics to worship, though some of them will use it for that purpose, at least until it falls down.

Nor was it built as an attempt to bribe God to deal charitably with the President when he dies, though I dare say Houph comforts himself with the possibility that that might work. Nor was it a guilt offering for all the wickedness of his life; as a matter of fact, as African dictators go, he is, and long has been, among the *least* tyrannical, arbitrary and cruel.

Why, then, put it up at all? Think; the Ivory Coast exports coffee and cocoa, pineapples and a few other items. It has a population of around ten million. As far as I know, it has never done anything to bring it to the world's attention, much less achieved something that affected the rest of the world. It has never held any balance of power, it has never arbitrated between warring countries and managed to bring them to a ceasefire. No world-famous poet has sprung from its shores, no string of Olympic gold medals has been hung round the necks of its athletes, no film company has used it for an epic remake of *Beau Geste*.

Well? Suppose you were the boss of it, as Houph actually is. Your people are very poor, but they are not dying of famine, and it is probable that they are not unhappy; they have no say in their own governance, but it does not seem that the lack of it is for them a burning shame. Well, then, how are you going to be remembered? How do you – foolishly, vainly, yet all too understandably – mark your passing through this world?

Change the country's name to yours? But your successor would change it to his. Write your autobiography? In vain the hope of the best-seller list. Find the largest diamond in the history of the world in the soil of the grounds of the presidential mansion? A bigger one will be found one day.

But if you build a basilica larger than St Peter's, it is possible that you will slip, at the last possible moment, into the history books, or at the very least the *Guinness Book of Records*. And after all, you can plead a superiority over Herostratus: he burned down the Temple of Diana at Ephesus to ensure that he would be remembered, even only in infamy: you at least have put up rather than pulled down.

In the end, of course, it won't matter either way, which is the truth that Houph fights every moment to keep at bay. Even if the basilica does not crumble, the world will sooner or later cease to attach his name to it, and his last hope of immortality will have gone. How does it begin? 'I met a traveller from an antique land . . .' And how does it finish?

> . . . Nothing beside remains.
> Round the decay
> Of that colossal wreck, boundless and bare
> The lone and level sands stretch far away.

The Times September 11th, 1989

Putting him on a pedestal

THERE IS A growing opinion that the wartime bunker at the Mall exit from Horse Guards Parade should be demolished. I have grown rather fond of it, I confess, as the years have mellowed it and bestrewn it with creeper, but I shall not lie down in the road if the bulldozers are whistled up. On the other hand, the proposal has been linked with the idea of replacing it with a monument commemorating Sir Winston Churchill, and on that I shall put my foot down.

London has long been in danger of sinking into the subsoil from the weight of dismal lumps of marble, bronze and stone which have, over the centuries, been carved or cast and set on a plinth, with the intention of commemorating for ever some distinguished booby, known in his lifetime only for losing three-quarters of an army through his military incompetence, and anyway entirely forgotten within a dozen years of his death, leaving nothing to mark his passage through the world other than an eyesore, an obstruction to the traffic and a perch for the pigeons.

It is true that since Mr Oscar Nemon is now dead, there is no danger of the commission for the proposed memorial being entrusted to him, but there are plenty of sculptors almost as bad, many of whom would be only too happy to disfigure yet another pretty corner of the town at very reasonable rates. It is also true that even if Michelangelo were to come out of retirement and offer to do the job for nothing, we should still be wise to hesitate, if only on the ground that Churchill, of all people, hardly needs another memorial, statue, mausoleum, obelisk or pyramid to keep his name and fame alive. Does anybody think it necessary to put up a second Nelson's Column?

I presume that the idea of replacing the bunker by a tangible tribute to Churchill involves not a straightforward statue of him (a bad enough idea, to be sure), but a much larger and more varied composition, possibly allegorical (an even worse idea). Yet the awful truth is only two or three hundred yards away, at the other end of the Mall; whoever dreamed up the Churchill-monument wheeze should have strolled along to Buckingham Palace where he would have found, smack in front of it, the Victoria Memorial, a monstrous white horror which provides conclusive proof that the queen's bedroom faces the other way, for if Her Majesty had been condemned to see that thing every morning as soon as she opened the curtains, she would have abdicated long ago.

Portrait sculpture goes back a very long way, certainly as far as Ancient Egypt and Assyria. But for a very long time it was confined largely, if not entirely, to the rulers, and presumably intended to symbolize their power and majesty; most were considerably bigger than life-size. We must, of course, add the representations of the ancient gods; I would love to know who modelled for the Parthenon statue of Pallas Athene.

When and where was the first portrait statue of an unroyal but outstanding citizen? Did Plato sit for his portrait in marble? Did Socrates? Was Miltiades immortalized in stone after Marathon? There were portrait busts galore, of course, that far back, but they were 'pure' sculpture, not designed to rebuke posterity for its belief that it invented greatness. (Brendan Behan used to say 'There was good men in Mountjoy before Kevin Barry I can tell you.') The dam burst with the Romans; it was not only the Caesars who had themselves immortalized in marble, though they surely led the field. (There is a haunting note in *Julius Caesar*. 'Marullus and Flavius, for pulling scarfs off Caesar's images are put to silence.')

Is there any evidence that the Incas made portraits with their gold? They made the most intricate and beautiful ornaments and models, so I don't see why not. But how can we think ourselves back into civilizations so utterly unlike our own? The Incas had a very complex and advanced knowledge of astronomy, but never discovered the wheel; perhaps they thought it sinful to create a *doppelgänger* for a real person. If they did, they were in good company; when did you last read the Third Commandment?

In this country, presumably, the habit of enshrining nonentities in stone was mainly of nineteenth-century origin. I am sure that there is a statue of Campbell-Bannerman somewhere in London, and another of Lord Salisbury, and even Spencer Perceval, though his sufficient monument should surely be the fact that he was the only prime minister of Britain to have been assassinated; I know of nothing else he ever did.

I suppose the Age of the Dictators gave rise to a greater tonnage of flattering marble than in all the rest of history put together. The giant Stalin monument in Budapest was toppled in the 1956 Revolution; there is a famous and unforgettable picture of the heroes pulling down their oppressor, and despite the failure of the rising, the statue was never rebuilt. An old 'Radio Armenia' joke concerns the competition for a statue of Lermontov to commemorate his centenary. Thousands of entries pour in; the winning design is a huge statue of Stalin, with a volume of Lermontov in hand.

Oddly enough, I cannot remember seeing a photograph of a bust of Hitler; did the Führer shun sculpture on superstitious grounds? Or did no statue of him survive the war? In the Third World there is another hazard; ephemeral regimes come and go too rapidly for their chroniclers to keep abreast of which statue should be erected in the main square, and which should be melted down to make way for it. (Prudence should dictate the removal, but not destruction, of such statues, for what happens if the former regime overthrows its overthrowers? Cries of 'Who's been pulling down *my* statue?' would be heard from the Presidential Palace.)

I sometimes wonder how anyone can have had the gall to sit for a public sculpture since *Ozymandias* was written, but perhaps the people with the gall have never read it. But the most grandiose proposal for a statue was turned down, and by Alexander the Great, too. His favourite architect proposed carving Mount Athos – the whole of it – into a statue of a man down on one knee; in the palm of the right hand there would be a city of 10,000 people, and through the left would flow a mighty river.

Mount Rushmore must be the nastiest idea ever thought of in the field of portrait sculpture. Schnozzle Durante used to say: 'Dey asked me to run for President, but I refused; my nose wouldn't fit on a postage stamp.' *Much* more modest.

Leave Churchill alone, and the bunker (I think its correct name is The Citadel) with him. Good wine needs no bush; if Churchill is remembered it will not be in stone, and if he is forgotten this country will have forgotten itself. Besides, what could the memorial consist of? A cigar? A Spitfire? A V-sign a couple of yards across? Worse, probably; the one thing that can be said with certainty about a project like this is that it will be tatty and unimaginative. Max Beerbohm had the right idea; he suggested that when it was desired to commemorate some lately-dead great man, it should be done not by unveiling a new statue, but by veiling an existing one.

The Times June 16th, 1988

Imagination 2:
The halt and the blind

Both these stories, the first from New York, the second from London, have been widely published; I therefore need only summarize them. In New York, a gang of youths set upon a 28-year-old woman who was jogging in an unfrequented part of Central Park. They attacked her with bricks, a metal pipe and a knife, then gang-raped her; she was found lying unconscious in a pool of her blood. Her injuries have apparently left her brain-damaged.*

In a British Rail train, going from Waterloo to Weybridge, a 22-year-old blind man, his white stick signalling his disability, was robbed, by three men, of all of the money he had on him, some £17. Having robbed him, they then beat him up, kicking and punching him; he suffered concussion, injuries to the face, stomach and kidneys, and two broken ribs. Before his assailants got off the train, they broke his white stick in half.

Not long ago, I read a powerful and singularly unpleasant novel by Duncan Fallowell, called *The Underbelly*. It ends in a revolting murder, the culmination of the opening of a series of Pandora's Boxes; the author's intent was presumably to show how near the surface lie the depths. But what is interesting in this context was a phrase from the blurb: '. . . a narrative no more shocking than can be found daily in newspapers.'

The claim is true; but of course that makes things worse, not better. However you interpret the crime figures, there can be little doubt that what is generally called gratuitous, random or meaningless violence is growing. There are, for instance, London gangs which beat into unconsciousness people who are complete strangers to them, and have given them no offence, not even the imaginary kind; these are in the habit of leaving a calling-card on the body of their victims recording, in cheery words, the gang's soubriquet.

Now somebody – perhaps Professor Laurie Taylor – will assert that there is nothing new in such horrors, and will cite, for instance, the Mohocks of the early eighteenth century, who performed horrible mutilations on their victims, without any thought of gain, revenge or other rational motive. Others will say that in totalitarian societies there are torturers who know neither pity nor remorse; the Holocaust will be cited, and Stalin's hecatombs. But I do not think any of these comparisons are useful.

First, what people did in bygone centuries is no guide to what we think about *our* time; it is not much of a boast to say that we are no worse than cavemen. Second, the ideological frenzy of killing is *sui generis*; it has nothing to do with what I am talking about. Third, the quantity of cruelty in the world has grown and is still growing; but that is not what I am talking about either.

The gang who destroyed the woman in New York, and the gang who beat up a blind man and broke his stick in Britain, have altogether shaken themselves loose from the human race. The difference is crucial, and can be seen in the terrible question that springs to mind of every fully human being: why did they want to do these things?

The New York gang, or some of them, have been arrested; among the comments they have made on the record is (of their victim): 'She was nothing,' and (in response to the question of why they did it): 'For fun.' The British gang have not yet been caught, but it is not difficult to deduce from what they did that their answers would be similar.

We are in trouble; a new kind of trouble. The time has gone

by for talking about social conditions (the New York gang
were from Harlem, but had stable homes with employed parents). Nor do I believe that the answer lies in the argument,
however rational, put forward by Barbara Amiel, which in
essence argued that if you tell people often enough that
they are deprived through no fault of their own, they
will eventually start to behave as though it were true. For
every one such creature from the deep there are thousands
whose lives are no less barren, hopeless and poor; many
of them will steal the wheels off your car if you leave it
parked, and knock you unconscious if you surprise them
doing it. But they won't brain-damage you for fun. In
this country, there are people who would think nothing of
robbing a blind man; but I maintain that not a divide, but
an entire universe, separates them from those who, having
robbed him, would smash his white stick. We are in trouble.

Now such people did not get that way from thinking about
nuclear war, the hole in the ozone layer or salmonella-ridden
eggs. 'Why did you smash in the head of that young woman
with bricks and then collectively rape her?' 'For fun.' 'And
you – why did you break his white stick?' So such a person
is capable of feeling pleasure (fun); he is not altogether a
deadened zombie. But he,

> Most ignorant of what he's most assur'd,
> His glassy essence, like an angry ape,
> Plays such fantastic tricks before high heaven,
> As make the angels weep.

What did Shakespeare mean by 'glassy essence'? And
why did he say that man's glassy essence is the thing he
could be most sure of, were it not for his ignorance?

I cannot read 'glassy essence' as other than imagination.
Without it, man is nothing but an angry ape, ignorant of
the most precious part of him, and therefore led to do
things that challenge heaven and make angels weep. And
consequently, I cannot read the accounts of these literally

dehumanized beings without concluding that it is imagination which they lack. For, of course, if the imagination had
not atrophied in them it would make them understand what
they are doing.

Is that the clue? Has our junk world of instant gratifica-
tion, uncoupled from any idea of consequences, destroyed
the capacity to change places, imaginatively, with another?
All culture – not just art – inculcates that act of imagination,
which puts one individual in the place of another. With it,
you can conjure up a bygone world; with it, you can be
Hamlet or Don Quixote, Danton or Columbus, Queen
Elizabeth the First or St Joan, your next-door neighbour
or Antigone. It is not necessary to be educated, or even
literate, to hear the inner voice that is imagination, 'But
whilst this muddy vesture of decay Doth close it in, we
cannot hear it.'

Is that what we have done? Have we made ourselves wholly
self-contained – *self*-contained – to the extent that we cannot
recognize other people as human ('She was nothing'), because
we have dehumanized ourselves? Look at the filth our cities
have become; look at those strangers, our neighbours; look
at what passes for art, food, music, reading matter, entertainment, nature, religion.

The Lascaux cave-paintings were done by beings whom
we would not recognize as of the same species as ourselves;
yet they understood the role and importance of the human
imagination. But where is there now space for imagination
to breathe? In what maze do people now wander, unable to
find the way out? In what imagination-trap, far more limiting
than any poverty-trap, are we held prisoner? What rough
beast, its hour come round at last, lays waste our golden
fields of imagination?

That is the best I can do; you are at liberty to do better.
But remember exactly what the task is. It is to explain how
human beings, not mad, not drugged, not hypnotized, can
break in pieces a woman in a park, and having broken her,

rape her*; and to explain also how other human beings half a world away, can savage a blind man and break his white stick as they go.

The Times May 15th, 1989

---

* As this book went to press, the trial of those accused of her assault was under way.

Island story

ONCE UPON A time, it is said, a great giant who had been angered by the Pacific Ocean decided to have his revenge. Armed with a huge club, he used it to prise up all the islands he came to as he roamed the ocean; he then flung them into the water, where they sank. Eventually, in his rampage, he came to a land known by various names, including 'the navel of the world', and began his work of destruction. He went round and round the island, breaking pieces off, so that it began to shrink in size. But when it was reduced to a triangle of which the longest side was no more than 13 miles, he found that this remaining scrap was made of some particularly hard rock, impervious to his attack. He strained and heaved to wrench it up, but it was too strong for him, and in the end his monstrous staff snapped in his hands; defeated, he went away.

Many centuries passed until, in 1722, a Dutch ship, with a captain by the name of Roggeveen, sighted the little triangle, a speck in an otherwise empty ocean. Roggeveen went ashore, and because it was the day when Christians celebrate the Resurrection, he named it Easter Island.

Easter Island is literally the most remote place in the entire world. No other piece of inhabited land is further away in any direction from the next nearest human habitation; Pitcairn Island lies some 1,400 miles to its west, and the coast of Peru 2,300 miles to its east. The rest is water; it is said that Easter Island's inhabitants are more familiar with the stars above them than with any other land on their own earth.

Not surprisingly, it is difficult to get to, and until, in the 1960s, an airport was built (this cannot take a jumbo, but can accommodate anything up to a 737), it was all but impossible, because the only connection with the rest of the world was a ship which visited it *once a year*. Even now, there are only two places which connect Easter Island by air; Tahiti on the west, and Santiago on the east. LanChile (Easter Island is a Chilean possession) flies a kind of shuttle service twice a week: Santiago, Easter Island, Tahiti, Easter Island, Santiago, Easter Island . . . The planes tend to be full, and early booking is wise. There is something called a hotel on the island, very rudimentary indeed; it is, however, run by very friendly and helpful people. Otherwise, the islanders will put up visitors; there is always a crowd at the airport to meet incoming planes and offer rooms. Do not expect *haute cuisine*.

You can hire bicycles to get about with, and horses; also cars, though with these you will certainly break both axles within the first hour. There are no paved roads, only earth tracks, and a Jeep or one of its cousins is the only safe version. I, who cannot ride a horse or a bicycle, or drive a car, engaged a young islander with a vehicle that could have climbed Everest. My Jehu clearly believed that the paths were only for scenic use and charged straight across country: since the island is made almost entirely of volcanic rock (it was that which did for the angry giant and his weapon), the rhythmic banging of my head on the roof could have been heard as far as Pitcairn, if not Sydney. But we proved once again the ancient and amazing truth that if two people who have not a single word of each other's language are sufficiently determined to communicate, they will manage to do so.

And what was I doing there? Like everyone else, I had seen photographs of those astounding, unique stone figures, and dreamed of a closer acquaintance. Since I had business in the Antipodes, I arranged to return home via the Pacific and across the United States. Tahiti seemed a good point for a week or two's basking in mid-journey, and the trip to Easter Island, for all that it is almost 3,000 miles away and I had to fly back to Tahiti to get to California, seemed logical. At any rate, it looked as though I would never have a better chance. (And Tahiti was delightful, not yet ruined by the tourist hotels. The little Gauguin museum, though sad, is worth a visit; the other one, of 'Tahiti et ses Iles', is among the most exciting and informative museums I have ever seen.)

I arrived at eight in the morning: Jehu was at once enlisted, and I got to work. The first shock had nothing to do with what I had come to see: it was the barren nature of the island. There are no trees, and even to my implacably urban eye it was apparent that almost none of the ground was good enough to support significant crops or even much grazing. I saw some herds of horses and a few flocks of sheep; these trades, now of course bolstered by tourism, seem to offer the only subsistence of the island. Still, in the tiny toy-town – there are no more than 2,000 inhabitants – nobody looked hungry, or for that matter unhappy. It has been, of course, part of the Pinochet regime, but the immense distance from the mainland must dissolve any feeling of oppression; there is a Chilean governor, but I doubt if he has anything to do. The airport was heavily policed, and hand baggage of *arriving* passengers was searched, but these days none of that is really surprising.

The second shock is one that the visitor does not recover from; I went about in an unbroken daze. As I say, we have all seen photographs of the stone figures, the *moai*; the pictures show single statues and groups of three or four, but I discovered that there are *hundreds*: the island is strewn with them. There is a superb map, a true masterpiece of modern cartography, which, in addition to everything other maps have, includes a black symbol, in the form of the familiar profile of one of the heads, marking where the figures are to be seen: the map looks as though it has had soot sprinkled over it.

The greatest concentration of the figures is at Ranu Raraku, near the eastern apex of the triangle. This was the quarry from which the stone was hewn for the making of the *moai* (and of the *ahu*, the stone platform, on which the figures stood), and it stuns the imagination thrice over. The first gasp is elicited by the profusion of the figures, in every state of making; there are fully-formed statues, plainly ready to be taken to their resting-place, and huge unshaped 'logs' of rock, waiting to be attacked with the stone adze which was the only tool the makers had, and figures in every stage between. To wander among them, looking into those impervious faces (there is one, in particular, lying on its back staring forever into the sky) is a haunting experience, though the word must be carefully interpreted; somehow, the figures are not eerie, nor threatening, yet they are certainly not passive. I felt that if they all suddenly got up and walked, I would not be frightened (or surprised).

The second thought that every visitor must have is: how? The figures are massive, some more than 30 feet tall (I measured the *nose* of one – it was two yards), and weighing up to 80 tons or more. They had to be transported over a distance of up to 10 miles. *How?*

It seems that the islanders, in the era of the statues' making, had not discovered the wheel. They had no metal. They had nothing with which to make rope. They had no kind of lifting gear. Yet they managed to move those immense, silent creatures over rough, unsmoothable terrain, until they got to the stone bases – the *ahus* – prepared for them. (We must pause here to contemplate those bases; some were almost two hundred yards long and eight yards high, and the gigantic blocks of stone, hewn with the same primitive tool as the sculptors used, and without any kind of grinding aid or fixative, were fitted together so perfectly that a knife-blade cannot be inserted between them.)

Very well: they had made the *ahus*; they had got the statues to them. How did they get the statue on to the *ahu*? And above all, how did they get it upright? Experts have deduced that the population of the island could never have been more than about 3,000: did they do nothing but hew and carve and build and haul? Was their entire existence the making and siting of the statues? Oh, if only they *would* get up and walk, provided that they talked as well!

For that brings me to the third and most powerful reflection that no visitor can escape. If the transport is given up with a shrug and a helpless 'How?', then the answers to the questions of 'What?' and 'Why?' contain mysteries so deep, so remote, so unfathomable that they can scare the daylights out of you.

For a start, who were they, these long-dead hewers of stone? Did they come from Polynesia on the west, or South America on the east? Or both? No one knows. And when? The experts offer dates from the 7th century to the 16th, a more than ample leeway. No one knows. But the further we go into the mystery, the darker becomes our ignorance. What *were* the statues? Were they gods to be worshipped? Or tutelary deities? Or a strange form of *lares et penates*? Or monuments to their ancestors? Or stylized portraits of historic figures? Or art? No one knows. And when they were finally standing on their massive pedestals, what rituals, what ceremonies, what offerings, did the islanders provide? No one knows. Boards, inscribed with an ideographic script, have been found, and there are beautiful and elaborate petroglyphs strewn about the island; scholars have pored over them for decades, trying to decipher the signs and thus learn the language. What did those people want to say to us? No one knows.

We do know a little about their history, but only from when it becomes part of ours. After Roggeveen, the Spaniards, the French, and – in the person of Captain Cook – the British, called at Easter Island. There was some wanton killing by the visitors, possibly in the mistaken belief that they were being attacked, later a good deal of more or less random slave-snatching, but the greatest crime against the people of

Easter Island was committed by Peru. At Christmas 1862, a Peruvian fleet put in and kidnapped a thousand of the islanders to be slaves in the guano islands. An enlightened prelate, the Bishop of Tahiti, protested at the crime and insisted that the victims should be repatriated, to such effect that they were. But 900 had already died; of the 100 who embarked on the return journey, 85 died on the voyage, and the 15 survivors, all unknowingly, brought smallpox with them. (Unknowing indeed; the people had never acquired an immunity from a disease that had not touched them, and the population fell to little more than 100.)

But the innermost mystery of this series of enigmas is: what happened? And why? For at some time, apparently on a single day, the islanders destroyed the entire work of their hands. In the quarry, tools were flung down; the figures, from the finished to the hardly started, were deliberately toppled, and throughout the island the *moai* which were being moved to their resting place were overthrown and abandoned, while the *ahus* and their rows of silent figures were smashed. Countless theories – invasion, apparition, *folie en masse*, civil war – have been put forward; these impenetrable stone faces, lying higgledy-piggledy where they were when disaster struck, still guard their secret. It now seems that no amount of study, from carbon-dating to excavation, will prise it loose from them, just as the giant failed to move the island's core.

At dusk, I went back among the statues at Ranu Raraku; they lay quietly, giving out no ominous or sinister feelings. The one lying on its back would soon be gazing at the stars, those friendly stars which for Easter Island are so much more real than their faraway neighbours. I sat on a fallen statue – they don't mind – and as the light faded, I contemplated what is perhaps the most strange, the most profound, the most echoing, the most eternally insoluble of all the mysteries of this ceaselessly mysterious place. Before the catastrophe, the island was ringed, right round its shores, with those mighty stone altars, each bearing a line of statues. The whole sea-girt scrap of an island was defended by the unwavering ranks of these silent sentinels. Yet every one of the figures on every plinth – every one – had its back to the sea.

The Times November 4th, 1989

Hop it

THE RECENT DEATH of Sir Frederick Ashton revives, in all its sharpness, my ballet problem. He was widely and generously mourned, and the obituaries and appreciations left no one in any doubt that he had made a unique contribution to ballet, and in particular to ballet in Britain. Yet, for all I ever gained from that contribution he might as well never have been born.

We all have, in the arts as well as other areas of life, though perhaps more obviously there, blind spots. I can derive nothing from El Greco other than a powerful suspicion that he must have been colour-blind, and the *St Matthew Passion* and *B-Minor Mass*, though I know they are among music's supreme masterpieces, leave me entirely outside their glory, feeling uncomfortable, guilty and bored.

Now I do not claim, when contemplating a work of art which moves me not at all, that I am right, and the rest of the world is wrong (with the exception of Frans Hals, the seventeenth century's Annigoni, flesh tints and all), and I truly suffer, from envy if nothing worse, at the knowledge that there are areas of joy and satisfaction before which, as I approach, there springs up an angel with a flaming sword in his hand.

Yes, but this problem normally bites with very selective teeth; if I cannot read Conrad, I can read Joyce Cary, and if you cannot abide Jane Austen, there are no fewer than three Brontës to choose from. What happens when we come up against an entire art form that, however carefully and faithfully tried, seems as null and pointless as tearing yesterday's newspaper into pieces one inch square?

I am, of course, assuming that the individual with this bit of his artistic response missing does have a feeling for art in general; the mystery of those who are entirely without that feeling is insoluble. But if a man who understood, and cared passionately for, the graphic arts and literature, were to tell me that he gets nothing at all from music – nay, that he detests music and thinks it beneath the notice of any civilized person – I should think he was very odd.

Well, where the ballet is concerned, that is me. I tried; you cannot accuse me of condemning what I have never experienced. For a good many years I went to the ballet, and sampled all sorts, from the most traditional to the most modern. I sat at the feet of Clive Barnes, than whom there was no one alive who knew and understood more about ballet, and who could have communicated his enthusiasm and the reasons for it to a haystack.

But he could not communicate them to me, and I disgraced myself irretrievably by going to the opening night of *Marguerite and Armand*, the ballet created by Ashton for Fonteyn and Nureyev, where tickets were changing hands on the pavement for £200 a go, and falling asleep.

But when I swore off ballet for ever, with no regret, I tried to analyse what it was about this form of art that repelled me. I think I can make a case.

Take the *Enigma Variations*. When I saw it, I had, of course, known the music for thirty years or more, and loved it, though I have never thought it a great masterpiece, or even among Elgar's finest work. But following that portrait gallery of the composer's friends 'pictured within' (don't bother with the hunt for the concealed theme) is always an enjoyable and touching experience. Well, all I can say is that so far from the prancing and pirouetting making the experience deeper and fuller, it just got in the way and diminished it; it was like those television sports commentators who carefully tell us what we have just seen.

★

Ballet, unlike the other arts, deliberately limits itself by eschewing the human voice, whether in speech or song. Once, in Canada, I saw a ballet which consisted of a ballet rehearsal. It was a charming and innocent work, and since it was only some twenty minutes long, it was within my ballet time-span, even if only just. At one point, the ballet-master motioned to the two principals to show him their *pas de deux*; he went to the ballerina, gestured with his stick to bring her forward out of the line, then repeated the action with her partner, then, with much gesturing with his head as well as his hands, he ushered them into the middle of the stage and indicated that they should start their demonstration.

Will somebody tell me why that is superior, indeed, why it is not manifestly inferior, to having the director say 'Mademoiselle X and Monsieur Y, kindly let me see your *pas de deux* now'? (Many operas, most of them dating from the nineteenth century when it was *de rigueur*, have ballets in them. With the exception of *Eugene Onegin*, I sit there wishing the dancers would go away and let the singers get on with their work. I could even dispense with the ballet in *Figaro* – which is significant in being set to the one musically weak passage to be found in that immortal score.)

Physical movement and gesture can be beautiful and even eloquent, but these are surely crude, in the matter of communicating a meaning, compared to drama and opera. Would anybody know what any narrative ballet is about, even roughly, if there was no synopsis in the programme? And the giveaway lies in what I have indicated in the Elgar business; the greater the existing music used for the ballet, the less the ballet contributes to the effect.

Has anyone ever done a ballet to the C-Major Quintet of Schubert, or the *Heilige Dankgesang* of Beethoven? There would be no point at all in even opening our eyes. And, incidentally, I said that movement and gesture *can* be beautiful, which brings me to the best-kept secret of ballet; the most familiar single moment of the art is the ballerina going up on her points, the truth about which action is that it is invariably hideous, suggesting nothing but an unpleasant kind of deformity.

Tell me, you ballet-lovers, why will not leading conductors, if they can help it, conduct for the ballet? For the same reason that they will not, if they can help it, conduct Donizetti or Bellini; they recognize that these works, entertaining and delightful though they are, simply do not contain the qualities and depths that alone would make the effort worth their while.

'Entertaining and delightful,' I said, and if the people of the ballet world were content with an encomium as modest as that, there would be no difference between us. But they aren't; though they have no answer to the conductor question, they insist that the ballet is every bit the equal of the other arts, and many of them are not above claiming that it is the greatest of them all.

One of the first ballets I ever saw, possibly the very first, was *Hamlet*, with Robert Helpmann; I think he was supposed to be experiencing 'what dreams may come, when we have shuffled off this mortal coil', and, even then, I felt (I can't remember what music was used) that I would rather be watching the play of the same name. A little later, I was much impressed by Kurt Jooss in *The Green Table*; after that came the absurdities of Martha Graham, and it is now many years since I went to a ballet of any kind. And if Terpischore and her sworn vassals are even now arming to tear me limb from limb, let them reflect that every seat I do not occupy at the ballet frees another for them, and be grateful.

The Times October 10th, 1988

You said a mouthful

THE OTHER DAY I bought a tube of toothpaste: 'Vademecum, the Swedish whitener'. The first thing I saw when I took it out of the box was a square of bright yellow, bordered in blue and with red capital lettering on the yellow; the thing leapt out at the eye, so sharp was the contrast with the white of the rest of the tube. The message which the manufacturers were so concerned to bring to the notice of the customers was the encouraging rubric 'Contains no dyes or phosphates'.

Well, good for Vademecum, thought I. Not only do they rigidly exclude dyes and phosphates from their wares, they go to great lengths to assure the users on that score.

We can set the domestic scene. 'Johnny, go and clean your teeth.' 'Shan't! Won't!' 'Why not?' ''Cos there may be dyes and phosphates in the toothpaste!' 'That's no excuse – there's a tube of Vademecum, the Swedish whitener, in the cabinet – use that.' 'Cor, mum, so there is – hurrah for Vademecum, the dentifrice which contains no dyes or phosphates!' (*Sounds of teeth being brushed, followed by cheerful whistling.*)

Johnny, evidently, did not turn the tube over. But I did. And there I learned, from a less striking message in smaller type, that although there was indeed nary a sniff of dyes or phosphates in the stuff, there were ample supplies of: water, calcium carbonate, sorbitol, glycerin, silica, sodium lauryl sulfate, natural flavorings, cellulose gum, poly methyl methacrylate, sodium chloride, methylparabin and sodium saccharin.

That, you may think, is what the man had in mind when he talked of straining at a gnat and swallowing a camel – or, more precisely, straining at dyes and phosphates and swallowing water, calcium carbonate, sorbitol, glycerin, silica, sodium lauryl sulfate, natural flavorings, cellulose gum, poly methyl methacrylate, sodium chloride, methylparabin and sodium saccharin.

I am perfectly ready to believe (though as of this writing I don't) that this monstrous catalogue of chemicals cannot, severally or collectively, do the user any harm at all, let alone make all his hair fall out and turn him into a werewolf at full moon. I am also willing to accept, if spoken to very nicely, that many of the ingredients listed are essential if the toothpaste is to do its work of cleaning the teeth – which, after all, is what we buy the stuff for.

But we do have a problem here. The increasing demand from consumers to know what they are buying is matched by the growth of legal requirements, imposed by governments, for exhaustive labelling of what is being sold, with listing of all ingredients. Whence the Vademecum catalogue and its feeble response with the cry 'Yes, but we have no dyes or phosphates!'

Yet on the very same shelf as the Vademecum there was another brand of toothpaste, called Rightfresh, which declared *its* ingredients as: water, tylenate of nacryl, absorbent thorium, ethyl viculite, milpenium, cadmide, phenic distellate, inert sodal, cyphinyl, anaphrite and refined sucrosan.

Now if I tell you that the second toothpaste is entirely imaginary, and that I invented all the ingredients as well as the name, you will, I think, feel uneasy, since you will realize that you had failed to tell the difference between the real list and the gibberish.

And if I now add – as I do – that I have deceived you twice, because the *first* list is the one in which I have invented everything but the brand name, and the *second* the one in which the brand name is invented but everything else is genuine, you will, I imagine, not only be disturbed, but will also have been brought, very forcibly and vividly, to the realization that the lists of ingredients which are required by law are entirely useless to any customer not-possessed of a higher degree in chemistry from a recognized university or polytechnic.

And yet the manufacturers do have a case. It is not their fault that the things they put in their toothpaste (and of course in thousands of other goods and substances) have names incomprehensible to the buyers; the proper names are attached to the genuine ingredients listed above, and it is no use demanding more information about them, because apart from the fact that the tube would have to be the size of the Rotherhithe tunnel, the only meaningful description of what, say, anaphrite and methylparabin actually *are* would have to be couched in similar language, which would get us no further.

Nor would it be enough to have on the packaging a statement to the effect that all the ingredients are non-toxic, nay, positively wholesome; there is nothing so pure that nobody, anywhere, could ever be allergic to it. I am allergic to one of the most common, familiar and useful substances ever made, but the trouble about allergies is that they are never predictable – the sufferer can only discover his unfortunate condition the hard way, which is what happened to me. (And happened, moreover, in so devastating a form that the world came very close indeed to losing an immeasurable quantity of instruction, entertainment and understanding.)

Until more or less our time, the problem would not have arisen. Science had not divorced itself from the familiar world, nor devised a language impenetrable to all but initiates. Moreover, we had not become so finicky, not to say terrified. When did you last hear anyone murmur the old adage 'We've got to eat a peck of dirt before we die'? Or rather, when did you last hear it without a list of busybodies,

including among others Mr Geoffrey Cannon and Mr David
Simpson, reporting the speaker to the police?

The manufacturers have played their part on this field,
too; when they discovered that a gullible public could be
impressed by an air of scientific hocus-pocus, they began to
trumpet their wares as full of health-giving substances utterly
lacking from their rivals' products; it served them right when
governments took them at their word and ordered them to
list everything they included, which I suppose is where we
came in. (I recall a *New Yorker* cartoon showing a group of
men round a boardroom table, to whom the chairman is
saying 'Well, which is it to be, gentlemen – "Our toothpaste
contains more misconal than any other brand", or "Our
toothpaste is guaranteed to contain no harmful misconal"?',
which is certainly where we came in.)

   Nor does *caveat emptor* help us here, for the reason I
gave when I started; it really isn't fair to say that, if the
ingredients are comprehensively listed, the purchaser should
have no redress if he takes it home and it poisons the lodger.
I suppose somebody (Johnny, for instance) will say that the
only way to get round the problem is not to clean our teeth
at all, but that would leave a million more substances for us
to ignore, one by one. Incidentally, I bought the toothpaste
which started me on this in New York. From nothing but
idle curiosity, I bought another tube, the other day, in
London. The latter carried neither the disclaimer on dyes
and phosphates nor any list of ingredients at all. Useless
though the list may be, why do you suppose that the makers
of Vademecum tell the Americans all and us nothing?

● PS I deceived you *thrice*. The first catalogue was entirely
genuine and the second entirely invented. *Or possibly the other
way round.*

The Times October 12th, 1989

Getting to know Mr Lear

That Singular Person Called Lear by Susan Chitty*
Edward Lear: Selected Letters edited by Vivien Noakes†
Edward Lear: The Corfu Years edited by Philip Sherrard‡
Edward Lear's Tennyson edited by Ruth Pitman**
Nonsensus compiled by Justin G. Schiller¶

T HE CENTENARY OF Lear's death (the Royal Academy
jumped the gun three years ago with an admirably comprehensive exhibition) has undammed a torrent of books tes-
tifying to his enduring appeal. Indeed, the last of this collection
hovers close to Lear-like parody, being no more than a col-
lation of the texts of various editions of his limericks, from
which we learn that in the 1848 edition of the 'Old Man of
Calcutta' 'Bread and butter' is printed 'Bread & Butter' and
that there is no agreement, in the 'Old Man of Leghorn', as to
whether, in the third line, 'snapped' should be 'snapt', authorities being hopelessly divided on the question. Nor is that the
oddest fate to befall him: not long ago there was an edition of
the nonsense verse which dispensed with Lear's illustrations
altogether and provided new ones.

Yet even from such marginalia two crucial facts
emerge: that the limericks and Nonsense ballads show
no sign at all of losing the hold they have had on children
and adults alike through so many generations, and that it is

*Weidenfeld & Nicolson, †Oxford University Press, ‡Denise Harvey, **Carcanet,
¶Catalpa Press, all published in 1988.

only these which ensure his immortality, not the prodigious quantity of landscapes he turned out (his own estimate was 8,000), nor even the marvellous ornithological studies, perhaps second only to Audubon.

He was deeply wounded when he overheard an Englishman at breakfast in a hotel tell his companion that the man they had been talking to the previous evening was 'nothing but a dirty landscape painter', but although he was not ashamed of the Nonsense (embarrassed for a time, perhaps), he certainly regarded himself as a serious painter of nature, and his life, which was rife with disappointments, ended in the realization that fashion had moved on, and forgotten him.

His life, reminiscent of Augustus Hare in its scarred childhood and stifled emotions (Lear travelled almost as much, too) was well done by Vivien Noakes, and Susan Chitty's given reason for doing it again consists mainly of her inclusion of a fuller account of Lear's homosexuality, though since her conclusion is that he was permanently celibate, it hardly carries matters much further. (He was also epileptic, incidentally, but managed to conceal the malady from almost everybody throughout his life.)

The real problem is that not enough happened to him to fill one substantial book, let alone two, for all that he gave drawing lessons to Queen Victoria, and Miss Chitty gets quite frantic for material sometimes, telling us that Lear eventually conquered his dislike of hard-boiled eggs, and that he once dropped his eraser and thus startled some passing Turks.

He made many friends, though he was not the first or last man to feel more lonely among those who loved him than in solitude, and when Miss Chitty says of a travelling party which he joined as a young man that it adopted him 'as a kind of pet' she is near to a definition of much of his life. But he was loyal: he hero-worshipped Tennyson, though they were never close, and struggled all his life to complete to his satisfaction an illustrated edition of the Laureate's work. Ruth Pitman's immensely detailed *catalogue raisonné* reproduces a complete set of one of the attempts, comprising 200 sketches, but they are mostly lifeless. Far better are the lavishly-strewn studies in Philip Sherrard's full account of Lear's travels in Corfu, which is given through Lear's own letters and diaries. He said, curiously, for he was not vain, that his life, letters and diaries would be interesting to posterity, 'quite as fit to read 100 years hence as anybody else's naughty biography'.

In his fifties he rallied his strength to get married. It was on and off for four years, but of course never came to anything. Ten years earlier, when a young lady had set her cap at him, he had written a moving epitaph for his hopes of marriage: '. . . we all know about the beautiful blue glass jar which was only a white one after all, only there was blue water inside it'.

The scrupulously edited letters enable us to hear him clearly, though he gives nothing away, not even his epilepsy: his oldest and closest friend, Franklin Lushington, the great homosexual love of Lear's life, learned of it only when, as Lear's legatee and executor, he was going through the diaries. Lear died as he had lived; the last letter in the selection, which was one of the last he wrote, is an account of the death of his beloved cat, Foss, who of course figures in one of his best-known and best-loved poems, 'How Pleasant to Know Mr Lear'.

> . . . whoever has known me for 30 years has known that for all that time my cat Foss has been party of my solitary life. Foss is dead; & I am glad to say did not suffer at all . . . tomorrow there will be a stone placed giving the date of his death and his age . . . All those friends who have known my life will understand that I grieve over this loss. As for myself I am much as usual, only suffering from a very bad fall I had . . .

There remains his monument, the limericks and the Nonsense verse. Some cannot abide any of it. But the usual

charge, that it is too whimsical, seems to me wholly mis-
placed. There is nothing like the simpering of A.A. Milne; on
the contrary, the haunting imagination which informs even
the slightest of the limericks has a mysterious, indeed sinister,
quality, a significantly large proportion end in disaster of one
kind or another, though without the frightening element of,
say, Struwwelpeter. It is clear that, consciously or not, Lear
put his true feelings, which in his life and his 'serious' work
were bound and gagged, where nobody would think to look
for them, in a series of apparently innocent jingles and naive
illustrations.

If you take the limericks and the ballads together, the
effect is of an overpowering melancholy, almost identical
to that which arises from Housman's verse. Both of these
self-isolated men ('I, a stranger and afraid/ In a world I never
made') were tormented by a sense of futility and waste. Miss
Chitty draws attention to the fact that of the ballads only 'The
Owl and the Pussy-Cat' has a happy ending, and she could
have gone further; the 'Yonghy-Bonghy-Bo', the 'Dong
with the Luminous Nose', 'Calico Pie' and 'The Pelican
Chorus' are all invested with a desperate pain, the pain
of separation and loss. Lear's outer life, for all the setbacks
and failures, was full, varied and enriching, bright with the
lights of welcome and loud with greetings, but those friends
who missed his epilepsy missed also the tragedy of a man
who could never understand why he had been born. True,
'He has many friends, laymen and clerical' but 'He weeps
by the side of the ocean/ He weeps on the top of the hill.'
How pleasant, then, to know Mr Lear: but how sad, how
sad.

Sunday Times July 24th, 1988

Of ale

As FAR AS I can recall, I haven't been really drunk since 1948 or thereabouts. But I am no Rechabite; many a glass of fine stuff, the finer the better, has soothed my tonsils and increased my well-being. I gave up spirits almost entirely a long time ago; the end of a long, hard day may be marked by a long, hard Bloody Mary or an aquavit, but it is many years since I tasted gin or whisky. Champagne is practically the only aperitif I touch, and if the food is conducive I can happily drink nothing else throughout a meal. Moreover, when that long, hard day is to precede a pleasant evening, a split of the same precious juice accompanies me to my bath.

Very well; I am neither a total abstainer nor a lush, and the same can be said of most people in this land, whatever their tipple. I am not unaware of the tragedies of which alcohol has been the instrument; a close friend drank himself to death. But it is silly to brand liquor as the *cause* of alcoholic self-destruction, when far more deep-rooted psychological problems or unbalances are responsible, with drink (and now, of course, drugs) being only the means.

Now, however, this pleasurable and health-giving custom (obviously, I speak of drinking beneficial liquor only, and in moderation) is under assault from a new and singularly repellent quarter. To be sure, in the old days, temperance societies and their like campaigned against drink; their efforts were, I believe, grounded in the horrors of the nineteenth century and the gin palaces. But they pressed their case with modesty and charity; there was little or nothing of the Single Issue Fanatic in their work, let alone persecution.

All of a sudden (and it *is* of a sudden) a new plague has broken out; today's wowsers are not concerned to point to the dangers of excessive drinking, or to urge moderation. No; for them, it is a Cause, and if there is one thing we know about Causes with a Capital Letter, it is that those who espouse them are suffocating in self-righteousness, convinced that to bring nearer The Day, harassment, interference and bullying are indispensable.

Here comes the Greater London Alcohol Advisory Service, whatever that might be, to demand for a start (oh, but not for a finish) that all cinema advertising of liquor should be banned, and that ultimately (I said the start wouldn't be the finish) it should be banned altogether on television as well.

It seems, moreover, that the cinemas, at least, are giving in with hardly a struggle, so that such advertising is expected to vanish within a year or so. The fact that many cinemas will disappear as well, because the lost advertising revenue will make the difference between profit and loss, does not concern the wowsers; provided their pestilent busybodying triumphs, it doesn't matter how many other freedoms are diminished.

The spokeswowser for this organization is a Mr Hatter, and he exhibits the stigmata of the SIF, as I shall demonstrate. The bodies charged with examining advertisements which may have a deleterious effect (on young people, for instance) have recently strengthened their rules; young actors are now not allowed to appear in television advertisements for alcohol, nor may such advertisements suggest that drinking alcohol is a specially manly practice; the new rules even restrict the use of humour to sell drink, presumably because impressionable people may be softened up by jokes into drinking more than they otherwise might. (I must say that between the hectoring of the SIF and the imbecilities of our guardians, there is less and less to choose as the days go by.)

Anyway, the rules have been made even more restrictive,

which you might think would have pleased Mr Hatter. Not a bit of it; he ululates thus: 'We put in 30 complaints to the ASA [Advertising Standards Authority] last year, and on all of them they ruled against us.' I said that Mr Hatter would typify the SIF; well, doesn't he? For what is the typical stance of this unattractive breed? It is, surely, a demand that the jury be picked by the accusers; it has plainly not occurred to him that the ASA may have rejected his complaints because they were without foundation, the advertisements in question being within the rules.

So much the worse for the rules, says the SIF; they shall be amended to ensure that whatever we want to happen must happen. The obvious analogy is, of course, with the smoking wowsers, but they, at least, have a case; smoking is in itself dangerous. The drinking, in moderation, of good wine or even pure spirit is in itself *not* dangerous, and indeed used wisely is beneficial.

The Rechabite says it is wrong to drink, and although I reject his claim, I can see, and even sympathize with, his point. He has, of course, forgotten what the First Miracle was about, which is naughty of him, since he bases his charge on scripture (Jeremiah, 35, 6), but although he wishes that we should all abstain, he does not see it as his duty to dragoon us into doing so.

Not so the Hatters. And now here comes Mr Derek Rutherford, of the Institute of Alcoholic Studies (how many more of these wowsers' covens are going to spring up before we rise in revolt and get the tar and feathers out of the cupboard?) who looks like joining his brother Hatter in the matter of packing the jury. *He* wants advertising controlled by a body set up by the Government and stuffed with 'members of the health lobby'.

The wowsers will deny it, but what they are really after is Prohibition, just as the smoking fanatics will not cease until the manufacture, sale and use of tobacco have been made illegal. But both of them start and finish at the same point; they are quite sure that they know what is good for us and what is bad for us. The fact that we dare to say that in our judgement they may be wrong in their assessment of it only inflames their certainty and strengthens their determination to call us all to heel.

I am a bachelor, but I am close to many children. I would never offer one of them a cigarette, and would gently ('gently' – the wowsers should look the word up in the dictionary, for they have certainly not encountered it before) try to stop them smoking if they have started. But I deem it nothing less than a duty to introduce them to good wine, which is one of the noblest and sweetest pleasures in life, and I am happy to say that one of the youngest has become something of a connoisseur of first-class champagne. He takes it in sips only, of course, for I stress again that moderation is an essential ingredient in drinking: but I hope and trust that he will learn more about wine as he grows older, and will appreciate it as one of nature's greatest gifts.

Meanwhile, the wowsers sow teeth and watch armed men spring up. Let us resolve to arm ourselves in turn, and do battle with those who hate pleasure but hate even more terribly the thought of those who enjoy it. Mud in their eye!

The Times February 13th, 1990

Of cakes

I TOLD YOU; you wouldn't believe me; now you're sorry. I said that when the wowsers have made smoking illegal, and then done the same to any liquor stronger than shandy-gaff, they will turn their attention to the food we eat. The pattern is identical; it starts with solemn shakings of the head and wagging of the finger; it goes on with harassment, increasingly unpleasant; finally it demands legislation.

What are they after now? Sugar, that's what. But see the way they go about it, in which can be seen the chief characteristic of the Single Issue Fanatic, or Nanny's Nanny. Demand investigation of whatever it is you want to suppress, and when it has been investigated, and the investigation shows that the fears are either groundless or much exaggerated, insist on a fresh investigation, this time with terms of reference that allow only a verdict of guilty.

For many years the food-wowsers could traduce sugar with impunity; it was widely believed to give you heart disease, diabetes, gallstones and cancer (to name but a few), while sceptics went on eating and drinking things stuffed with it. Finally, it was time to find out.

The finding was entrusted to the Committee on Medical Aspects of Food Policy (with the enchanting acronym Coma), which sat for two years, and reported recently. Its findings, cautious and scrupulously couched, declared that the most serious charges against sugar were unproven; there was no direct link between sugar consumption and heart disease or diabetes, and little evidence of such a link with cancer. On the other hand, the report recommended reduced sugar intake for all, and urged manufacturers of foodstuffs to label their products with the sugar-content; they also pointed out that excess sugar can lead to obesity, and that obesity is widely agreed to play a part in a number of ailments. And the chairman of the Coma investigation, Professor Harry Keen, said that although it would be 'almost mischievous' to argue that sugar was a direct cause of heart disease, 'If people are trying to reduce weight gain, especially because obesity affects blood fats and they want to protect their coronary arteries, then reducing sugar would be a good idea.'

A most sober, fair and well-founded verdict, you would say? But you reckon without the wowsers and their implacable determination to reject any findings, however thoroughly researched and however meticulously framed, that do not correspond entirely and exactly to the wowsers' demands. And if all else fails, try questioning somebody's integrity.

At which point, as so often in these matters, Mr Geoffrey Cannon enters the argument. As Life President, Great Panjandrum and Sugarfinder-General of the Incorporated Society of Food-Wowsers, he has devised a new kind of slur for those who do not agree with him; the method he uses I call 'the pre-retracted libel', and he is very fond of it. To show how it works I cannot do better than quote him verbatim. *Before* seeing the Coma report, he seems to have sniffed the wind and concluded that it would not be what he wanted. This is what he said about Coma and its members: .

> Professor Harry Keen, chairman of the committee, and Professor John Durnin, the deputy, have both, before their appointment to the committee, spoken on sugar industry platforms in defence of sugar and it is matter of record that Professor Keen has had research funded by the sugar industry for over 10 years.
>
> This is not a comment on the integrity of the two professors, both of whom believe sugar is relatively harmless.

You see what I mean? If you don't, I can do better –

or rather, he can. Also before he had read the report, he managed to get *five* of his pre-retracted libels into a single article.

> . . . the Medical Research Council . . . give[s] a low priority to research into food and public health. The chairman of the MRC is Earl Jellicoe, a director and ex-chairman of Tate & Lyle. This is not a reflection on Earl Jellicoe . . . Scientists who believe that sugar is harmless . . . are liable to accept sugar industry funding. One example is Professor Harry Keen . . . Sir Donald Acheson, chief medical officer at the Department of Health, appointed Professor Keen chairman of the Coma Committee . . . Similarly, this is not a reflection on Professor Keen . . . Sir Donald was untroubled by the fact that two other members of the committee, its vice-chairman, Professor John Durnin, and Professor Don Naismith, had spoken in defence of sugar at . . . meetings organized by the Sugar Bureau . . . They are entitled to their views . . .

Is this story not a very definition of the Single Issue Fanatic and the belief that they, and they alone, have the truth, so that anyone who disputes their belief must be in the pay of the enemy? But that is only the fruit; it is the tree that is most dangerous. And we must look at the roots of the tree.

The wowsers always start with the conviction (sometimes correct) that certain perfectly legal activities are harmful. They then see a great light in the sky, in which is framed an angel with a fiery sword, who tells them that they must go and stop it; and long before they have rubbished an honourable professor or two (or in this case three, not counting Sir Donald Acheson and Earl Jellicoe) they have forgotten their original impulse, which was, after all, to stop us harming ourselves.

That, though, is why I called the food-wowsers not just Nannies, but Nannies' Nannies. Smoking and drinking are peripheral to life, whatever pleasure their users find in them; but food is essential to our survival. If the wowsers, therefore, can harass and traduce us into conforming to their demands at table, they will have managed to control a central element of our lives. I believe there is a clue here to the abuse I receive whenever I describe a fine meal I have had; I have plainly slipped the leash by eating Bise's *poulet à l'estragon* or Pic's *foie de canard au marc*, to say nothing of the four-pound lobster I consumed all by myself a few months ago at the Arbutus Lodge near Cork, followed by an immense slice of chocolate gateau. It is not just that they are puritans and busybodies, but that they cannot rest until they have chained me down and put me on a diet of carrot-juice and vegetarian cheese.

Come; if you were worried about your children eating too many things with sugar in them, because you feared it would harm their teeth, which would you do – stop the Mars bars or ensure that they brushed their teeth thoroughly? You would vote for the toothbrush? Well, the food-wowsers would vote the other way, and that is how you know them.

Incidentally, Mr Cannon gets a lot of money from newspapers and publishers for writing articles and books denouncing certain foods. This is not, of course, a reflection on Mr Cannon.

The Times February 15th, 1990

Uneasy lies the head

IF YOU ARE surprised to find me today writing about the Royal Family, be assured that you are not nearly so surprised as I am. It is not that the subject has no interest for me; so significant a part of our constitution, entirely ceremonial yet vital to the workings of our democracy in its role as a stabilizer, is well worth exploring. The trouble is that today it is discussed only in terms of weary triviality or sickening gush (including hostile sickening gush), and anyone trying to be even half serious on the subject will most likely be drowned in the triviality and gush as soon as he opens his mouth. Here goes, though.

Let us start with a word of comfort for the Duchess of York, aka Fergie. At present, she can do nothing right, at least in the eyes of the less expensive newspapers; she is painted as a monster of callousness and indifference, neglecting her duties and her baby (it's a mercy she hasn't been accused of battering the poor thing) in the search for pleasure and entertainment, a search which involves dragging her royal husband away from his ship, so that instead of spending his time sinking the Swiss Navy he is always following her to Klosters.

How, then, is she to be comforted? By realizing that the attacks on her, however odious and painful, are entirely impersonal. That, she may say as she scans headlines reading 'Fergie Ate my Pet Rabbit' or 'Fergie Forgets to put her Knickers on' is a rather quaint way of looking at it. But it is true.

For a reason I do not fully understand, there has to be, at

any time, one 'bad royal'. The choice is entirely arbitrary, and bears no relation at all to the personal qualities or conduct of the chosen victim; that is what I mean when I say that the attacks on the Duchess of York are impersonal.

If she doesn't believe me, she should slip over to Kensington Palace and take tea with Princess Michael of Kent. Princess Michael? I can hear the start of surprise from one end of the country to the other, as my readers suddenly realize that there hasn't been a word about her in the press for well over a year, though for two or three years before that it was she who occupied, just as implausibly and irrelevantly, headlines asserting that 'Princess Michael was Nazi Death-camp Guard' or 'Princess Michael has her Bottom Tattooed'. There was nothing meaningful, let alone sinister, behind it, though I dare say she would take quite a lot of convincing of that; it was only that she had been selected, through some mysterious process, as the current bad royal.

As it happens, the campaign against Princess Michael was much nastier than that directed at the Duchess of York (though I imagine the Duchess would take as much convincing of *that*), but that was because Princess Michael made the ultimate mistake: she answered back. Even so, the time came when she was displaced from the role of Wicked Royal Fairy to make way for Her Inexcusable Ferginess. What nobody but me remembers, or will believe, is who held the post before Princess Michael: it was Princess Anne.

You find that difficult to swallow? But that is precisely because the whole thing is spurious and random. Today, the Princess Royal has been canonized as a secular saint, for her truly admirable international work on behalf of the Save the Children Fund. Her dedication and concern are beyond doubt, but she didn't catch them like measles.

She is the same woman, albeit now somewhat older, who in her turn used to inspire (and inspiration was the word, or perhaps it should be imagination) headlines like 'Princess Anne kicks Stableboy to Death' and 'Anne to Divorce and

Marry Claus von Bulow'. She was so provoked on one occasion that mere remonstrance was not enough; she *swore* at the *paparazzi*. I suspect that that was the moment at which it was decided to remove her from the Pedestal of Shame, on the grounds that there could be no greater achievement than provoking the Queen's daughter to audible profanity, and therefore there was no more to be got out of baiting her.

If I am right, there is hope for the Duchess of York; all she has to do is to go further than her sister-in-law (who only, after all, used one word, and that a euphemism – 'Naff off!' – for the real thing), and let fly with both barrels of the most fishwifely obscenities. Of course, the girl doesn't know such words, but Prince Andrew must be acquainted with a chief petty officer or two, and if *they* can't come up with a full range, we might as well scuttle the whole fleet, for all the use it would be.

But we can go further back still, for the thing did not start with Princess Anne, either; before her there was Princess Margaret. She, too, was attacked for going on holiday, and indeed for putting on weight, but the main charges, which seem almost incredible today, concerned her choice of men friends – and after, not before, her divorce. (But if you haven't discovered that even the most hardboiled tabloid reporter who ever wore a dirty raincoat is, beneath his assumed toughness, a milksop and a prude, you cannot understand my profession. Do you actually know James Whitaker? I do.)

Then we go back to the Duke of Edinburgh; I recall an amazingly ridiculous campaign against him because, on a visit to India, he was invited to go tiger-shooting (such an invitation is a great honour there), and after a few days of the newspapers back home yelling and screaming and jumping up and down, he had to pretend that he had a whitlow on his trigger-finger and so couldn't shoot anything, not even a tabloid journalist.

Before the Duke, there was nobody. The present Queen

has always been greatly loved, and of course her mother is the most popular figure in the land; those who remember George VI will also remember the immense affection in which he was held, and not only because of the faultless inspiration he and his wife offered the country, in parallel with the leadership of Churchill, throughout the war. (Did you know that the King pleaded with his Prime Minister to be allowed to sail with the D-Day invasion fleet and go ashore with his troops? The PM said no.)

The absurd game of the 'bad royal' may be a subconscious recoil from the ghastly slobbering over royalty in general, which shames the nation and must sicken the recipients of it. It seems almost impossible for us to see the Royal Family straight, so that they are not wholly mythical figures on the one hand or just like your auntie on the other. The appetite for news of them and their activities is plainly insatiable; there are magazines entirely devoted to them, and I doubt if for decades there has ever been a day in which nothing about them has appeared in the newspapers.

Yet there is no sign that the monarchy is viewed as an anachronism, as it is in, say, Sweden, where the Royal Family go about on bicycles. (Norman St John-Stevas put it well once, when he said: 'We can have a grand monarchy, or we can have no monarchy, but we can't have a mean monarchy.') If we could only wipe away the poisoned molasses and truly understand the role and value of such a focus for our national life as the monarchy provides, we might not only restore the cohesion of our fast-fragmenting society but achieve an adult attitude to the Royal Family which would benefit both us and them, instead of the unwavering imbecility that is the only product of our present view of them as partly divine, partly film stars, partly football hooligans and partly chocolate boxes.

I return to my starting point: the hounding of the Duchess of York and its meaning. It has no meaning; it is a ritual comparable to some of those still practised by religions so ancient and primitive that it is impossible for the adherents even to guess at their original purpose. All the Duchess has to do is wait, and I believe not for very long. A year from now the headlines will say 'Fergie in Midnight Dash to Save Toddler's Train-set'. But I have a nasty suspicion that there is a bad time coming for Prince Edward.

The Times January 23rd, 1989

Unsocial climber

WE ALL ADMIRE the people who can do things that are entirely beyond us. So we should; unless we turn it into envy or mere daydream, it is proper to look up to those with great gifts or powers, 'For emulation hath a thousand sons That one by one pursue'. There is, to be sure, a dangerous bridge to cross; if what we yearn for is within our grasp, so that unremitting labour would bring it to hand, we have no right to aspire to a condition that we could create for ourselves.

Only if we are truly crying for the moon does it work. It would please me very greatly to be able to play the piano as well as Alfred Brendel, to write novels as good as Dostoevsky's, or for that matter to master the art of the doorman's whistle with two fingers in the corners of my mouth; but none of these elevated states can ever be mine. So, as my rule dictates, I bow before those who can do what I cannot.

These reflections are prompted by reading a recently published book by Al Alvarez, *Feeding the Rat* (Bloomsbury). We'll come to the rat in due course, but first I must issue a warning to prospective readers; we have all read (or stopped reading) books of which we say colloquially that 'It made me sick,' but this is the only book I have ever had in my hands of which that could almost be said in literal truth; more than once I was on the point of leaving my chair for the bathroom and the old heave-ho.

Before anyone concludes that Mr Alvarez has written a book describing a variety of more than ordinarily recondite

sexual practices or a lavishly illustrated study of disembow-
elling through the ages, I had better say that there is nothing
in it that could bring a blush to even the most sensitive cheek.
But a ghastly pallor, yes.

The sub-title is 'Profile of a Climber'. The climber in
question is called Mo Anthoine, and I might as well say
now as later that he is plainly raving mad. If you want the
evidence, here it is:

Mo . . . had watched the accident, appalled, from the
ice-cave, knowing there was nothing they could do in
the dark. At dawn, Mo . . . traversed across to help the
others . . . The major problem was that they were about
9,000 vertical feet above their base camp, and . . . they
had eaten up nearly all their food . . . they decided that
. . . their safest way off the mountain was to climb back
to the top . . . They ate the last of their food and spent an
uneasy night trying to block the entrance of the ice-cave
. . . next morning . . . Mo . . . had lost all sensation in
his hands; it was so cold that his eyelids froze to his
eyeballs . . . their food was gone, they had only one gas
canister left with which to melt the snow for drinks, and
they knew . . . they would soon be too weak to move
at all . . . Mo . . . left a note to say he was going on to
Askole . . . he had already been going for twelve hours.
The distance to Askole was about thirty-five miles . . . A
couple of times, Mo fell asleep and woke to find himself
still walking . . . He kept walking all the next day . . .
he walked into Askole at seven o'clock the next morning
. . .

Now my contention that Mr Anthoine is a very long
way indeed round the twist does not stem from that tale of
horror (very much condensed, I must say); terrible things
can happen to anybody. The proof lies in the fact that he
not only did all that deliberately, he did it *for fun*. And what
is more, when he looked back on it, he concluded *that it had
indeed been fun, enormous fun.*

I suffer badly from vertigo; I can get dizzy climbing into a taxi. But the nausea was not confined to my shuddering imagination peering over the edge with Anthoine and Alvarez; the vicarious fear was so powerful that even when they were stuck to a vertical rock-face like wasps to a fly-paper, I didn't have to think of looking down (which is the killer for the vertiginous) to be so terrified that I had to hold on to the arm of the sofa, and a few minutes later I had become convinced that the bay-windowed wall in which the sofa stands was going to fall out – window, sofa and I – and deliver the lot to the ground, four storeys below. A second warning; this book can make you as crazy as its subject.

The secret of life, I have long been convinced, is to know what you cannot do. I cannot do things that call for great physical endeavour, and it is no use telling me that I ought to be ashamed of myself. But when it gets to the kind of courage, fortitude and brute strength that the people in this book display, the old head, as Bertie Wooster would say, swims.

We live in a sedentary age, and I am more sedentary than most. I don't know how I would behave if I were pitched into a situation of great physical danger – facing a madman with a gun, say, or trapped under the ruins of a bombed building, or in a shipwreck. But that is the point; I *don't* know how I would behave, and I hope I shall never need to find out. The difference between me and the mountaineers is that they go into the ordeal deliberately, matching themselves against not only the known hazards but the ones (like the injury that set off the events of my quotation) that cannot be guarded against.

But there is a further dimension to my problem. Mo Anthoine is entirely beyond me; he is the physical Brendel to my physical incapacity. But Al Alvarez, whom I have known and admired for many years, is a writer, a journalist, a poet; damnation, he is an *intellectual*, and so am I.

What right has he to be so brave, so hardy and so strong? (What makes it all the more galling, incidentally, is that the writing in this book is as beautiful as it is thrilling.)

You see what I am getting at. There are those who can climb mountains in impossible conditions, and there are those who have read and remembered thousands of books. Mo Anthoine is in the first category, and I am in the second. But Alvarez, rot him, is in both.

Rot him because he reminds us that human beings are riven not only by the Cartesian split but also by a more obvious duality; we have both a body and a mind, and we were given both for a reason. We make a very serious mistake if we believe that the body is nothing but a receptacle for our minds, yet the mistake is made a million times a day.

If you tell me that I should take exercise, you have already missed the point; keeping fit (I *am* fit, and not overweight, either) is not what I am talking about. I am talking about the duty of every one of us to use the body to its full, as the mind is used. And using the body to the full means giving it challenges to meet and overcome.

These challenges need not be as extreme as those devised by the mad mountaineer; they need not be extreme at all. But they must demand the full potential of the body in meeting them, and the attainment of the Greek ideal of the harmony of mind, body and spirit is farther away than ever, not just for me but for most people in countries such as ours.

Oh, yes, the rat of the book's title. Feeding the rat means precisely what I have been describing; a deep need to seek, and to be involved in, the body's exertions. Mo Anthoine's rat is a voracious and insatiable creature; for my part I would rather eat the rat than feed it in the way he does. But I know that in making that choice I am limiting my life, and the fact that I have long come to terms with my sedentary nature is little consolation. Anyone for tennis?

The Times June 30th, 1988

Visionary position

I F, AMONG MY readers today, there is a sociology graduate with first class honours seeking a subject for a dissertation, I offer him without charge (well, if it's ever published he might dedicate it to me) the connection between extreme political views and sexual scandal.

I started thinking about the combination when South African tongues began to wag concerning the melodiously-named Mr Terre Blanche, who runs a neo-Nazi coven dedicated equally to keeping South Africa white and beating up their opponents. Mind you, from the photographs of the Führerkin that I have seen, he seems to have suspiciously pointed ears; I wouldn't half laugh if it turned out that he had a touch of the tarbrush. (Even if he hasn't, how does he square his *echt* South African white supremacist views with his frog name?)

The more extreme the politics (left as well as right, I must stress), the more the True Believers insist on purity and fidelity, if not total celibacy, and it is easy to see why. We, the faithful, have the keys of the kingdom; we, and we alone, know how the world should be, and we are only awaiting the signal to remould it to our hearts' desire. Meanwhile, though we can stop ourselves from getting rusty by knocking in the teeth of those who disagree with us, we must keep ourselves clean in thought, word and deed, *mens insana in corpore sano*, to be worthy, when the call comes, of entering into our inheritance.

Two things follow. First, and most obviously, it doesn't work; only a few real ascetics can curb their fleshly desires

solely for political reasons. Just as I believe that among the
ranks of the strictest vegetarians there will always be some
who from time to time can't stand the thought of any more
lentils, and nip round to the Berni Inn, when nobody's looking, for a T-bone steak done rare, so – indeed much more so
– members of the more extreme political *groupuscules*, though
they have taken a thousand vows of chastity, are regularly
found a-mollicking when the sukebind is out.

The second fallacy concerns the leaders, who are destined
to carry the flag, when the whistle blows, into the citadel.
Since it is they who lay down the rules of conduct, they must
set an example to the weaker members, and the consequent
strain inevitably means that when they finally come off the
rails they do so in a truly spectacular manner. Far be it from
me to come between Vanessa and her Loonies (I would as lief
step between Mr Tyson and Mr Bruno), but if a quarter of
the conquests attributed to Mr Gerry Healy (Vanessa's *chef
de cabinet*) were real, he must have spent very considerably
more time at, er, bonking than at planning the expropriation
of the capitalist hyenas, which may account for the fact that
the capitalist hyenas are still unexpropriated.

The Nazis had enough sexual weirdos to keep Krafft-Ebing
busy for a century; Streicher is not known to have read anything other than pornographic magazines; and what Röhm
got up to with his entourage of strapping young Brownshirts
hardly bears thinking about. The question of whether Hitler
had any sexual relations at all, or even the capacity for them,
will never be finally answered, Eva Braun or no Eva Braun;
we certainly cannot rely on the familiar song which, set to
the tune of 'Colonel Bogey', begins 'Hitler, he's only got
one' – but perhaps we had better leave it there. Our own
dear fascist Leader, Oswald Mosley, was an adulterer of
considerable assiduity; he even scored with his sister-in-law.

Lenin wasn't interested, but there were dark stories about
Stalin and thirteen-year-old girls, probably true; Beria had
a reputation as a rapist, which wouldn't be surprising. But

the *histoire amoureuse* of the Soviet Union's leading figures would, I guess, be a pretty fat volume.

Pushing out the boundaries just a little, the American TV evangelists have a fairly impressive record of clutching a Bible in one hand and various things in the other; it seems, not surprisingly, that extremism in religion puts the same strain on the chief extremists as political fanaticism does on its own leaders, quite apart from the fact that some of the tellygodmen are zealots every bit as politically bigoted as the straight politico-fanatics.

Some of the sects that sprang up at the end of our Civil War, and waxed powerful, or at least loud, during the Interregnum, handily combined the most extreme religious principles with the advocacy of total sexual licence; they got their kicks, you might say, both coming and going. And what, now you mention it, about Rasputin?

It's South Africa's turn now. Mr Terre Blanche and his rivals in the organization are following the usual – indeed invariable – pattern among *groupuscules*; they are sub-dividing the membership into ever smaller *groupuscules*, each of which expels and anathematizes all the others. (There is always one figure who, while this is going on, makes off with the funds.) Actually, the misdemeanours of which Mr Terre Blanche is accused are very mild stuff, going no further than a liaison with a newspaper political columnist. (Thou canst not say I did it, never shake thy gory locks at me.) But South African standards in these matters are naturally more extreme than elsewhere, and the upshot will be that where there was one organization of kaffirbashers, singing a hideous but reasonably united song, there will now be six, each determined to shout all the others down. Good; noisy, but good.

I could never be a fanatic, even if I felt fanatical, because I am too impatient. Imagine waiting, year after year, decade after decade, generation after generation, for the trumpet to sound, only to see around you the same couple of dozen comrades, going as grey as you are and, though never wavering, no nearer to the goal. That is why – no joke, this – I cannot withhold my admiration for Vanessa and her heroic band. The organization – I dare not call it anything but Vanessa's Loonies, because I would quite certainly get it wrong, if only because it must have changed its name yet again – never did comprise more than a few hundred members, most of them her brother, and since the Great Split Forward it probably has to be numbered only in scores, if not dozens. Yet they are perfectly certain that any day now the British people will rise in revolt, hang their oppressors from the lamp-posts, and proclaim the Loon Republic. (Vanessa herself, incidentally, leads a perfectly respectable life.)

Mr Terre Blanche is not quite so badly off as that; he sails a sea that he knows is full of ships manned by people sympathetic to his views. If there are genuine moves towards equality in South Africa, many thousands will flock to the neo-Nazi banner, which is, among other things, the perfect excuse for Botha to do nothing – an excuse used with great success and satisfaction. But at any rate, those thousands rushing to join the crowd pushing the gates shut will have to decide whether they can associate with a man (and who says that Terre Blanche was the only one?) who has been caught at nookie.

As I have suggested, boredom must rank high among the ingredients in the extremism-and-sex cake-mixture. Very few participants in hopeless causes can put in a full and active day undermining the foundations of society, only to find next morning that the foundations of society are as sound as ever, and then put in another such exhausting day. What better antidote to boredom and disappointment alike could there be than the solace to be found in the arms of a member of the opposite sex – or the same sex, for that matter?

You can see that I have only touched upon a few of the very complex questions into which my sociology student will have to inquire. And I leave him to the task with one final question: can the boredom factor activate the explosion in the absence of the fanaticism factor? If it can, we can look forward, as more years of disappointment pass, to an epidemic of sexual shenanigans among the leading figures of the Labour Party. It won't touch Kinnock, of course, and Benn could give lessons in resisting temptation to Mother Teresa. But oh! Wouldn't it be wonderful if Gerald Kaufman ran amok!

The Times January 20th, 1989

Les neiges d'antan

I AM SORRY that *The Baker's Wife*, a musical directed by Trevor Nunn, has folded after a brief run at the Phoenix Theatre. I didn't get to see it, so I am in no position to say whether *vox populi* judged it correctly or not. But I must confess that when I say I didn't get to see it, it would be more accurate to say that I was reluctant to do so.

My lack of enthusiasm for a visit had nothing to do with the director, whom I hold in the very highest esteem, nor with the cast; and of the music and lyrics I naturally knew nothing. My problem was nostalgia, for I remember, and remember well, the film on which the show was based: Marcel Pagnol's *La Femme du Boulanger*. If you have handkerchiefs, prepare to wet them now.

Has there ever been a cinematic Golden Age to touch the years in France between, roughly, 1930 and 1945? I am no cinema buff, but I should be very surprised to hear of a challenger. The names alone constitute a roll of artistic honour which anywhere else would have taken half a century to match, not just a dozen years. The directors: René Clair, Julien Duvivier, Marcel Pagnol, Jean Renoir, Jacques Feyder, Marcel Carné. The players: Arletty, Raimu, Pierre Fresnay, Michèle Morgan, Fernandel, Louis Jouvet, Françoise Rosay, Jean Gabin, Michel Simon, Pierre Brasseur, Jean-Louis Barrault. The films: *Un Carnet de Bal, Hotel du Nord, Drôle de Drame, Pepé le Moko, Quai des Brumes, Le Jour se Lève, Les Bas Fonds, A Nous la Liberté, La Kermesse Héroique*, the trilogy of *Marius, Fanny, César, La Grande Illusion, La Règle du Jeu, Les Enfants du Paradis*.

Hindsight tugs at the sleeve; after all, even I am not old enough to have seen the films as they came out. But in the years immediately after the war they were to be seen in cinemas such as the Hampstead Everyman, and I gradually collected them all. I suppose you can get the lot on video these days.

The Thirties in France were rotten, corrupt years, worse even than in Britain. Our politicians were creatures without vision, courage or even competence; theirs mostly were in the pay of anyone who would fork out, from Stavisky to Hitler. Our generals were useless boneheads; theirs were thirsting to destroy *la putain République*. Our fascists were led by rubbish like Oswald Mosley; theirs by one of their greatest writers. (Do you know what Maurras cried out when, at the end of his trial for treason in 1946, he was pronounced guilty? '*C'est la revanche de Dreyfus!*')

The arts can never get far away from their time; inevitably the French cinema mirrored French society and its quality. But the approach was from an oblique angle. There was nothing political in such films, though *La Règle du Jeu* did paint the French upper classes in acid (Renoir rightly guessed that they would be too stupid to realize how they were being mocked), but there was a remarkable prescience in much of their finest work. You cannot fail to hear the note of something coming to an end; in film after film, the fragility of the world around the makers is at the heart of the work, and the shadows are closing in. I do not believe it is a coincidence that so many of the love films end in tragedy, or at the least in loss.

It is as though they knew that the world was done for; the elegiac, autumnal melancholy that pervades many of these masterpieces says so clearly. If so, there was another irony to come; many of the actors and film-makers got out of France before the fall (of these, most went to Hollywood, but few prospered there), but some stayed, and went on making films throughout the Occupation. Carné was finishing *Les Enfants du Paradis* even as the liberating armies rolled on towards Paris; I have heard said that half the Resistance were in the crowd scenes, impenetrably disguised as the poor of 1830 and ready to drop everything and fight as soon as the word came.

It came; but nothing since those years could match what had gone before. I saw a few films of the post-war French *nouvelle vague*; wretched, thin and lazy I thought them, and saw no more. And why should I, when I had such memories? There was a dire stage musical called *Fanny*, based on the Pagnol Marseilles trilogy, which I went to much later; it was at Drury Lane, and a stupendous flop. (One of the actors in it told me that at a weekday matinée just before it closed there were only sixty people in the house. Imagine that vast shell holding only that tiny handful of grains of sand!)

Of all that wonderful galaxy, surely Arletty was the greatest star of all. Her beauty – not just of face and form, but voice as well – was like something out of a great Renaissance painting, instead of the manufactured, empty artefacts of the Hollywood make-up rooms. I was dining once with Alan Moorehead; alone at a table on the other side of the restaurant there sat a beauty, no longer young. Alan said nothing, but went over and embraced her; the unheard dialogue ended in her shaking her head, gently, gracefully. Alan came back and said it was Arletty, whom he knew well, and the shake of the head was her reply to his invitation to join us. (Mind you; once, on the stroke of the midnight that ushered in a New Year, I kissed Ingrid Bergman.)

I suppose that *La Règle du Jeu*, if there is to be a choice of one masterpiece among many, is the greatest of all those creations. My own personal love, though (and I think it is most people's), is *Les Enfants du Paradis*, for the richness of the unfolding story, the artistry with which all the plots and sub-plots are woven, the perfect casting, above all the passion and love and heart with which it is filled. If the pre-war films announced the end of the world, Carné's war-end epic says 'I told you so.'

A crazy attempt to film an English farce, *The Lunatic at Large*, which ended up as *Drôle de Drame*, is the only one of my list that was pure comedy, though *A Nous la Liberté* (my own runner-up) is very funny; *La Grande Illusion*, Renoir's great shout of pity for mankind's delight in war (the shout was soon stifled in his throat – the film came out in 1937) manages to avoid the obviousness and didacticism which have sunk many such attempts to indict war; the Pagnol trilogy will survive for ever not because of the love story but for the antics of the Marseillais who frequent Raimu's bar; *Le Jour se Lève* (Gabin at his best) is the one which has the most intense form of the twilight I have described. Ah, the alarm clock in the final seconds! (I am not spoiling it for you; long before you get to the end you will have been so gripped by the story that you will have forgotten all about alarm clocks. I invariably have.)

I am sorry I didn't see *The Baker's Wife*, and I wish Trevor a huge success in whatever he does next; it's the least I can do in return for the memories he has awakened in me today. Incidentally, who played the dwarf in *La Kermesse Héroique*? And *was* he a dwarf?

The Times February 9th, 1990

From spark to furnace

Among the treasures of theatrical legend, there is one about a historical play in which a character has to rush on to the stage crying 'The Thirty Years War has broken out!' Let me be the origin of another such anecdote, as I rush on to the stage with a cry of 'The Russian Revolution has broken out!'

It has indeed. Thousands of journalists, politicians, commentators and historians have written and broadcast millions upon millions of words about the momentous events in Eastern Europe, yet the picture is still moving so fast that it is pointless to try to fix a label on it, and few have ventured to predict what may happen in the next few days, let alone years. How can we know what rough beast, its hour come round at last, is hurrying to Moscow to be born?

I, however, have no such inhibitions, and for a very good reason; if evidence of the past may be admitted when the present and future are to be considered, I insist on being consulted. For I once made a remarkable prediction, and I am now living through the last days of its incarnation. Hark.

In 1968, I was writing a column (five days a week!) for the *Daily Mail*. On this occasion I was abroad on holiday in Austria; I remember vividly the weird experience I had there (made all the more weird, for some reason, because it was my birthday). I was having breakfast in the dining-room of my hotel, and heard two men at the next table discussing, in German, some sensational thing that had happened. But since they both already knew what the sensational thing was, they had no need to describe it, and they confined their conversation to comment and opinion on it, from which it was impossible for me to deduce, without the key, what had happened. Feeling that if I leaned over and said sharply 'What are you two Krauts talking about?' I might be misunderstood, I got up and asked the concierge for the morning newspaper, where I learned that the Czech Spring had been crushed by Soviet troops.

When I got home, I picked up my column where I had left off; I naturally wrote many times about those dark and wicked days. And I ended one such comment with these words: 'Within twenty years, the Soviet Union will be free.' I think I am going to be a couple of years out in my prophecy, but these things cannot be exactly delineated, and I trust that my readers today will allow for a margin of error.

I am not clairvoyant; I am not a spy; I am not even cleverer than everybody else, or anyway not much. Whence, then, my certainty?

I based it first on something that nobody seemed to have spotted; at least nobody had spotted its enormous significance. I argued as follows. All the leaders of that heroic attempt to move the world from its orbit had come up through the Czechoslovak Communist Party; most were senior figures in the politburo, and all were, as far as could (or can) be discovered, orthodox members of it: Dubcek, Kriegel, Goldstuker, Svoboda, Sik and the rest sat round the table of power, while Pelikan presumably paced up and down outside. And at some point, they all looked at each other, and all realized that every impassive face they saw was impassive because its owner was waiting for somebody to speak.

Somebody spoke. Beside that colossal gesture of hope, faith, courage, vision and truth, the fact that a few months later it was brought to a brutal end counted, and still counts, for nothing; another one in the eye for the Manichee. Of course, the man who has the guns commands the action;

but whatever the force that guides the universe, it knows that, however long the waiting, guns will rust. From the moment I realized that the heroes of Prague were *not* secret conspirators or undercover agents or men longing for martyrdom, I knew without doubt that sooner or later, and my prophecy was for sooner, much sooner, there would be an equivalent, in some form, in the Soviet Union.

Why did I think that, and think it inevitable? There were several tangible reasons, and a single, overwhelming, intangible one. First, the practical considerations. For everybody other than the fellow travellers who simply lied about it, the obvious truth about the Soviet Union was, and is, that its system was, and is, incapable of feeding its people, housing its people, healing its people, transporting its people (except, alas, to prisons and concentration camps), keeping its people informed, teaching its people, even entertaining its people, and above all incapable of trusting its people. It could not, and today still cannot, keep its people clothed, warm, clean, hopeful, industrious, healthy, comfortable, honest or sober. Moreover, the system of lying as a way of life meant that however merciless the rulers, the massive pillars of the system were hollow, and thus could not stand for ever.

I remember a perfect proof of that contention. A group of West Germans, moved by a charitable impulse, began to send food parcels to an area of the Soviet Union in which there lived a substantial number of Soviet citizens of German descent. The parcels were confiscated, but that would have surprised nobody; even I was surprised at the nature of the regime's propaganda in response to what had happened. It was based on a campaign of scorn for the German well-wishers, who were pictured as sending a few miserable bits of coke to a coal-rich Newcastle; why should Soviet citizens, enjoying a lavish plenty of fresh, wholesome food at absurdly low prices, want the powdered egg (that, as I recall, was one of the goodies in the parcels) which those poor wretches in West Germany, hardly able to keep themselves in bread, insisted on sending?

Now the Soviet recipients of the charity knew better than the Germans or anyone else how bitter was their life, how empty were their stomachs, how bare the shops, how unimaginably exciting and lush the treasures in such parcels. Yet the propaganda did not simply tell them to shut up and refuse the charity; it told those pitiful beggars that they were, in fact, not pitiful beggars but rich burghers. That was, for me, another conclusive confirmation of the truth; a society which tells a man with red hair that in fact he has white hair, must sooner or later rot from within, its constitution diseased by the mad unreality it is obliged to proclaim.

The Soviet Union was indeed rotting from within. But I knew from my analogy with the Czechoslovaks that within the decay, my semi-mythical figure was steadily, patiently, working his way up through the system; he was doing any work, however dirty, that he was called upon to undertake; making any speeches, however lunatic, that he was called upon to deliver; agreeing with any course of action, however obviously ruinous, that he was called upon to support. And I realized that it mattered not at all whether the avatar was coming to free the Soviet Union or to make the Soviet Union efficient, or indeed whether he knew which course he intended to follow; I knew that whichever it was, it was doom for the system, and I knew that that doom was the ineluctable precursor of freedom.

I still don't know, or much care, what Mr Gorbachev wants to do; indeed, I don't even know whether he is the man of my prediction, or only the herald and trumpeter for the real thing. What matters – *and matters more than anything else in the world* – is that he has put his boot through the hollow pillars; the rest is, or will be, history.

The moment Mr Gorbachev made clear that whatever happened in the evil empire he would not lift a finger to help the colonial rulers, he had done the deed – the irreversible deed – that would put paid to communism not only in its colonies but in the mother country itself. For the wind of liberation, now blowing with hurricane force through the Eastern marches, cannot be diverted or tamed.

There was an amusing scene in the Soviet parliament (well, it's a sort of parliament) the other day: a number of deputies wanted to remove from the new constitution the section which made clear that the Communist Party would always rule, and that those who wanted a real Opposition would not be permitted to create one. I call it an amusing scene because although Mr Gorbachev got his way, so that the perpetuation of communist rule is now officially assured, the barrier to a multi-party system will – here is another prophecy – have collapsed long before the end of 1990.

But I promised you two reasons for the certainty with which I announced my prophecy twenty years ago; one, the tangible, I have now given in some detail. The other, however, is far more important, despite the impossibility of demonstrating its effect, or even its existence. Yet it does exist, and its effect is one of the very greatest truths of the world, as can be seen, at this moment, anywhere in Eastern Europe.

It is the fact that the longing for freedom is not just embedded in every true soul's heart. It is embedded so deep that it can only be part of evolution, so that a man or woman who is born without it is as strange as one born without a head, even though there are those who stifle it in themselves (such people have ruled the Soviet empire, and at this moment are having that rule prised from their grip).

The explosion of peaceful, mass revolt which has ended Soviet rule from Berlin to Bucharest – *and will shortly end it also from Lvov to Vladivostok* – was set off not by the eloquence of charismatic leaders, not by hatred of the oppressors, not by hope of gain, but by that tiny yet searing flame which is in us all, and which no Niagara of oppression, hunger or torture can ever extinguish. It was my belief in the power of that flame which, two decades ago, led me to my prediction, a prediction which is now coming true with a speed and completeness almost impossible to believe.

The captive nations believed in the power of the flame, and were not confounded; we who believed with them even in the darkest times salute and embrace them as our brothers and sisters in freedom. They bore the brunt; they tended the spark; to them goes the palm. Let them take it, as the sun climbs up their sky, in the words of Charles James Fox, himself an honoured member of the Company of the Flame: 'How much the greatest event it is that ever happened in the world! and how much the best!'

The Times December 26th, 1989

The fifth quartet

THE INCREASINGLY BIZARRE controversy over the T.S. Eliot Centenary Fund would hardly be complete without a contribution from me calculated to exacerbate feelings on all sides of the question. In case there is anyone who has not yet entered the maze, the few necessary facts can be quickly established. That indispensable institution the London Library is soliciting funds – a target of £100,000 has been mentioned – to set up a trust which would enable young or needy writers and researchers to make use of the library, because in the ordinary way there is a subscription which for some would be hard to meet. Because Eliot was the president of the London Library for thirteen years, and himself instrumental in starting a similar fund, the present appeal bears his name.

It also bears, among the list of patrons of the appeal, the names of some very distinguished Jews, including Sir Isaiah Berlin and Lord Goodman, and shortly after it was launched mutterings were heard suggesting that it was inappropriate for such people to be associated with such a cause, because Eliot was anti-Semitic.

That was the first damned silly thing said on the subject (not the last, alas), since it implies that you have to be Jewish to deplore anti-Semitism. As soon as this idea was mooted, however, everybody forgot what the money was *for*; I would not be surprised to learn that some people are now convinced that it is to buy jackboots for retired SS officers of limited means.

The next slice of baloney consisted of a claim that Eliot was *not* anti-Semitic, and indeed that (ah, what scents not of lavender rise from the familiar old phrase, unheard now for decades!) some of Eliot's best friends were Jews. Well, anti-Semitic he was – not, of course, in the Mosley-rabble mode, though not in the robust Chesterton or slimy Belloc manner either; his anti-Semitism was what I would call the genteel-demented. The anti-Semitic references in his work, which are sufficiently unambiguous to convict him of the charge, suggest that Jews are an alien, corrupt and debasing influence, a kind of impurity or bacillus in the blood of the body politic, allied with all those who in societies like ours, 'worm-eaten with liberalism', cannot be trusted to uphold the ancient virtues. (In his fascinating article on this page last week, Mr Anthony Julius quoted Eliot as claiming that since he was a Christian he couldn't be an anti-Semite, because that would be a sin. I look forward to the first burglar who declares that he cannot have done what the prosecution alleges, because that would have been a crime.)

As it happens, I have a soft spot for Eliot, because, more than thirty years ago, he wrote me a fan letter, and what is more, it began (as all fan letters do) 'I do not often write fan letters, but I am impelled . . .' I had hardly started on my illustrious career at the time, and you can imagine what I felt when I got that from the Great Cham of the day.

At this point, most sensible people will conclude that Eliot was anti-Semitic, but that the excellent cause to which his name has been attached by the London Library is in no way tainted by that fact, any more than would have been the case if they had chosen another past president, the late Michael Astor, and belatedly discovered that his mother had been a teetotaller.

But I want to go somewhat further, since there is an aspect of this story which is rarely discussed, and which has bedevilled consideration of anti-Semitism for many years now. I think it was Maitland who said that one of the problems of establishing historical truth was that we forget that things now in the past were once in the future. If you put Eliot's anti-Semitism in its historical context, you are likely to get a surprise.

I take it that there will be no dissent from my view that anti-Semitism is wrong and vile, whether practised by St John Chrysostom and Martin Luther or Dostoevsky and R*ch**d W*gn*r. But, hard though it is to say, not all anti-Semitisms are equal, and some are less culpable than others. Anti-Semitism, from the earliest ages till three quarters of the way through the eighteenth century, then again (at any rate in Russia) at the end of the nineteenth, and finally from the Nazis onward, is wholly inexcusable. The reason is that those who fanned the flames of *Judenhass* in those eras knew that the flames could and did destroy human beings, which of course was frequently the intention of the men who plied the bellows. Nobody knows how many Jews died in the pogroms through the centuries until Hitler came to put it into scientific practice: tens of thousands? Hundreds of thousands? Millions?

Anyway, it gradually died out; the Enlightenment helped, and Napoleon still more – so much so that the horrors of late Tsarist Russia must have seemed a dreadful throwback to less civilized times. This is not to say that anti-Semitism had disappeared; only that massacre was no longer the inevitable result of it. Discrimination and hostility remained; but Jews in all civilized countries, and a surprisingly large number of uncivilized ones, no longer went in fear of their lives.

It was in the lull before the final, terrible storm that Eliot and his like were free to express what they felt about Jews, *with no social disapproval*. If you read at all widely in the literature of, say, the period from the end of the First World War to the beginning of the Second, you will find, frequently in the writings of the wisest and gentlest of men, let alone the less so, expressions and attitudes about Jews which would today rule out their authors from decent society. The point is that decent society, in those days, was filled with people who had forgotten what anti-Semitism *had* led to, and who could not guess what it *would* lead to.

Indeed, the situation was stranger still; the prevalence of casual anti-Semitism was such that its use became quite unconscious; John Buchan has been accused of it, and defended stoutly, but both sides have missed the point. Buchan would have been genuinely indignant if he had been accused of anti-Semitism, for he would not have recognized the references in his work for what they were.

Much, much worse was Sapper. The Bulldog Drummond stories, which I hugely enjoyed in my youth, oozed anti-Semitism, but I am sure he had no intention of expressing a considered view of Jews; such attitudes were in him because they were all around him. Best-sellers like *The Constant Nymph* contained anti-Semitic attitudes, certainly without any considered thought. (Evelyn Waugh *was* an anti-Semite.)

In that atmosphere, anti-Semitic feelings could be expressed without embarrassment or guilt across almost any dinner table – even a table with Jews at it.

Remember that well-informed and sympathetic men, when the Holocaust was under way, could not believe the reports that were coming out of Occupied Europe; how much more difficult it was – indeed, it was impossible – to imagine it ten or twenty years before it happened.

For Eliot's generation the expression of anti-Semitic feelings was *safe*, therefore it was expressed. Now, we have no excuse; we know what it has led to, in the heart of Europe, in the lifetime of men and women not yet middle-aged. Those who strike matches today are playing with fire; yesterday, the world was non-flammable.

But I cannot find it in my heart to condemn Eliot and the others (Harold Nicolson was another) who thought that it was all right because they used only safety matches. There are, of course, no safety matches where anti-Semitism is concerned, but we must not judge the ignorant past by the knowing present.

Anti-Semitism is one of the oldest of the world's plagues; I doubt if it will ever be wholly eradicated. No two theories

as to its cause are the same, and no lasting cure is in sight.
But while the search for a vaccine is pursued, let not the
London Library fund suffer for doing no more than attach
T.S. Eliot's name to a most worthy project.

After all, perhaps one of those researchers who cannot
afford the library's subscription, and whose work will be paid
for by the fund, will there find the cure for anti–Semitism that
has eluded mankind for so many centuries.

The Times August 15th, 1988

Do you sincerely want to be swindled?

THERE IS AN amazing man on the *Sunday Times* called
Tony Hetherington (I presume he is not the DPP of
the same name, picking up something handy to eke out his
pension) whose job it is to deal with the financial queries and
problems of readers; it is something like the *FT*'s 'Briefcase',
only very much less genteel. *Very* much less genteel, for the
bulk of his work consists of chasing fly-by-night rogues who
have sweet-talked the customers into investing in a scheme
for pulling down St Paul's to get at the immense quantities
of gold, diamonds and oil which the salesman has no doubt
at all are to be found there for the trifling cost of the opencast
mining that will be all that is necessary.

I say that Mr Hetherington is amazing because his
technique, as far as I can see, is to bustle off, whenever
another such scam comes to light, find the perpetrators, and
bite them in the leg, having first thoughtfully coated his teeth
in that deadly arrow-poison of the South American Indians
so beloved by the thriller writers of yesteryear.

Where you and I, or at any rate you, would use
terms like 'dubious', 'thin ice', 'regrettable' and 'under investigation', he cheerfully sprinkles the fruits of his
researches with 'crooks', 'swindlers', 'rip-off', 'disappeared
with the money', 'ought to be in jail' and 'blatant forgery'.

More power to his elbow; it is not, however, Mr
Hetherington's answers that I wish to discuss today,
but his readers' questions. For this intrepid financial sleuth,
despite the gaiety of his style, cannot wholly disguise his
incredulity at the folly, ignorance, haste, carelessness, naïvety

and greed revealed by some of those who have come, weeping, to seek his assistance.

Almost all of us want to be richer than we are, even if we are very rich indeed. To be sure, there are exceptions; saints, ascetics, those who travel light and will not add even the weight of a wallet, a few whose material ambitions are fully satisfied and who therefore truly want nothing further. But the rest of us want more than we have, and the specially thoughtful sometimes wonder whether there could ever come a time when we didn't.

The crucial question, though, leaving out of consideration the exempted categories, is: what are we willing to do to increase our wealth? There is a wide spectrum available; at one end those who do nothing but sit on their bottoms and glower in envy at those better off, at the other end pickpockets and burglars. In between there is a substantial variety of options: hard work, gambling, exceptional ability, luck. And – perhaps covering the widest single band on the spectrum – gullibility.

Again and again in Mr Hetherington's column, and of course elsewhere (notably the courts), there is material a-plenty to demonstrate that the old truth needs bringing up to date: a fool and his money are indeed soon parted, and not only soon but very easily, too. In one of Mr Hetherington's recent revelations, it transpired that the company which was promising untold wealth was registered in the Dutch Antilles, and by the time it had collapsed, those who wanted their money back were obliged to seek it in the Turks and Caicos Islands (where, in any case, it was not to be found).

Now I have nothing against the Dutch Antilles or the Turks and Caicos Islands, other than that I have no idea where they are, but even if the prospectus bore the genuine signatures of two dozen assorted bishops, the least touch of prudence would surely cause me to wonder whether, if anything went wrong, it would be easy to deal, in the subsequent negotiations, with people so far away that a single exchange of letters might take a couple of months and, with the return half, arrive with some very exotic-looking stamps on the envelope.

Not only that; the shares had started life in Belgium under the name of Mercantile Benedict, but subsequently did a moonlight – indeed, a couple of moonlights – to Geneva and Barcelona, changing names on the wing to Textech NV, Textech Decorations, Marathon Financial and Grand Prix.

What did the investors in that shambles think they were doing, as the malodorous steam rose from it? I can tell you; they thought they were going to become rich. Some thought they would become *very* rich; some thought they would become millionaires, billionaires, trillionaires. Not one of them thought they might be ruined.

Why not? Even the least sophisticated racegoer who ever put a fiver on a horse did so in the full knowledge that the beast might run more slowly than its fellows; apparently, though, those who invested in Mercantile Benedict or any of its aliases gave no thought at all to the possibility that the business might fail, even if it wasn't run by a bunch of crooks. You may say that everybody recognizes a horse, whether fast or slow, but those who know nothing of companies and shares and high finance would not have understood a word of the talk that persuaded them to stump up.

But that is precisely the point. They not only knew nothing; they *knew* they knew nothing. Yet they signed because they wanted to be rich; and because they wanted to be rich, they persuaded themselves that their signature alone would achieve the riches they yearned for.

'They wanted to be rich'; as I wrote those words, an echo sounded in my head. 'Do you sincerely want to be rich?' was the slogan of Bernie Cornfeld, who was among the biggest thimble-riggers of the modern world; by the time his house of cards subsided with an unmelodious clatter, he had

raked in a billion pounds – a billion in 1970 money. Cornfeld
had a kind of twisted genius, and certainly a silver tongue;
he also recruited conmen in his own image (it was to them
that the famous question was addressed). Moreover, many
who should have known better – City analysts, financial
journalists – were not only taken in by him but seemed
positively eager to be taken in.

Well, they shouldn't have been. I am appallingly
ignorant of such matters; the Stock Exchange itself
is a mystery to me. Yet it was apparent to me from the
very first stirrings of Cornfeld's public appearance that no
one with fewer than six excellent new cars in the garage
should even consider buying a second-hand one from him,
even – which would have been unlikely – if it came with
a real engine under the bonnet and a slightly foxed MOT
certificate in the glove compartment, together with a pair
of gloves.

As I say, I know nothing of wheeler-dealers and their
wheels. I do, however, know a little about human
beings, and a lot about the English language, and I needed
no more than that to button my back-pocket in case Mr
Cornfeld went by. A rough and ready test, certainly; but
at least I realized that a test would be required.

That, no doubt, brands me as one who does *not*
sincerely want to be rich, but I plead not guilty. I *do*
want to be rich, enormously rich, stupendously rich; but I
know that I cannot become so without certain very great
talents that I do not have, together with an unremitting
application that I am not willing to embark upon.

In other words, my desire for riches is subservient
to my reason. You may say that I am cleverer than the
poor devils who put their life savings into Upintheclouds
Investments Pty, registered in Pitcairn Island; no, I am not,
or if I am it is irrelevant. You don't need to be a genius or
a sage to realize – realize, not know, let alone work out –
that there is no easy path to great wealth (or to anything

useful) because if there were, the poor would be in a very small minority, and everybody else would be stinking rich.

That is manifestly not so. Yet the glitter from a heap of gold blinds thousands – millions – to the obvious truth. I look forward to many more entertaining Sundays reading Mr Hetherington's column. But you will never find me in it.*

The Times March 23rd, 1989

---

*Some eight or nine months after Mr Hetherington's account of the company which fetched up in the Turks and Caicos Islands, calling itself Grand Prix, a reader wrote to him to say that *he* had bought for £2,177 shares in Grand Prix *over the telephone*, and then, in the next few months, invested further sums in Grand Prix, viz., £4,056, £20,787 and £37,088, but could now not get an answer from the company, not even over the telephone.

Two firkins make a Gill

THE RECENTLY PUBLISHED life of Eric Gill, by Fiona MacCarthy, has led to two interesting debates. Neither concerns the quality of her research, writing or balance; it is a comprehensive and understanding work, full of insight and interest, and the general opinion among the reviewers, which I fully share, is that it is a considerable addition to modern biography.

What, then, are the two arguments about? Only the second one interests me much, but some reference to the first is essential. Miss MacCarthy tells us that she has been widely criticized, not least by members of Gill's family, because she disclosed for the first time the full pattern of his sexual life and thus violated Solon's Law, the tradition which bids us speak only good of the dead. She defends herself spiritedly, even waspishly, but she really had no need to; the convention has long ceased to serve any useful or honest purpose, and anyway there is nothing titillating or lubricious in her book, and she handles the more *outré* side of Gill's life with tact and discretion.

Of those who have thus accused her, she says this:

> One mistake they make is in thinking biography judgemental when it is fundamentally descriptive and creative. I am there to record things which actually happened. I am there to capture people *as they were*.

And so say all of us, at any rate those of us who know what biography and biographers are for.

But if the code of practice for biographers precludes

them from being judgemental, I have to insist on the right
of readers to be as judgemental as they please; indeed, I
would go almost as far as to say that they had a *duty* to
judge.

Gill was indeed an artist: sculptor, engraver, portraitist.
His work was uneven, but at its best was very good indeed,
and as a craftsman – designer, woodworker, stonemason,
typographer – he was close to genius. His works of art are
in museums and galleries; his works of craft are still widely
in use. Without doubt, he contributed substantially to the
beauty in the world.

He was also given to having sexual intercourse with his
pubescent daughters, including what are called 'unnatural
practices', to incest with many of his large number of sisters,
to bestiality (in the legal meaning), to exercising the *droit de
seigneur* with young female servants, and to the seduction of
most of his female acquaintance, whether married or not.
Oh, I almost forgot; he also had intercourse with his wife.
Eric Gill must have been one of the most extreme cases of
satyriasis known to sexual psychopathology.

It is hardly his fault, or his biographer's, that these revelations have been made while the Cleveland affair continues
to reverberate; still, we can count, and by my reckoning Gill
could have notched up a total of several hundred years in prison, not counting the stretches for his homosexual activities,
which were then illegal.

He obviously bore a charmed life, for he was never exposed
(er – that is, he was never found out); it is difficult to believe,
though it must be so, that none of his partners or victims
ever got sufficiently resentful to shop him. But what makes
Gill not just a lecher beyond compare, but one of the most
frightful hypocrites in history, is that he professed a devout
Catholicism (he was a convert), and life in the communes he
ran was crammed to bursting with religious practices; Gill
himself was, or thought he was, a lay Dominican friar, and
wore beneath his habit a symbolic cord known, so help me,

as 'the girdle of chastity'. God knows how Miss MacCarthy, after all that, comes to the conclusion that he was not a humbug, indeed that he was 'a tragic figure'.

History is replete with great artists who were very badly flawed human beings, and there have been many arguments about how much of the flaw should be condoned for the art, though the answer is obviously none; the two categories, though they inhabit the same person, must be judged separately.

Yet I have been amazed at the way Gill has been treated by the book reviewers. The tone of many has been equivocal, with at most a curt dismissal of his iniquity and the implication that his practices were mere trifles which should hardly count in estimating him. And such opinions are not even based on the Dubedat theory; Shaw's artist-villain certainly thought that his art excused his behaviour, but few of the reviewers have taken refuge in that argument. No; they simply shrug it into a minor matter in itself. Of the couple of dozen reviews I have read, only David Pryce-Jones says plainly that the book 'puts paid to any idea that Gill might have been either lovable or great'.

But it is Mr Patrick Nuttgens, the reviewer in *The Tablet* (the Catholic weekly), who seems to sum up the kind of *tout pardonner* monocular morality which is still floating around in our society, presumably marking time before the abolition of morality altogether. Mr Nuttgens's family knew Gill well; though he was only ten when Gill died, he clearly has many first-hand memories, and many more trustworthy second-hand ones. Carefully weighing the evidence of Gill's diaries (they recorded his sexual activities, including the criminal ones), Mr Nuttgens asks: 'Was he, the celebrated Catholic *paterfamilias*, founder of the cell of good living and pronouncer of morality, simply a humbug and a hypocrite?' And he answers his own question thus: 'I think not. He was far too honest, with himself and ultimately with God . . . His sexual behaviour was never violent, it was an expression of love.' And he ends his review with a striking passage; of the book, he says that:

> It does not change what anyone like me, growing up in the midst of the Gill ethos, learned at first hand – that life is to be seen not in terms of good and bad, nice and nasty, fresh and foul, but enjoyed as a wonderful, glorious and often hilarious totality.

Well, I don't know. You *could* say that a man who does what I have described to his teenage daughter is enjoying a wonderful, glorious and often hilarious totality, and even that the practice is to be seen not in terms of good and bad, nice and nasty, fresh and foul; indeed, you might go so far as to say that the action was an expression of love. But if you do, it is hard to see how you could call anything at all wrong, in any circumstances. Mr Nuttgens goes quite close to taking that very view, and I am tempted to ask him – well, I shall succumb to the temptation – whether he thinks that sexual abuse as in the recent events should carry no penalty if it was an expression of love. (I forbear to ask him how the jury is to know.)

We are all frail; all sinners; all no holier than thou. But there are degrees of sin, and some of the degrees amount to wickedness, and not a few to evil. Yet it seems that because a biographer refrains from judgement, nobody else may point out that the subject of the biography was a revolting criminal. It is claimed by Miss MacCarthy, and I am in no position to dispute it, that the children Gill abused did not grow up psychologically damaged; it is interesting to see how many reviewers seemed to cling to that claim in order to avoid judgement, though nobody could now be sure. (And what about the sisters with whom he committed incest?)

Everything, I shall be told, is relative. So much the worse for everything. Eric Gill was a fine artist; he was also a scoundrel. But it is only possible to say so if there are real standards against which to measure his behaviour. I think there are; imperfect, leaky and fuzzy round the edges, but real. Instinctively, we know and recognize them, and we know also that if they fall, the integument of the world will fly asunder, and chaos will come again. And that is why I thought it worth saying these things today, even at the risk of being told that I have failed to enjoy life as a wonderful, glorious and often hilarious totality, and failed also to realize that there is more than one way (if you see what I mean) of expressing love.

The Times March 13th, 1989

Camouflaging the dead

FEW TODAY WILL dispute the familiar claim: war is hell. Perhaps, though, the definition should be further refined. As all the history of warfare testifies, there are circles in hell, and the deeper the circle, the greater the torment of the damned. And surely the lowest depths of war are reached with the remorse felt by those who, in error or confusion, have killed their own comrades.

Call back yesterday, bid time return; the plea is made in vain when the hideous realization dawns upon those who have shelled their own side's position, or fired in the dark at a shadowy figure who turned out to be a returning scout.

It is safe to say that there has never been a war without these fatal errors; Miltiades' troops at Marathon must have made as many such tragic blunders as did the armies of Iraq and Iran only the other day. And however brief are the hostilities, there is always time for an irretrievable mistake.

The Falklands conflict was no exception. We shall never know, any more than Argentina will, how many deaths were caused by mistaking a friend for an enemy. But as it happens, we know – or, more precisely, we *now* know – the details of one such incident. And I think it is worth discussing, not so much because of what happened in the split second of accidental death, but because of what happened in the six years that followed it.

The facts are few, and conclusive. On June 6th, 1982 (the anniversary of D-Day, which must have had its own share of irretrievable mistakes), Major Michael Forge, Staff Sergeant John Baker, Staff Sergeant Christopher Griffin and

Lance-Corporal Simon Cockton were flying by helicopter to establish a signal station ahead of the British troops advancing on Port Stanley. They were forbidden to use radio contact in the air, as a precaution. Not far away, the helicopter showed on the radar screen of HMS *Cardiff*. It was close to a flight path used by the Argentine forces ferrying supplies; as the *Cardiff*'s officers had no information about British air movements in the vicinity, and the radar blip did not respond to attempts at contact, the order was given to fire at it. Two missiles were launched; the second blew the helicopter and the four men in it to pieces.

Now one thing must be made clear immediately; nobody on the ship was incompetent, nobody was negligent, nobody was lazy, nobody was drunk. The rules of engagement, and the circumstances, obliged the *Cardiff*'s officers to take the action they did. Later that day, they learned indirectly that friendly aircraft had been in the vicinity at the time they had fired, and later still that an army helicopter had been lost.

When such things happen, it is rightly deemed unwise for the authorities to publicize the details immediately; the effect on morale can be devastating. In this case, however, the tragedy took place only eight days before the Argentine surrender. A reasonable further lapse of time could properly have been added, and thereafter we might assume that the details could, should and would be disclosed. The grief of the families and friends of the dead would inevitably have been made more bitter, but the knowledge that no one had been negligent, and the episode a true tragedy, would have helped to assuage their pain.

But that is not what happened; not what happened at all. The Ministry of Defence, for reasons that have still not been explained, decided on a cover-up. For six years it prevaricated and delayed, dissembled when it could and lied when it couldn't, and if it had not been for the tenacity of one elderly lady, it would be doing so still. She is Mrs Winifred Cockton, mother of the lance-corporal who died, and she was determined that the truth about her son's death would be known.

It is not clear exactly why she became suspicious. Soon after the Falklands war ended there was an inquest on her son and the three others who died; the MoD claimed that the helicopter had been shot down by an Argentine Sidewinder missile. Perhaps the ministry's earlier claim that it had crashed in bad weather – whereas it was discovered that the weather was fine – had alerted her not to take on trust the word of those who could so smoothly change their story.

Some of those who gave evidence at the first inquest seem truly to have believed that it was an enemy missile that hit the helicopter, but when Mrs Cockton's single-handed campaign finally forced the setting up of a board of inquiry, *four years* later, the truth oozed out. Yet still the MoD plied the mop, and it took another two years before a second inquest – ordered by the High Court – revealed the truth. (Among other revelations it uncovered was the testimony of the expert witness who had taken part in the earlier investigation; he said he had been 'severely hampered' and subjected to 'pressure' to say it *was* an Argentine missile.)

As far as I know, nobody has been dismissed or reprimanded, let alone prosecuted, for organizing or taking part in the six years of deceit. Mrs Cockton says she is not interested in being reimbursed for the £7,000 she has spent in her campaign to unveil the truth, though as far as I know she has not yet been offered it. But just as I have not concentrated on the tragedy itself, I am not concerned to demand retribution either. What I want to know is: why?

Why, that is, did not the MoD and the Army face, and tell, the truth? No one was trying to protect a guilty friend, for there were no guilty friends. No one could have feared a court-martial, for any such tribunal would have acquitted anyone charged. No one could have believed that what happened was so shockingly unprecedented that it should never see the light of day, for something of the sort must have happened in every battle in history.

We all find it hard to admit that we have made a mistake. But not even that will explain what happened, because the mistake was made in the Falklands, and the cover-up was organized in London.

There is no evidence that the *Cardiff*'s officers would not have shouldered the tragic blame if the facts had been presented to them, but the words of the officer who took the fatal decision are significant:

'We said we had shot something down in the Stanley area and received a signal back saying an Army Air Corps helicopter had been lost in that area at that time. *But that was the last I heard of the affair until the Board of Inquiry in 1986.*'

My italics. And they draw me towards a conclusion. The disease of secrecy, which spreads like dry rot in an old house, has so infected the people involved in this story that they cannot see why what they did was unnecessary as well as disgraceful. Something happened which should not have happened; it was nobody's fault, and it had happened thousands of times in the past, but because it *should not* have happened, the lie that it *didn't* happen must be told.

Must? Yes, in the minds of those responsible. Something has gone wrong, therefore we must conceal it. If we must conceal it, it must be important. Blankets, please, gentlemen.

The impending secrecy legislation announced by the Government will be coming up shortly. Mr Richard Shepherd, the Conservative backbencher, and his courageous band, who were so narrowly beaten (only 37 votes) in their attempt to introduce a real Freedom of Information Bill, will naturally fight hard for their principles and our liberties.

And they had better, because one thing I know beyond conjecture is that somewhere in the Government's legislation there will be a clause which would make forever impossible Mrs Winifred Cockton's six-year campaign to find and reveal the truth about the death of her only son. May his memorial be its defeat.*

The Times November 1st, 1988

*There was no excuse or reply from the Ministry of Defence or any other official source, let alone apology. And the legislation was passed unamended.

Thoughts from the darkness

MANY YEARS AGO, I predicted that one day, Wagner's laundry-lists would be found in an attic, whereupon a vast industry would spring up; Wagner scholars would busy themselves with the publication of annotated, facsimile and Variorum editions, and within a few years there would be monographs and Ph.D. theses discussing such themes as *Symbolism and Meaning in Wagner's Collars* or *Lohengrin and Underpants. New Sources of Wagner's Inspiration*.

I thought I was joking, but I arrived in Bayreuth for the new *Ring* to learn that the *laundry-lists have been found*. They take the form of a vast sub-Shakespearian drama, combining the themes of *Hamlet* and *Macbeth* (and a good deal else), which Wagner wrote between the ages of thirteen and fifteen. Well, many precocious schoolboys scribble romantic rubbish as adolescence begins, but only in the case of Wagner is it taken seriously 160 years later.

Taken seriously? The programme-book for *The Mastersingers* devotes 167 pages to it; it starts with an essay by Isolde Vetter, adorned with forty-eight footnotes and couched in that ghastly jargon which passes for learning in Wagner studies, and ends with the entire text of the work (*sics* and all), which is called *Leubald*. It is to be published by Schott's in the autumn, and a critical edition will be included in volume 31 of Wagner's *Collected Works*. (I fought my way right through *Leubald*; I put it like that because the play is, quite literally, unreadable.)

Let me dwell a little longer on those programme-books. There is one for each opera of the season, and they are without question the most beautifully, lavishly and scrupulously produced theatrical programmes in the world. Unfortunately, the esoteric twaddle of which they largely consist makes me wish, every time, that either Richard Wagner or I (but not both) had never been born. This year, the torment is made worse by the inclusion of thirty-seven opinions of *The Ring* by writers from all over the world, almost all of them weird nonentities, culminating in Marion Bradley, who says she was *thrilled* to be asked, because she never thought her opinion would be worth anything. Oh gosh, girlie, it isn't.

In other words, the sickening tide of the cult of Richard Wagner, which began in his lifetime, still flows unabated – indeed, more strongly than ever. There are, of course, detailed studies of the works and lives of his few equals; the literature on Beethoven, Mozart, Schubert, Bach, is very substantial. But the Wagner library is *much* larger than all of those together.

Why is it that the ore of the Wagner-mines alone is inexhaustible, and the efforts of the miners likewise? Alas, there is an answer, and it covers those who cannot break free of his spell as well as those who hate him and every bar of his music. It is that he alone in all genius knows all our most terrible secrets, and forces us to know ourselves as we are – or, worse, as we might be. Wagner is Honorary Psychiatrist Extraordinary to the art of music, and you will find him in the third scene of *Das Rheingold*, under the name of Alberich, wielding a whip over the workers in his power (including his brother) as they dig deeper and deeper to tear out of the innocent earth the truth about human beings. He does it by dealing impartially and implacably with the most sublime of humanity's attributes – love, heroism, nobility, truth – and also the darkest of humanity's secrets – hate, treachery, incest, murder. And what moves both those who are his slaves and those who are his declared enemies is his iron insistence on the most dreadful truth of all – that good and evil are equally available to all, entwined like the rope

of the Norns in *Götterdämmerung*. Steeling myself, I stood in
front of the Festpielhaus bookstall and began to count the
books by and about him: I ran, shrieking for a sausage and a
beer, when I got to eighty-seven. *My* dissertation will be
called *Sausages and Phallic Symbolism in the Works of Wagner*.

There is, I fear, some galumphingly obvious sexual symbolism in Harry Kupfer's production; Siegfried waggles the
sword about between his legs, and Brünnhilde launches a
violent lesbian assault on her sister Waltraute (my *dear*, those
Valkyries, whatever *next*!). The cast spend most of their time
running about or crawling – nobody is allowed to walk or
stand still; Siegfried wears a boiler suit, which I suppose is
reasonable since in Act One he is living in an abandoned
boiler; the gods all carry transparent suitcases, which are all
empty. (Yes, Mr Kupfer, we do get the point; can we eat
our buns now?)

The *Ride of the Valkyries* is accompanied by the progress
upstage of a multitude of hideously mummified figures (I
never knew that Valhalla was supposed to be a leprosar-
ium); Siegfried and Brünnhilde live in a coal cellar, the
Norns spin their rope among a forest of television aerials
planted at the entrance to a multi-storey carpark; as for the
Family Hunding, their rough hut was clearly furnished at
pre-Conran Heal's, with a marked Japanese influence in the
pitched roof and the wallpaper. Only the Porsche is missing.

It is not all like that; Kupfer, though a wretchedly limited
man, is an ingenious one, and some things came off splen-
didly; the use of lasers was exciting, the gantries and catwalks
of Nibelheim worked well, even in British Telecom yellow;
the giants were a triumph – fully 14 feet high, and moving
on invisible wheels – at one point, Froh had to skip nimbly
out of harm's way. ('Cause of death: run over by mechanized
giant.') And the Woodbird appeared in a dangerously unca-
nonical but most striking form, though a world-renowned
authority on songbirds whom I met in the interval assured
me that the whole scene was based on a fallacy; apparently
they do not sing while flying, only when they come to rest.

(Presumably the production will be panned in the *Ornitho-logical Quarterly*.)

But in the end, it won't do, if only because Kupfer, when-ever faced with a real difficulty, runs away from it. Take those giants; because the men inside them can do nothing but sing, they cannot pick up the gold, let alone quarrel over it, so there is no visible reason for Fafner to murder his brother. There is no attempt to deal with the problem – the people out there are only the audience, and what do they matter? So the production gets progressively lazier and more contemptuous, till it peters out in the clichés of the day before yesteryear, which Kupfer doubtless thinks the last word in modernity; where he comes from, it probably is.

He comes from East Germany. Now the physical brutality of Siegfried towards Mime in Kupfer's production is more marked than any I have ever seen; perhaps he has a brother in the Vopos, who showed him how it is done. Very well; but if there is one opera-house in the world where it should not be permitted for a production to have a character representing a Master Race seize a member of a race he is shown as hating and despising *and make to thrust him into a furnace*, then that opera-house is Bayreuth. Millions of a despised race went into furnaces by the order of the Wagner family's most loved and honoured regular patron; if Kupfer, next year, has not removed this filthy gesture from his production, Wolfgang, who will remember the honoured guest, no doubt with mixed feelings, as Onkel Adolf, had better do so for him. (Jeremy Isaacs told me that when the scene took place, the man sitting behind him laughed.)

And yet, musically, this came very close to the *Ring* of my dreams. Barenboim, whose first *Ring* it is, has cleared out the old guard almost completely; I cannot remember a year with so many leading roles taken by singers new to Bayreuth – with, I am happy to say, the Brits to the fore: John Tomlinson was a Wotan of formidable power and

beauty of tone, Graham Clark a deadly, ice-cold Loge and
an amazingly acrobatic and mellifluous Mime; Linda Finnie
a Fricka more human and intimate than most (and she threw
in a Norn and a Valkyrie as well).

More to the point, Siegfried Jerusalem is the conquering
hero the world's opera-houses, as well as Brünnhilde, have
been waiting patiently for; he is so far singing only the
Siegfried Siegfried, but when he has mastered the *Götterdämmerung* one as well, the role is his wherever he wants to
sing it – the voice is beautiful, ringing and equal to all the
tasks Wagner set it. (But he may be called to higher things.
He fielded his bouquet – they are flung from the end of the
front row – with sensational skill; it crossed in front of his
body shin-high, and he had the light in his eyes as he dived
for a brilliant left-handed catch. Bayreuth be damned; this
man is needed in the slips for the MCC.) There is also a
sensational new Korean Hagen, Philip Kang, and an equally
exciting new Alberich, Günter von Kannen, with a voice
almost too rich and fine for the character's evil. (Brünnhilde?
Hm.) As for the conductor, Barenboim had been criticized
for uncertain tempi; by the time I got there they had largely
settled down, and his loving, rich but restrained version
reminded me of the years with Kempe at Covent Garden,
and none the worse for that.

At Bayreuth, the mustard for those sausages is provided in a
bucket – a large, green plastic bucket. Well, it is not the only
thing that comes by the bucketful in Wagner's opera-house.
I begin to think it is time for me to pack up the entire box of
tricks, cut the puppet-master's strings, and free myself from
lifelong bondage. For great genius that he was, perhaps the
most original figure in all art, he was nevertheless a man of
his time, which was the second half of the nineteenth century.

What do I want all that musical mahogany for, what
do I want with the horrible *Stabreim*, that never was talked
by land or by sea, why do I tolerate the entire Wagnerian
system of the *leitmotivs* (I think it was Saint-Saens who

said it was like meeting a lunatic at a party who keeps giving you his visiting-card), why do I put up with the gibberish, the reverence, the interminable hours in Stygian darkness while the characters review the plot and ask each other idiotic riddles? (There is only one laugh in the *Ring*; it is unintentional, and you have to wait from Tuesday to Friday for it. It is also not very funny.)

There is damnable darkness in these works; what in God's name am I doing, wallowing where Hitler wallowed? Even the audience demonstrates the triumph of the Manichee; did you know that booing, by however few, can always be heard over cheering, by however many? Why don't I just *retire* from Wagner, and spend the rest of my life with Mozart and Schubert, who show me the way to a real heaven, not that gimcrack Valhalla, and with Beethoven, who tells me that for the brave there is heaven even on earth?

Because I stayed on for *The Mastersingers* (another success for the Brits – Alan Opie as a marvellously bureaucratic Beckmesser), and the glorious human goodness of that tremendous score not only soothed my soul to quiet, but told me that my ravings about the *Ring* will dissolve instantly every time, as soon as that E flat steals out into the darkness. And so they will; because for all the fear and cruelty and beastliness it contains and all the beauty and passion and excitement, as well as all the intolerable demands it makes of us over those sixteen hours, it is among the world's profoundest and most certainly eternal masterpieces, forever challenging us to confront and absorb it. And because, finally, it tells us, in sounds utterly different from anything else in music, that those creatures from the depths of the human psyche are in us all, and that unless we face that truth, as Siegfried faces the fire, we shall never heal the split that rives us, and be whole. Believe me; when I say I shall never come to Bayreuth again, I lie.

The Times September 3rd, 1988

Dilemmas of life and death

HAVE YOU EVER wondered what would have happened at the Judgement of Solomon if neither woman had said a word? Would Solomon have cut the child in two? We would hope not; but remember that the decision had been handed down, and it was stayed only because the real mother withdrew her claim. Would the King's logic have compelled him to carry out the sacrifice?

This question is neither so abstruse nor so irrelevant as you might think, let alone wish. It is beginning to agitate the people of the United States, and before it is decided it will have agitated them a good deal more. In its modern form, it is the case of the State of Massachusetts *v.* David and Ginger Twitchell, of Boston; the charge is manslaughter, and the defendants have pleaded not guilty. Only the first formalities have been completed; the case proper starts on June 1st. But the bones of it are clear, and stark bones they are, too.

The Twitchells are charged with the manslaughter of their two-year-old son, Robyn, who died from a bowel obstruction. When he became ill, they refused to seek medical advice or treatment because they are both Christian Scientists, rejecting the very concept of illness as it is generally understood. Instead of calling a doctor or taking the child to hospital, they called in two Christian Scientist spiritual healers, who prayed over the boy. Their prayers proved inefficacious, and he died.

Some twenty years ago there was a similar case in Massachusetts. A woman follower of Christian Science was charged with manslaughter in similar conditions when her child died without medical attention. She was convicted, and the fierce public debate that then ensued ended in legislation in these terms: 'A child shall not be deemed neglected or to lack proper physical care for the sole reason that he is being provided remedial treatment by spiritual means alone in accordance with the tenets and practice of a recognized church or religious denomination by a duly accredited practitioner thereof.'

The defendants will rely on that clause; the prosecution insists that the statute did not relieve them of their responsibility when the child's life was in danger.

The first thing to be said is that anyone who came at once to a firm conclusion, one way or the other, on no more knowledge of the case than my exposition, should be ignored. This tale is a tragedy in two senses, not one; the death of the child is obviously a tragedy, but the dilemma makes it a double one, and it is the dilemma that I wish to discuss, precisely because it *is* a dilemma.

Let us get one or two things out of the way quickly. The achievements of spiritual healing, even allowing for a substantial number of charlatans engaged in it, are manifold; to anyone with a mind not locked and barred against any idea sufficiently unusual to cause fear in that mind, the evidence is conclusive. But, like conventional medicine, it is not infallible. It might have worked with the Twitchells' infant; however, it didn't.

Few, I think, would deny the Twitchells' right to refuse orthodox treatment *for themselves*, even at the cost of their lives. But has anyone the right to deny the ministrations of secular science to those who are too young, or ill, or lacking in understanding, to make their own choice? There is, of course, no certainty that orthodox medicine will succeed when unorthodox has failed. But in this case, it was not given a chance.

It is not for us to interpret the laws of Massachusetts; that will be done in due course by the appropriate authorities. But the moral verdict is another matter, and it here has to deal with the claims of religion. Does profoundly held belief entitle anyone to risk or cause harm to another?

There is an obvious *reductio*: what about someone who insists that he is a committed Aztec, and that his religion demands that he should undertake human sacrifice? Absurd; but would you like the job of drawing the line between the Aztec's claims and those of Christian Science? And if you would, where would you get a pencil with a point sufficiently fine to do the job?

The Jews, I believe, are in no doubt; any dietary or sabbatical or similar practice enjoined by their religion is waived in a matter of life and death. (Very pragmatic people, the Jews.) I take it that no one would refuse the right of vegetarian parents to bring up their children without meat; but what if their vegetarianism is rooted in profound spiritual beliefs concerning the right to life of all sentient creatures, and one of the vegetarian children develops a rare medical condition curable only by drinking the blood of newly killed chickens?

If you argue that no parents have the right to harm their children, what is your answer if the parents declare that to harm their immortal souls is a much greater wrong than to harm their ephemeral bodies? Can you prove such parents mistaken? We could, of course, propose a compromise; the devout parents might try prayer, and then, if it doesn't work, fall back on the doctors. But what if the child dies anyway – would the parents not consider themselves accurst for ever more, believing, as they undoubtedly would, that the child's death followed from their breaking the rules? (And suppose they were right in that belief?)

Think about those rules. Most of us would think it sinful (or whatever term would be used by those who become nervous at the very word) to neglect any possibility of saving a life. But have we the right to outlaw those for whom, in certain circumstances, it is sinful to use certain means for saving the same life? Can we distinguish between the two feelings of sin? If so, how? Certainly not by counting heads; mere majorities cannot establish such categories.

And there is another argument for the defence, though only the boldest Christian Scientist, I suspect, would use it. What about those people who trust in orthodox medicine for their dependants as well as themselves, and are told by the doctors that a condition for which treatment is sought is incurable and fatal? If they accept the verdict and reconcile themselves to the imminent death of a child, are they not culpable in failing to seek an alternative remedy in the ministrations of spiritual healers?

There are other echoes. One of the reasons we may find the Christian Scientist's stand alarming, or even abhorrent, is that we have come to put our trust wholly in the hands of the doctors, and persuaded ourselves that they are gods who have only to utter the sacred mantra ('Keep taking the tablets', for instance) to bring the moribund, if not the dead themselves, back to full health. Many of the doctors know what dangerous nonsense that is, and are weary of telling the truth to those who will not listen; but I cannot see the notion being eradicated in a mere century or two.

If you have followed me this far, you will have noticed a striking lack of certainty in my views. But, as I have said, certainty in a matter so uncertain is deeply suspect. The only thing I *am* sure of is that I am glad I do not have to sit on the Massachusetts jury who will try the case. King Solomon didn't know when he was well off.

The Times May 9th, 1988

Last post

IN BOOK VIII, Herodotus, describing the messengers of the Great King, said these memorable words: 'Neither snow, nor rain, nor gloom of night stays these couriers from the swift conclusion of their appointed rounds.' The words are inscribed on the General Post Office building in New York; they are not, however, inscribed on the General Post Office building in London, and I think I have just discovered why.

A few months ago, the postal delivery service where I live collapsed abruptly, completely and disastrously. Before the collapse, I could reckon on receiving my first post nearer 8 a.m. than 8.30; on Saturdays it was usually somewhat earlier, and on Mondays somewhat later, for obvious reasons. From the moment the Martian spaceships struck, however, the change was literally from one day to the next. And it was no mere trivial change; the post *never* came before 10 a.m., rarely before 11, and often not until well into the afternoon. On Saturdays, it sometimes didn't come at all.

Now before you all draw attention to the fact that the Outer Hebrides are a long way away, and I should be grateful to get any post at all, considering the gales the postman has to contend with, I must point out that I live not only in central London, but in a part of London so central that you could make the hole in a gramophone record out of it; besides, I was not yearning for improvement, only for the service I had had without fail for many years.

You will not be surprised, if you know our beloved Post Office, to learn that no advance warning of any kind was given; nor, of course, was any explanation provided *post facto* (if you see what I mean). No matter; if an explanation is not forthcoming of its own accord, it will be, I reasoned, only a moment's labour to ask for one and get it.

Most politely, I wrote to the central post office for my area (West London District, it is called), to ask what had happened, and why. I discovered that the department to write to was called 'Customer Care', a most promising title; I had visions of rows and rows of Post Office officials, sitting at desks, caring like anything for their customers. I sat back and awaited my ration of care.

This, I should say, was about a month after the disaster had struck. I wrote on February 9th, silence ensued. I wrote again on February 21st, enclosing a copy of my earlier letter; a week or two later, I received a letter from Messrs Care, Like and Billy-o. It revealed that the writer had not the slightest idea that the delivery service now compared unfavourably with that in up-country Burundi (this, I would remind you, was now a good while after Pearl Harbour); clearly, Mr Care was not in cahoots with Mr Customer, or with anybody else for that matter. But he did promise that he would 'look into' the situation, and let me know what was – or, more precisely, was not – going on.

On March 13th I received a letter from the old firm, only from a different member of it. To avoid any but collective blushes, let us call my first correspondent Mr Joe Carefrightfully and my second Mr Fred Careterribly. Fred actually began by apologizing for the problems; aha, I said, all is, or shortly will be, well. Alas, he spoilt the impression of the first sentence in the second. 'As you are aware,' he wrote, 'we have just undertaken a major revision.'

Why he thought I was 'aware', since neither he nor anybody else had seen fit to tell me anything at all (including Joe Carefrightfully, who at least had the excuse that he wasn't aware himself), was not at all clear. He then went on to say – oh, well, I might as well quote the whole thing, together with my parenthetical comments:

. . . inevitably problems will occur [*actually, the problems had already occurred*], but in the long term these will be eliminated [*ah, but how long is a term?*] and as a result the standard of service achieved will be improved. [*At this point, a man less temperate in speech than I might have said that the standard of service recently achieved could hardly deteriorate.*] In the interim [*all right, how long is an interim?*] while your Postman is settling down [*which of you lot unsettled him, and why?*] and any unforeseen problems are ironed out, I have asked that every available assistance be given to ensure that your mail is delivered as early in the day as possible. I do hope you see an improvement shortly. Please accept my apologies for the obvious annoyance and inconvenience you have been caused.

Let it not be said that Levin's heart is so stony that it cannot respond to a plea like that. I do indeed accept Fred's apologies, and I truly value the action he has taken to ensure that my mail is delivered as early in the day as possible. Only, you see, I am writing this at 11.10 in the morning, and the post hasn't come yet. What *has* come (a couple of days ago) is a letter from Joe, my original correspondent; it seems that they care in pairs at Rathbone Place, or possibly nobody has thought fit to introduce them to each other.

This is what *he* says: 'Thank you for your enquiry of March 17th concerning your deliveries. I am now looking into the matter, and I will be in touch with you again as soon as possible.'

My letter of March 17th was the one I wrote in response to Fred's apologia; remaining scrupulously polite, at the risk of grinding all the fillings out of my teeth, I had asked him to explain to me what he was talking about, since his letter didn't actually tell me anything at all. Joe now assures me that he is looking into the matter, which is very kind and helpful, or would be if he hadn't sworn, Scout's honour, a couple of months ago, that he was *already* looking into it, and what I want to know is whose telescope is he using to do his looking – Nelson's?

It will be seen that the situation has not altered since *Der Tag*; not altered, that is, in two senses. First, the problems have been neither eliminated nor ironed out; second, I still don't know why. I must say that I have no reason to believe that whatever has happened is the postmen's fault; the tenor of Fred's letter suggests, in so far as it suggests anything, which is not very far, that it is all because of Major Revision, a bogus officer if ever I saw one.

Why such a figure should have been employed in the first place I don't know; the service was excellent, and nobody had anything to complain about. Of course, the late Pat Hutber's great and indisputable statement of profound truth – 'Progress means deterioration' – is as valid as ever, and may well be in operation here. That, however, only *describes* what has happened; it does not explain it. But nor do the ranks of Customer Care, or anybody else.

There was a jingle in my youth, which went 'Don't care was made to care, Don't care was sorry.' It is more than five weeks ago that I wrote to Customer Care specifically asking for an explanation of the disappearance of our postal service, and to this day I have not received one. Strictly speaking, it is not to 'this day', only to last Friday, but since last Saturday's delivery was omitted altogether, and I don't suppose that my doorbell is ringing as you read these words, it comes to the same thing, which is more than my post does.

The Times April 24th, 1989

Playing silly burgers

YOU HAVE HEARD of wife-swapping, of house-swapping, of schoolboy stamp-swapping? Now you must learn of hamburger-swapping, and if you have tears, prepare to shed them now, though they will not be induced by the onions accompanying the celebrated *plat du jour et nuit*.

In Oxford, of all places, there is a branch of McDonald's; I have not tried its fare, feeling that for another few minutes down the road I can eat at Le Manoir aux Quat' Saisons, which is more in my line; I am, however, willing to believe that the Big Mac is as succulent as its advertising insists, and that the supply of ketchup is most unlikely to dry up. What I didn't know was that McDonald's also sells – or at least dishes up – some of the greasiest staff-regulations that ever deserved to be condemned as unfit for human consumption.

It all began with the deputy manager at the Oxford branch, Mr Tony Maslin; if any firm or organization has a vacancy for a managerial post, and would like to fill it with a trained man who has the additional virtue of possessing some common sense, they need look no further, particularly because Mr Maslin was out of work when last heard from, having been sacked by McDonald's.

And for what was he sacked? For fiddling the books? Perish the thought. For injecting the hamburgers with salmonella? Heaven forbid. For bad timekeeping, falling asleep on the job, pinching the female customers' bottoms? By no means; even McDonald's admitted that he was in all respects but one a model employee. Now listen while I tell you, in the teeth of your incredulity, what flaw it was that brought him down.

It seems that the governors of McDonald's, properly mindful of their position *in loco parentis* to their workers, provide each of them with a free lunch every day, in the form of – well, obviously – a hamburger. Mr Maslin qualified for this bounty, and indeed had been thus eating off the company for four years, which suggests that prospective employers of him should note that his c.v. includes – or should – *un foie de fer*.

Now it so chanced that next door to McDonald's there was a branch of a scarcely less famous fast-food chain; Pizzaland. One day, a girl who worked there marched into the McDonald's with a pizza and asked Mr Maslin if she could swap it for a hamburger. You and I, being real human beings, would see this as a suggestion both sensible and friendly; we would hardly be able to refrain from thinking that if the leaders of the world's great powers could act similarly, we would all lie more safely in bed o'nights. Mr Maslin, being no less human than we, and in addition feeling that he was, as he put it, 'sick and tired of hamburgers', traded his courtesy lunch for the tempting pizza.

Let us record the score before we go on. A man with a hamburger he didn't want met a lady with an equally redundant pizza; they exchanged the goods, to their mutual satisfaction; neither McDonald's nor Pizzaland had been put to any extra cost or trouble; plainly, the sum of human satisfaction had increased, with nothing at all in the debit column. This simple, reasonable and doubly beneficial form of barter went on for five months, at the end of which McDonald's found out what their admirable Mr Maslin had been doing, AND SACKED HIM.

That is how I came to know about it; he took his case, pleading unjust dismissal, to an industrial tribunal, and Mr Jamie Pyat recorded the proceedings for posterity in the pages of our dear sister, the *Sun*.

It transpired that the McDonald's handbook (I bet you didn't know McDonald's had a handbook – I certainly didn't) lays down that the staff may not give the food away, but Mr Maslin said that there was nothing in the sacred scripture forbidding the staff to *exchange* it. A Mr Fenwick, representing McDonald's at the hearing, declared that the swap amounted to 'gross misconduct'; it's a mercy he didn't say it amounted to breaking and entering, grievous bodily harm and kerb-crawling.

Keith Waterhouse not long ago drew the nation's attention to the Great Umbrella Case. It had abruptly come on to rain, and people were sheltering under Selfridges' awning, when one of those enterprising small businessmen whom all parties applaud arrived with a suitcaseful of umbrellas, which he proceeded to sell at astonishingly reasonable prices to grateful customers. Did he get an OBE? No, he was arrested, and subsequently fined. I remember thinking at the time that the policeman who fingered his collar, and the magistrate who fined him, should both be boiled, though it never occurred to me to specify what in. Now, of course, I have no doubt; it should have been in whatever cooking fat McDonald's uses, and they should be joined in the pot by the entire McDonald's senior management. And also, I may say, the members of the industrial tribunal to which Mr Maslin appealed; their decision was that he had been unfairly dismissed, but that he had contributed two-thirds of his fate because of the swapping.

It is a well known truth of legislation that manifestly daft laws will not be obeyed; in the end, if they are not repealed, they are simply ignored by the law-breakers and the law-enforcers alike. It seems that McDonald's are made of sterner stuff (though no doubt they would claim that their hamburger meat is of the softest and most tender), for their statute book allows of no sensible compromise, no spirit of live and let live; at the hearing, a Mr Taylor, head of McDonald's in the Midlands, praised Mr Maslin's work, but added: 'We are a business, firm but fair.' I suppose it says, in The Golden

Book of McDonald, that hamburger-swapping is punishable by death, and no employee can plead that he didn't know, particularly because there is a gibbet (no, not a giblet, you idiot) just inside the door of each of the chain's premises, with a coil of stout rope lying to hand. The black cap, please, usher.

And yet sense, though it be hanged five fathoms high and then buried in quicklime, will rise from the grave to point a ghostly finger at people who think that hamburgers are important, merely because they have provided vast profits, and will go on making more such profits until we all become vegetarian.

'People who think that hamburgers are important'; there lies the reason Mr Maslin needs a job, but there lie also many of the most characteristic aspects of our society. Hamburgers fill a need; so does pop music; so does the advertising industry; so do fashionable photographers; so does Beauchamp Place. None of them, however, has any real substance, let alone roots, and a puff of economic wind would blow the lot away like dandelion clocks. Yet they are all taken seriously, and the hamburgers perhaps the most; I wouldn't be surprised to learn that the very customers at McDonald's, if they heard of the incident, nodded their heads gravely and agreed that the outcome was hard on Mr Maslin, but rules are rules, and what would happen if all the employees started swapping their handout hamburgers for pizzas, eh?

I have no information about the fate of the girl next door, nor what the Analects of Pizzaland have to say about pizza-swapping, though I take comfort from the fact that the pizza was invented in Italy, a land where pomposity, self-righteousness, meanness of spirit and the rigid adherence to a wholly imaginary duty are unknown. But as for McDonald's, whoever presides over its fortunes, and who is therefore ultimately responsible for this affair, should swap his head for one of Colonel Sanders's chickens. I don't think anybody would notice.

The Times March 9th, 1989

On second thoughts

THERE WAS AN auction of musical autographs at Sotheby's not long ago at which the original manuscript of the Schumann Piano Concerto fetched £880,000 (by far the highest sum paid at the sale), not only because it was obviously an exceptional treasure, but because the experts have found substantial traces of Clara's hand in the autograph score; so substantial, indeed, that it seems we may have to call it the Schumanns Piano Concerto in future.

The same sale included a number of Beethoven items, *crowned by a sketch for the first movement of the Ninth Symphony*. The very thought of such an item makes me tremble; to look over Beethoven's shoulder as he wrestled with that unique and astounding opening would be as close to God as we sinners are likely to get:

> In what distant deeps or skies
> Burnt the fire of thine eyes?
> On what wings dare he aspire
> What the hand dare seize the fire?

There was also a Schubert *ms*, of a Magnificat, described as 'lost', leaving it unclear whether it was only the *ms* that had been lost and was now found, or whether the work itself had hitherto never been known about. If the latter, I trust the new owner will have it published; to think of even a fragment of Schubert left unplayed, let alone a complete addition to his catalogue, would be unbearable.

Mind you, I have held in my hands the original score of the *Coriolan* overture; perhaps not among Beethoven's

best-loved masterpieces as, for instance, *Egmont* is, but surely one of his most characteristic creations, in its numerous
unexpectednesses, the most unexpected being that strange
finish with the four ghostly chords, like some set of great
folios shutting. (The museum which let me touch the
Beethoven *ms* drew the line at their Gutenberg Bible. Still,
many years ago I turned the pages of the Kelmscott Chaucer;
it was going for £900, and I didn't buy it, fool that I must
have been.)

There is, I think, something much deeper than curiosity
in the wish to see the hand actually at work; what wouldn't
we give for a volume, a page, a line, of Shakespeare's! For
one thing, we could see how the first attempts turn gradually
into the finished passage; oh, I know Ben Jonson said 'He
never blotted a line', but that was surely an exaggeration,
understandable in a tribute to a dead friend and colleague.
But to see the ink he dipped his pen in, rusting now on the
page, would be a magical experience.

Berlioz said of the second movement of Beethoven's
Eighth Symphony that 'It was conceived in an instant and
written down in a single sitting.' And that is what we all
feel when we hear it, so magically complete and perfect is
it. But Berlioz was wrong; Beethoven's sketch-books show
that he worked long and hard, changing his mind over and
over again, until at last he was satisfied, if indeed Beethoven
could ever be satisfied. *Ars est celare artem.*

For that matter, Beethoven's most notable change of
mind is *Fidelio* in its entirety. If you compare the original
work, which failed in the theatre, with his second thoughts,
you will find that every time he made an alteration it was for
the better, and the result is not only one of the greatest operas
ever written, but one of the most profound statements about
love, truth, courage, justice and deliverance ever made in any
form.

It is now said, with much plausibility, that the age of
manuscript is coming to an end; I ran into a tiny example

of the plausibility not long ago, when someone wrote to ask for the original manuscript or typescript of a particular column (in which my correspondent had been mentioned). I was obliged to reply that there was no such physical reality; the article had been 'typed' on the green glass of my Atex VDU, and once I had pressed the appropriate button (I am very good at pressing the *in*appropriate button), it went on its way into *The Times*' system, untouched by human hand.

This in turn led to another, more mysterious, question. I mentioned the episode to friends not versed in computer typesetting and similarly arcane matters; I explained that my words are stored automatically until I want to work on them again, whereupon the right button will bring the entire text to the screen. 'But where', asked one of the company, 'are your words *before* you bring them back to the screen?' I realized that not only was I unable to answer the question; there was a sense in which I couldn't even understand it.

I can make noises, of course: 'The words are stored as electrical impulses.' But for all that actually means to me, I might as well say that they are written down by an angel with a golden pen. It is all very well to be assured that the medium is *not* the message, and the contents are still supreme, but I don't trust this world; I fear that one day I shall wake up and find that the last bottle of ink has been emptied.

Let us go back for a moment to where we started. There are computers which can copy music as easily as words; suppose Beethoven had had one of them. You can say that he would have written the same music. But we should never have had the evidence to confute Berlioz over the Eighth Symphony, and we would never be certain which version of *Fidelio* was the better, because Beethoven would have wiped the earlier version.

What is more, we would have lost something very valuable from our idea of Mozart. For he *did* conceive of masterpieces in an instant; with some of his greatest works the fair copy exactly matches the sketch, indeed *is* the sketch. We have to believe it, from the incontrovertible evidence of the manuscripts, which was the last straw for Shaffer's Salieri ('Tonight at an inn somewhere in this city stands a giggling child who can put on paper, without actually setting down his billiard cue, casual notes which turn my most considered ones into lifeless scratches.') But if those casual notes had had no existence other than as part of a machine's electronic innards, the argument could never have ended, or even started.

All is not yet lost, though, as I can testify. I possess the original manuscript score of a work dedicated to me, in fact written for me, by a young composer of great gifts, Richard Blackford. (He also, without actually setting down his billiard cue, wrote the music for my last two television travel series.)

It is a fantasia for wind quintet (flute, oboe, clarinet, horn and bassoon) on themes from *The Mastersingers*, and is called *Portrait of Hans Sachs*. It was presented to me first in a surprise performance; the circumstances were festive, and reminiscent of Wagner's birthday present to Cosima, the surprise of the *Siegfried Idyll*. I would not part with my manuscript for ninety-nine times the sum that bought the Schumann Concerto *ms*, and it is no use your waiting until I die and going to the auction of my effects, for I shall have bequeathed it to one who loves music and Richard as much as I do.

The Times February 1st, 1990

The last hurrah

WE ALL KNOW where we were when President Kennedy was shot. I think it is time we wondered where we would be if he hadn't been.

Well, in the first place we would not be bracing ourselves for yet another deluge of rubbish demonstrating that he was killed not by Lee Harvey Oswald but in a conspiracy organized by the Mersey Docks and Harbour Board under the direction of the Pope. There are many reasons why I wish he had not died that day in Dallas, all of them much more important, but the products of the 'Who killed Kennedy?' industry constitute one of the most depressing.

Kennedy's posthumous reputation has undergone an extraordinary series of metamorphoses. As could have been predicted, the first revaluation of his character and achievement was almost as depressing as the conspiracy theories; his *histoire amoureuse* was being touted around before the first blade of grass had grown on his grave, and fairly soon every whore in America was announcing that he had enjoyed her favours. (A few even had books written for them to that end, by what may be called secondary whores.)

These revelations did his memory a disservice but no harm; most were too obviously mendacious and self-seeking to be taken seriously, and the rest were greeted, if at all, with a shrug.

The next use of Kennedy's brief ascendancy was as a club with which to belabour Lyndon Johnson. When Camelot was pulled down and a more homely White House built on its ruins, the intellectual *beau monde* took offence, particularly when Johnson made clear that he had little need for them, whereupon they rallied round Kennedy's brother Robert until he was shot – by a conspiracy, of course. The indignation engendered in them by Johnson's own Presidency was such that Nixon managed to win two Presidential elections while they were still seething, but that didn't matter, as Nixon was beyond the pale for them anyway.

Then, subtly, the image of John Kennedy began to change in itself, rather than in relation to a rival totem. Think back to the hopes engendered by his brief Presidency, starting with his inaugural address, in which he declared that 'the torch has passed to a new generation', and made clear that that generation saw the world through younger and less tradition-clouded eyes. Remember his pledge to 'pay any price, bear any burden', his appeal to his fellow Americans to ask what they could do for their country, not what their country could do for them. Call to mind the last important speech he made, the venue – Berlin – shortly to become, when the shots rang out in Dallas, retrospectively symbolic, standing as it did on the frontier between East and West. Hear again his cry '*Ich bin ein Berliner*', which summed up both the pledge and the appeal.

And none so poor to do it reverence. What happened? Surely something did, for that portrait of Kennedy can hardly be recognized from the version we have today. He is now widely thought of, when he is thought of at all, as either an earlier model of President Carter, all goodwill and muddle, or a belligerent adventurer likely to follow the Bay of Pigs fiasco with an unprovoked nuclear strike on Moscow. Was it all show and froth, good looks and rhetoric?

I do not believe it. In the first place, Kennedy was not a liberal in the Carter mode (let alone the Dukakis version); it would almost be closer to the reality to say that he was a liberal in the sense of the Manchester school. Remember that he was a Boston Irishman; remember, also, to what lengths he went to get the crown.

He should be classified with the toughs like Nixon and Johnson and Thatcher, instead of the romantics like Stevenson and Reagan and Foot. But he was a Manchester liberal and a Boston tough with a vision, and the strength which had carried him to the White House was deployed with a steely, measured calm in the Cuba missile crisis of 1962, when he stood firm while so many of America's allies were squealing for surrender, and many of his own advisers were singing the same song. I have never had any doubt that Kennedy's stand on that occasion kept not only the immediate peace but the long-term one; the years that followed the fall of Khrushchev were dangerous enough, but they would have been hideously more so if it had not been for Kennedy's unwavering confidence.

Whoever is the President of the United States is, ex officio, the leader of the free world, which is one of the reasons that the recent Presidential election was so depressing an experience for most of us. But Kennedy showed true leadership in his three years; those who had eyes to see realized that the torch had been passed into hands not only younger but firmer. Both Nixon and Reagan followed the path Kennedy cut, and the world is the safer for it; for one thing, I doubt if the Grenada invasion would have taken place, Reagan or no Reagan, if Kennedy had not set the agenda for international action all those years before. (The Truman Doctrine had been looking very woebegone for a long time.)

Of course, the international scene has not been one of confrontation only; I believe that the current of Western European integration would have gone faster and more smoothly if the dynamism of a Kennedy had been available to power the engine. He understood the way the world might work and did work; his youth was his greatest advantage, because it meant that he was not bent double with the weight of tradition, precedence and caution on his back. It is not at all fanciful to think that even South Africa might have moved towards decency if Kennedy had lived and served two full terms.

Domestically, I cannot believe that the United States would have remained still while a President Kennedy was so active internationally. Kennedy's death left Lyndon Johnson to force through the civil rights legislation; Johnson worked on Congress with cunning and force, but Kennedy might well have made it a crusade, and one with more rapid results. Moreover, to think of Kennedy as a Democrat in the interventionist mould would be a profound mistake; that is what I meant when I said he was a liberal in the nineteenth century meaning. I believe that the appalling (and growing) urban poverty which stains the United States would at least have been attacked with less blunt weapons; it is not inconceivable that even the drug problem might look very different.

Or perhaps not. Perhaps it was all an illusion, made out of skilful publicity and a response owing more to a reaction against the Eisenhower years (I forget who said, when Kennedy was elected, 'The Goths have left the White House') than any feeling of excitement stemming from the challenge that Kennedy offered. Perhaps; but I am old enough to recall not only the state of the world and of America a quarter of a century ago, but also the real excitement which Kennedy generated, and the feeling of desolation, as though a light had blown out and left only darkness, when he was killed. If he had lived, I believe that the world would look, and be, a brighter, more courageous, safer, wiser, more prosperous place, better-tempered, more adventurous, less introspective, even happier. The torch of youth, determination and courage did pass to him, but it fell to the ground with his body, and no one since has been able to seize it and lighten our darkness with it. Those shots in Dallas sounded two knells, not one.

The Times November 21st, 1988

What price glory?

THE OTHER DAY, at Heathrow, in Terminal Four, I was waiting for my flight to be called; I wandered about the concourse and came upon the duty-free shops. I have never seen the point of this absurd concession, have never used it, and was delighted to learn that the goods in question can be bought more cheaply at the shopper's destination. But some of the goods are pretty, and worth a glance. As it happens, I had need of such glancing; I had left my belt behind, and I felt that it might excite comment if I boarded the plane with my trousers round my ankles; besides, I find aesthetically unpleasing the sight of the empty belt-loops at the waist.

So I strolled into a shop which sold such items, and came upon a rack of belts, many of them sufficiently handsome to serve in the cause of keeping me tidy. In such matters, I go for the plain rather than the decorated, and I plucked from its hook a suitable brown job by Dunhill; my feeble eyes could not make out the price on the label, so I took it over to the cash-desk and asked what it cost. See this wet, see this dry? The answer was £78.50.

Now you all know, or should, that Lavish Jack Levin, last of the big spenders, recks not the cost of keeping himself the glass of fashion and the mould of form; if the Levin trousers must hang just *so*, then an appropriate belt must be acquired to see that they do. On the other hand, not even in a dim light could I be mistaken for the Sultan of Brunei, and I replaced the belt in its place on the rack.

Intrigued by what can only be properly described as a diabolical bleeding liberty, I ran my eye over the other belts

on offer, this time putting on my reading-specs to make sure
I could see the figures. There was a Dior one, in a particularly
nasty design, which cost £78.95; two from Allders, the first
at £71.50, and the second at £29.95, doubtless designed for
cheapskates; and so on, *pro rata.*

I went over to the ties; these were all by Dunhill, and
all were of identical material and style, though there was a
very wide variety of patterns. There was also a single price
for each: it was £38.95.

It was time to go aboard; as I walked towards the gate
I passed a little kiosk selling sweets, T-shirts and the like,
and on impulse asked if they stocked belts. Yes, came the
answer, over there. Over there were indeed belts; I homed
in on a smart one which was two-toned, being reversible
with the use of an ingenious buckle. In fairness, I must say
that the Dunhill one that had had me backing out of the
shop making the sign against the Evil Eye was almost as
smart and supple as this one. Mine was, of course, of real
leather, but, again, so was Dunhill's.

All in all, the two were not to be distinguished by sight,
feel or quality. But they could certainly be told apart by the
wallet; the belt in the corner set me back a cool £5.95, and
if you meet me in the street I shall be perfectly happy to
unbutton my jacket and let you have a look at it.

Honour where honour is due; the one that cost me not
quite 7.6 per cent of what was asked for Alf's scam was
made in Italy; its brand name is Montecarlo Im (dunno what
the Im stands for). But the episode set me thinking.

Economists have identified a concept called negative, or
reverse, elasticity. The elasticity of demand, as the technical
term has it, is measured by changes in price: if purchases
of one item that has become more expensive fall off more
than another item that has been raised in price by the same
proportion, it is said that the former has a greater elasticity
than the latter. The point about economics, as you may
know, is that it only tells you things you know already,

like the above. But there are a few exceptions, and reverse elasticity is one.

It means that demand *increases* when the price goes up. It is very difficult to think, unprompted, of anything that fits the definition; at least, it was until recently, and most of us would have thought that common sense would ensure that examples would be few, and those very peculiar. But for all I know, if the belt I rejected had cost £100 instead of £78.50, there might have been a queue of customers for it.

More fools they. But I have just thought of an exact parallel to the belt nonsense, and one which is much more widespread; if I had had another few minutes at the airport I bet I could have compiled a long list of 'men's toiletries' exhibiting all the stigmata of reverse elasticity. You can buy perfectly satisfactory and pleasantly scented deodorants, after-shave lotions, talcs, colognes and the like for two or three pounds a go; you can also, if you are daft enough, fork out anything up to twenty-five quid for something exactly the same.

Many years ago, somebody coined the term 'ilth', as a reversed echo of 'wealth'; he meant it for certain kinds of conspicuous consumption. The kind of thing I am discussing did not exist then in that form, but the principle cannot have changed, though my experience at Heathrow suggests that it is being much more skilfully and effectively employed.

It wouldn't be difficult to devise an experiment. Here are two items in identical blank containers; no brand names, but price tags, one of which is fifteen times the other. The subject can examine both to his heart's content, and after admitting that he can find no difference, he plumps for the higher price *only because* it is higher.

There are, of course, a few areas in which his method would work; if you are going to the theatre, and want the best seats, you simply buy the highest-priced ones. And for that matter, two oranges will rightly cost more than one. But our world has now got to the point at which one orange will be bought for vastly more than the very next orange on the barrow, though the barrow-boy will be hard put to it to stifle his amazement, not to say giggles.

And the result is very big business indeed; ilth is lord of all. I don't think this is a moral question: throwing money away is foolish, not sinful. But I am intrigued by those who do the throwing, and their motives.

I can only make a guess; it is that the enormous incomes which today accrue in professions which were once poorly paid (these are the years that the hairdressers have eaten), or – more subtly – which now pay starting salaries that would once have been earned only after a dozen or more years spent slowly rising in the firm, have bred a strain of spenders with no idea of value or restraint.

This is the impostume of much wealth and peace,
Which inward breaks, and shows no sign without
Why the man dies.

If you go to the Campo San Geremia, in Venice, you will find, in the corner, the Palazzo Labia; if you can wheedle your way upstairs (the palace is now the Venice headquarters of the Italian broadcasting service), you will see a magnificent room decorated by Tiepolo at the height of his powers, with a *trompe-l'oeil* ceiling that will stop your breath.

Generations ago, the head of the Labia family gave a huge banquet, at which the guests feasted off massive gold plates. At the end of the meal, all the precious plates and utensils were gathered up, and he threw the lot into the Grand Canal, to demonstrate his enormous wealth and extravagance. He had, however, taken the precaution of fixing nets under the surface of the water, so that when his guests had gone marvelling home, it could all be hauled up again. I think that he and our modern yuppies who spend for the sake of spending can reasonably be called very silly. But I think they are sillier than he was.

The Times October 27th, 1988

First impressions

O F ALL THE absurd self-justifications of our time, the worst and most dishonest is the one ruling in the arts. If anyone says (though as far as I can see nobody except me actually does) that Schrecklich's 439th Symphony is bilge, and that the other 438 are bilge also, or that the Ordure Gallery's exhibition of the most recent works of Knotworth-Fawpentz is exactly what you would expect from a man so spectacularly untalented, or that the new 870-page novel by Clarence Brokentupperware has the same effect as a lethal dose of Nembutal, or that all sensible men, hearing that Mr Howard Brenton is sickening for another play demonstrating that this country is rotten, diseased, wicked, corrupt and beyond hope, will at once don impenetrable disguise and flee the country, the reply is invariably the same: 'They jeered at the Impressionists, they mocked James Joyce, they drove Mozart to penury and despair, *therefore* our works are as good as those of the Impressionists, Joyce and Mozart (or better, actually).'

It is the 'therefore' which sticks in the gullet, and must be fished out before we all perish in a welter of relativism, unable or afraid to say that some things are unacceptable still, that some things are *better* than others.

On the other hand, they *did* jeer at the Impressionists. Apart from the loathsome Alfred Munnings, they gave up jeering (and cooled their blushes) about half a century ago, though I am by no means sure that the present state of affairs, in which Impressionists fetch sums rather larger than the GNP of Switzerland, is a whole lot better.

But in one sense, neither situation matters at all, nor

indeed does the rubbish produced today and the way it is boomed and boosted; the proof of this claim will be found until well into August in the Diploma Galleries of the Royal Academy, in the exhibition entitled *Cézanne, The Early Years, 1859-1872*.

The problem of Cézanne, which we who only want to feast on his pictures can happily leave to the experts, is how to classify him. To start with, was he an Impressionist at all? He said himself that his aim was 'To make of Impressionism something solid and durable . . .', which suggests that he was not altogether at home in a world where everything dissolves, and if he was the true precursor of Cubism, that would further distance him from the 'true' Impressionists, though his Cubism was all his own, and it didn't last long anyway.

A fig for all this taxonomy; go to the Academy and stand in front of No. 17, 'View of Bonnières'. Better still, get yourself a camp-stool and *sit* in front of it. If you stay there long enough you will see the picture change before your eyes, first becoming Impressionist, and then sliding imperceptibly into Cubist. What you are watching through these metamorphoses is Cézanne becoming Cézanne – no, Cézanne making himself Cézanne, wrenching his genius apart to see how it works and how it can be put back together and remade.

Of course it is true of any great artist that you can see or hear in the seed the mighty tree that it is to become. Schubert wrote the 'Erlkönig' at the age of seventeen; well, Schubert sprang fully armed from the brow of Zeus, and though there is virtually nothing of his that can be called juvenilia, the example need not be so sensational. What Mozart wrote at the age of eight was amazing, though mainly because he was eight.

But this exhibition demonstrates that Cézanne's progress was virtually a level line, however many phases he moved through. And what is so extraordinary is the variety of techniques, styles and approaches which, never suggesting that he was trying his wings, come off every time.

Look at the series of palette-knife paintings of Uncle Dominique; in some of them the impasto is so thick that if you peer too closely you can break your nose on it. You *can't* call this experimenting; it is genius full-fledged, and he started the series no later than 1866, when he was twenty-seven. Or look at the three self-portraits, Nos 2, 15 and 63. The first, based on a photograph (included in the excellent catalogue), is of a man burning with mingled doubt and certainty, his eyes hypnotically fixed upon the viewer, his skin sallow, his mouth set. If you come upon it unawares, you will gasp; but what will you do, having gasped, when you meet the second of the trio, where he is almost invisible in the darkness like a parody of the late Rembrandt?

He was twenty-two when he painted the first, twenty-six the second, thirty-three the third. This last one is in fact the first picture you see as you enter the exhibition, immediately beside the door. He looks furious, and the catalogue-note (the notes are by Sir Lawrence Gowing) is worth quoting:

> The art of Cézanne's twenties was a dream from which he awoke in the furious temper that he portrayed in this picture – awoke from a nightmare of loneliness and sexual aggression to insist on being reconciled with life. He was wakened not only by the grace of Hortense, the colossal humility of Pissarro and the beneficent faithfulness of truth to sensations; he was wakened by the clear sight of genius, which at the crucial moment does actually know its greatness.

What a good phrase that is, 'the beneficent faithfulness of truth to sensations,' though the very attentive viewer will not need those words. On the Academy's walls the faithfulness of truth-to-sensations leaps out; the man is as honest as Vermeer, asking not 'Is it beautiful?', 'Is it powerful?', not even 'Is it real?', but 'On the Day of Judgement, when my soul stands in the balance, can I say that that was *exactly* how I felt it?'

He can. But that doesn't even begin to exhaust the treasures (at least two thirds of them, I must say, unknown to me) of this exhibition. There is, for instance, an astounding paraphrase on Manet's *Le Déjeuner sur l'herbe*.

The label suggests that it was a conscious rejection of Manet and his style (and, presumably, those who followed him), and so it may have been, but if, like me, you have no great wish to know such things, you will see a picture exactly like a dream landscape, for all that he has borrowed the elements from the older artist; in fact, I am convinced that it *was* a dream literally, of Manet's *chef d'oeuvre*, for the differences and distortions are just what a dream does to reality.

Cézanne was a close friend of Zola, but his realism is very different from the writer's; it is a mysterious penetration of the aspect which the world turns towards those content to believe that what the world shows *is* the world. Cézanne knew better; inside the walls there are deep, echoing mines of another reality altogether, and he worked on those mines by hewing at the coalface with an unimaginable strength.

The result can be seen at the Academy, in some 70-odd pictures from the first dozen years of his life as an artist, as remarkable a portrait of young genius bursting its bonds as we can hope to see.

When I was there, there was a living artist – one of the few real ones we have – sketching from *Young Girl at the Piano*. He shook his head in wonder and joy, and murmured: 'Once in a lifetime, once in a lifetime.' He meant the exhibition, and he was right.

The Times June 27th, 1988

There's nowt so queer as volk

WILL EVERYBODY PLEASE keep calm; this is not going to be about Wagner, however ominous the evidence.

Not long ago, as I was going into the theatre for Scottish Opera's excellent new production of *Das Rheingold* (keep *calm* – have I ever lied to you?), I saw by the door a handful of people who were giving out leaflets. There was a man looking like a helpful bus conductor, and a lady resembling an assistant in the curtains department at a large haberdasher's, and at first I assumed that they were bent on some theatrical enterprise of their own, and were sensibly taking this opportunity to advertise it among the music-goers.

I took a leaflet, and at once realized that my guess had been wrong. For the piece of paper (a suspicious green) was headed, in very large type, 'Wagner Betrayed . . .' (I shall not say it again: *keep calm*.) I read on, and was instantly transfixed. These were the next words:

> Many admirers of Wagner's *Rheingold* may not be aware that the religion and worship of Wotan (or Odin) continues to flourish and grow in the modern world, in this country and abroad, amongst people who look for their spiritual inspiration to the original living faith of our heathen fore-bears.

That, you must admit, was promising stuff. I could not immediately recall exactly what the worship of Wotan entailed, though I knew that the fourth day of the week is called after him, and I had a vision of this meek band horsing

around in Epping Forest every Wednesday, wearing ridiculous garments. Moreover, they all looked as though nothing
stronger than cocoa had ever passed their lips, whereas I
certainly knew that Wotan and his mates were into the
quaffing business in a large way. What is more, the most
striking of the Wotan legends is the one which records his
auto-crucifixion; he stuck his own spear into himself, then
hung himself on a tree for nine days and nights. Well, all
right if you like that kind of thing, provided you keep the
children out of the way, but the leaflet brigade looked pretty
vegetarian to me, and again I couldn't quite see them getting
up to such extravagant monkeyshines, Wotan or no Wotan.
Besides, where did the betrayal of Wagner come in? I read
on, in search of understanding, and all too quickly got it.
For this is how the second paragraph ran:

> Those responsible for the present production of *Rheingold*,
> who have cast a black man to portray Wotan, have clearly
> failed to appreciate the real significance of the myths on
> which Wagner's operas are based. Wotan, the god of
> spirit, genius and poetry [first I've heard of the poetry
> bit], is the archetype of the Northern race's collective
> unconscious, the repository and manifestation of the folk
> soul . . . In this production Wotan has been parodied and
> Wagner betrayed.

Facts first. Yes, the Wotan was black, and a very fine
Wotan he made. (His name, just to add to the gaiety
of the occasion, is White.) But if there is one thing that
sticks in my craw, and I should think in the craws of most
people, it is talk about 'the northern race' and its 'folk soul'.
I don't want to be indelicate, and anyway my regular readers
will know of my regard, sympathy and admiration for the
Federal Republic, but people who go about suggesting that
a black man, solely by virtue of his blackness, is unworthy
to represent a Wagnerian hero straight out of the northern
race and its folk soul, ought to have their mouths washed

out with soap and water; that's dirty soldier's talk, that is, and another word of it and you'll be going to bed without any supper.

You will observe that I am trying not to make heavy weather of all this; the daft lot distributing the leaflets were so respectable (the next paragraph disclaimed any desire for the banning of the performance and insisted that 'we are not casting aspersions on anyone's artistic capabilities') that in trying to imagine them unleashing the *furor teutonicus*, with the haberdasher lady's breasts bared to the elements and the bus-conductor gent roaring his fearsome battle-cry – 'Fares please' – it is hard not to giggle. Yet there is something ugly here, for all the harmless idiocy it is clad in.

I doubt if Wagner ever set eyes on a black man in his life. But where the 'northern race' makes an appearance there are other varieties of submen to be looked down upon. Wagner may not have had a thing about blacks, but he more than made up for the omission by taking it out on certain people nearer to hand. What, I wonder, would our Wotan-worshippers say to a Jewish Siegfried? (Don't rush to answer; the surname of the present leading singer of the role is Jerusalem. Mind you, he looks as blond and heroic as any Wotanist could wish.) And would it be all right if Willard White had been singing one of the villains, Fafner or Alberich? Come; I don't want to upset the Wotan-lovers too much, but the most recent *Parsifal* at Covent Garden had *two* black singers, and one of them was portraying Amfortas, who is the keeper of the Holy Grail, no less. (I was about to say that Christ wouldn't have minded, when I remembered that the Wotanists thought Christianity a pretty namby-pamby outfit, to say nothing of their inevitable suspicion of your man's complexion.)

O Castor and Pollux! Just stop and think for a moment about those members of the 'northern race' we know all too well. There goes Heinrich Himmler, for instance, with his broad shoulders, his manly bearing, his keen blue eyes beneath his shock of golden hair. Or Northern Racer Joseph

Goebbels, striding out ahead of his troops, towering over the tallest of them. Or Ernst Röhm, one glance from whose eyes would make any maiden swoon. Or the Führer himself, the curly-haired rascal, wrestling bears just for the fun of it. Be proud of your exemplars, Wotanists, and tend the sacred flame with reverence!

Alternatively, stop playing grown-ups. There is no such thing as a 'northern race', or a 'folk soul' either. And even if such categories existed, we can be sure that art knows no boundaries except the ones which enclose talent; Bayreuth itself pioneered the defiance of this Wotanic nonsense, when it cast Grace Bumbry as Venus in *Tannhäuser*.

It was Chesterton who said that if you want to know why Christianity is special, try thinking of something blasphemous to say about Thor. These Wotanists are plainly harmless; they say of their religion that 'it is a mystical and spiritual awareness of nature that underpins a wholesome and noble lifestyle', and of those who have 'betrayed the spirit of Wagner's intentions' that they should 'exercise a more discriminating artistic judgement' and 'think more deeply about the spiritual meaning of the myths'.

Well, *they* aren't going to start pogroms. Still, they think it wrong for anyone not a member of the 'northern race' to take part in Wagner's *echt* northern-race works. I must therefore reveal to them that the composer entrusted the first performance of *Parsifal* – *Parsifal* itself! – to the Jewish conductor Hermann Levi, whose only hope of qualifying for the northern race would have been to go to Aintree and watch the Grand National. What do they say to that? I know: 'Good Wotan!', 'Wotan help us!' and 'Wotan Almighty!'

The Times April 27th, 1989

Is there a doctor in the house?

AT A TIME when voices are being raised, not all of them in the Saloon Bar and one or two on the Bench, to demand castration for rapists, child-abusers and other sexual offenders, it comes as less of a surprise than it once would to learn that the practice seems to be taking place already. And the fact that the instrument used is not a knife but a hypodermic needle does not greatly reassure me.

The facts were recently set out in detail by Denise Winn in the *Sunday Times*; for those who missed her article, I shall summarize them. After sexual behaviour which led to his detention in a mental hospital, a man is to be treated, *without his consent*, to a course of chemical injections which it is believed (mark well those last three words) will diminish his sexual urge and make him impotent. This has come about because of a High Court decision in a different case; that judge ruled that the drug to be used is not covered by Section 57 of the Mental Health Act, which forbids treatment against a patient's will. Instead, the drug was classified under Section 58, which covers treatment that may be given to patients whether they agree or not.

The 'wonder drug' was developed for use in cancer of the prostate, and Miss Winn mercilessly pointed out that its effects on patients not suffering from that condition are unknown; she also demonstrated that the drug, as a means of chemical castration, is almost certainly quite useless anyway. (That, I may say, will not stop some judges I know, and some doctors I don't wish to know, from prescribing its use.) I am obviously not qualified to take part in the medical argument; but that, in any case, is not my concern. What I want to discuss are the moral considerations.

The combination of judicial ignorance and medical zeal has frequently had catastrophic results, and sometimes lethal ones. Alan Turing, one of the two men who invented the computer, also made a huge contribution to the Allied cause in the Second World War, in the field of cryptanalysis; a man to be honoured in his lifetime if ever there was one. But he was a homosexual, and was prosecuted for having unorthodox relations with another man. He was 'sentenced' by a judge whose vocation should have been burning witches, and 'treated' by a doctor who would have been more at home diagnosing his patients' ailments by examining the entrails of a freshly killed chicken, to a course of hormone injections which were supposed to correct his abnormal sexual propensities. Turing committed suicide.

We have to assume, therefore, that we shall get no help, if we are seeking to establish or defend a right to be protected from hazardous medical experiments, from the judges. There may well be situations in which treatment without consent is permissible or even necessary; say, the sedation of a dangerously violent mental patient who is incapable of giving or withholding consent, or for that matter the quarantining of typhoid carriers. (And there have been authenticated instances, at least in the United States, of Aids carriers deliberately infecting sexual partners.) But all this is far from the case described, which consists of a man being forcibly treated with a drug which was designed for an altogether different disorder, which has never been tested for the effects of the new use, and which is roundly condemned by leading experts in this field as not only inefficacious in its proposed purpose, but quite likely to make worse the condition that it is supposed to alleviate.

I did not think that I should have so soon returned to the Fallacy of the Altered Standpoint. But what better demonstration of the Fallacy could there be than what has happened in this case? Let us put out of our minds the horror-novel figure of the mad doctor performing hideous experiments on victims he has kidnapped; let us acquit the judiciary of intending the harm they so often cause. Let us just examine the Fallacy at work.

First, we note an apparently substantial rise in the incidence of sexual crime; I say 'apparently' because there is much dispute as to whether what has increased is only the willingness on the part of the victims to report such crimes. But whichever it is, public anger is increasingly aroused, with a corresponding increase in demands for harsher penalties; after that – well, in medieval ages men were castrated for various reasons, but only in very recent times has the practice been seriously advocated anew.

Are we collectively losing our reason? Do we no longer believe that civilization is supposed to elevate us on to higher and higher planes of thought, conduct and action? Is superstition now to be regarded as the basis of our law, medicine and social relations? I can hear the cries now: 'Wicked man! Wicked man! Quick, quick – cut his thingies off and he won't be wicked any more!' Does nobody today stop to think that wickedness is seated in the mind and soul, not the genitals? You will think I am jesting, and in poor taste, too, when I predict that not more than three years from this date there will be serious and ostensibly responsible people advocating the amputation of the right hand of persistent thieves.

Science-fiction? Let me tell you that injecting chemicals into legally helpless men, with no idea of what the effects may be, can be called by a more homely name: mumbo-jumbo. We bow down today to men in white coats, whether they have come to mend our broken bones or our minds or our television sets; in each case we are unlikely to understand what they are doing, and quite possibly they don't either. And it is useless to appeal to the General Medical Council on ethical grounds.

The public have a right to be protected from criminals and from those unfortunates whose minds are so twisted or damaged that they cannot help acting in a criminal way. Members of both categories may have to be locked up for the public safety, but oddly enough, when they are, the criminals have more protection against unconsenting medical treatment than the unfortunates. Is there perhaps a tendency – it would be another result of the Fallacy – to think of those whose minds are not normal as inert objects, to whom anything may be done in the name of science, provided it is done with good intentions?

The mad have rights, particularly when they are so mad that they cannot claim those rights, or even understand what they are. There are safeguards in the Mental Health Acts; for instance, a second doctor, who has not been involved in treating the patient, must agree that the treatment is proper. It is not clear whether a second doctor, or even a first, has given this case such an imprimatur, but it is difficult to see how any reputable medical man can authorize treatment with a drug of wholly unknown potential. And we should remember that even the judges have been careful to give convicted offenders an option: probation or a suspended sentence *if they consent* to treatment.

Perhaps this is another form of the ancient search for the one true elixir which will cure all ills; superstition indeed. More likely, it is a product of the modern version – the belief that whatever ails you, from ingrowing toenails to death, there is a pill, preferably made in a strikingly vivid colour, that will instantly relieve what ails you, so that with a sufficiently wide variety of tablets you will become immortal. Or possibly we should read Samuel Butler's *Erewhon*, where the only crime is to be ill. Incidentally, is there any evidence that the wonder drug under discussion is of any use in treating the condition – cancer of the prostate – for which it was manufactured?

The Times September 5th, 1988

And a smutty New Year

I T WAS KING Lear who pointed out that 'the worst is not, So long as we can say "This is the worst"', and it may be that what I am about to reveal has long been familiar to my readers, and even that the more blasé among them can cap it with ease. So be it: but did *you* know that you can now buy obscene Christmas cards? I found some when I was browsing through a shop selling seasonal stationery, and I am not sure whether the fact that the themes of the cards are of an almost unimaginable witlessness and the drawings of an equally striking lack of artistic talent makes matters better or worse.

I should say that they are nowhere near the level that might invite prosecution, and if they were I would not name the shop; I find the idea peculiarly repellent, as I shall shortly demonstrate rather vigorously, but if there are people who wish to send or receive such things I do not propose to set myself up as a jobbing censor, let alone a stoolpigeon. Only nowadays I do sometimes find myself cocking an eye at the heavens not for rain but for fire and brimstone.

For the thousandth time: I am not a Christian, and I am aware that when I meddle in Christian matters it is open to any Christian who disagrees with me to tell me to go back where I came from. (Fitzroy Square Synagogue, in case you're interested, and the rabbi did *not* look like Julia Neuberger.) Still, very few Christmas cards today have any pictorial or verbal connection with the birth of Christ, and I dare say that an opinion poll would reveal a substantial proportion of respondents who have no idea what the 25th of

December is supposed to commemorate. I have long enjoyed
the innocence of those gift shops which sell a wide range of
Christmas cards and label one rack 'Religious', but I do not
buy my cards from that section, as I think it an impertinence
on my part to do so.

Very well; but there is plenty of room between the
Adoration of the Magi and Santa Claus (an actual example)
using his traditional fur-trimmed red bonnet as a condom.
If Christmas is not about the birth of Christ, as for most
people it plainly isn't, then it is about friendship and families,
goodwill on earth, the exchanging of presents, the sharing of
meals, the giving of alms – but let Scrooge's nephew take up
the catalogue:

> '. . . a good time; a kind, forgiving, charitable, pleasant
> time; the only time I know of, in the long calendar of
> the year, when men and women seem by one consent to
> open their shut-up hearts freely, and to think of people
> below them as if they really were fellow-passengers to
> the grave, and not another race of creatures bound on
> other journeys. And therefore, uncle, though it has never
> put a scrap of gold or silver in my pocket, I believe that
> it *has* done me good, and *will* do me good; and I say, God
> bless it!'

To which Scrooge retorts that Fred ought to go into Parliament, but he doesn't accompany his sarcasm by knocking
off a lightning sketch of (another genuine instance) Santa
sitting on the lavatory.

I have never believed that Gresham's Law applied to
anything but money; to admit it into any other area is to
surrender to the Manichee. For instance, however empty,
debased or simian most popular music is today, it leaves
the Schubert Octet untouched; similarly, dirty pictures for
Christmas will not damage even the secular majority among
Christmases, let alone the ones that seek to mark the birth
of the Saviour of the world. Yet we are diminished by such
things; though they cannot defile the spirit of Christmas, the

very fact that they try to do so admits another enemy through the lines.

Let us try, however difficult and otiose the task, to enter into the thought processes of the people who drew these pictures, who commissioned them and who stocked them. Presumably, all three categories thought that the cards would sell, and presumably at least those in charge of the shop paused to wonder whether some potential customers might be offended, only to conclude that the people who would be delighted would greatly outnumber the offended ones. But was there no room at all in their weighings-up for the possibility that something both lawful and profitable might nevertheless be better left alone?

Here, a sharp lawyer could do wonders with a charge of inconsistency; obscene birthday cards have been with us for many years, and I have never publicly complained. Where's the difference? The difference lies in the fact that sending a smutty card to old Jack makes no comment on anything or anybody other than old Jack; a smutty Christmas card makes a comment about Christmas, and it is a comment which denies any meaning at all to the season, even in its most secular guise. If Christmas weighs exactly the same as old Jack, there is something seriously wrong with the scales.

Back comes the sharp lawyer. Have you not, Mr Levin, seen lewd caricatures of the Royal Family (yes, Sir Travers), of Parliament (oh, *yes*, Sir Travers), of Adam and Eve (all right, all right)? What's the difference?

Look here, I have in my time seen an obscene photographic parody of the Crucifixion, though perhaps I shouldn't have mentioned it, lest some even more enterprising firm starts to turn out a frightfully amusing line in those.

My point is that although I would not suggest that anybody in this business should wonder whether what they are doing is in good taste, I think that they might ponder for a moment on a similar but not identical question: are there such things as bounds, and if so does an indecent Christmas card go beyond them? And if it does, why?

Well, why are there *decent* Christmas cards? Why do the images which decorate them – the three kings, the star in the East, the manger, the babe in arms, the holly and the ivy, the carol singers – why do these icons go on resonating after so many centuries? Because they correspond to something buried deep in even the least observant family, whose imagination will stretch no further than the silver coin in the pudding.

Whether you take it or leave it, the Christian story is so colossal in its telling, its course and its promise, that those who live in even an ostensibly Christian society cannot but be moved by it. The child who comes home from school bursting to tell his parents about the crib he has helped to make may be greeted with blank stares, or even condescending smiles; but the little child has got hold of more of the truth – as, indeed, the central figure in the Christmas story was more than once impelled to point out when he grew up. And it is not only images; it is also phrases. Glad tidings . . . the shepherds abiding in the fields . . . no room at the inn . . . Christians awake . . . O come let us adore him . . . these words have dug themselves as deeply in Christian-based cultures as have the famous pictures.

The answer takes shape. Whether or not you accept the Christmas message, if it is soiled something in you is soiled. If the Nativity is what Christians believe it to be, it is no joke; and if it isn't what Christians think it, it is still no joke. And even if it were a joke, it certainly wouldn't be a dirty one.

Those in charge of the shop where all this started may retort that the cards in question have nothing to do with religion or Messiahs or Holy Families or Virgin Births, but are meant only for those who do not care a fig about such matters, and who merely want something to convey

Christmas greetings to their like-minded family and friends.
Er . . . *what*mas greetings?

The Times November 12th, 1988

Intimations of immortality

I HAD LITTLE interest in John Lennon when he was alive, and I have somewhat less now that he is dead. But there is a new biography of him out (*The Lives of John Lennon* by Albert Goldman, published by Bantam Books), and I have been reading the substantial excerpts in the *Daily Mail*, where it has been serialized. In almost every paragraph it has what might be called the ring of inauthenticity, and indeed some of those close to Lennon, notably Mr Paul McCartney, have denounced it as mendacious trash. I am in no position to adjudicate, nor do I care one way or the other, but two trivial coincidences, one on each side of the book's serialization, have led me to a comment.

The first was an item in the 'Pop Music' column in the *Spectator* – and those who are surprised to learn that the *Spectator* has a pop music column may rest assured that they are not half so surprised as I am. From it I learn (*nihil humanum* . . .) that there is a new kind of pop music, called 'hip-hop', which is said by the writer, Marcus Berkmann, to be worse than another recent kind of pop music, called 'house', but not as bad as an even newer kind called 'Balearic Beat'.

Moreover, there is yet another variety, called 'acid house' (not the same, it seems, as 'house' *tout court*), and it is this that fastened itself upon my attention. For Mr Berkmann, who is plainly an expert in all these matters, explains in words simple enough for even people like me to understand what acid house is. But he begins his account like this:

. . . the Capital Radio disc jockey Graham Dene, when confronted on air with the term 'acid house', had no idea what it meant – a career-limiting move if ever I heard one.

I shall come back to Mr Dene's problem in a moment, but first, I would like to share my newly won knowledge of acid house music; I offer it in Mr Berkmann's terms:

Acid house is . . . repetitive, mainly electronic and based almost entirely around complex percussion patterns . . . It's an astonishingly odd music, impossible to listen to . . . Its almost hypnotic effect, combined with the rather psychedelic lighting that always seems to accompany it, make acid house an ideal backdrop to the ingestion of . . . 'recreational drugs'.

Mr Berkmann goes on to advertise and extol two of these drugs by name and effect, with their current prices; it is perhaps worth pointing out that one of them is among the most dangerous drugs, which has led to psychosis, suicide and murder.

I shall leave the editor of the *Spectator* to pick the bones out of that; my own interest starts further back. It is the impending fate of Mr Graham Dene, the Capital Radio disc jockey who – I think I must tip my hat to Bateman here, and break into capital letters – was The Man Who Had No Idea of What Acid House Meant, and Thus Had His Career Limited. And what I want to say about Mr Dene is that if that was all it took to limit it, then before the calamity fell upon him he must have had one hell of a career.

Now for the other linked but separate item. Among those who have come to the rescue of John Lennon's posthumous reputation is Mr Ray Coleman, formerly editor-in-chief of *Melody Maker* (the sheer grandeur of the posts held by the people in this story is beginning to give me the creeps). He plainly knew Lennon very well. And in an editorial footnote to his article (in the *Sunday Times*) it was revealed that he 'has written a definitive biography of Brian Epstein'.

I think this is what we journalists call a 'hot flash', not just *any* biography of Brian Epstein, but a definitive one. I can see it now; eleven pages of Acknowledgements, seventeen of Bibliography and forty-four of source-notes, with a massive Index and a promise in the Introduction of a forthcoming edition of the Letters in six volumes. Looking sick, Holroyd, are you? I'm not surprised.

Well, there are my three coconuts; revelations about Lennon, the last word on Brian Epstein, and the career, poised on the brink of the abyss, of Graham Dene. Let's have a shy.

Young people today want music of a kind very different indeed from the traditional forms which, though of course constantly changing, held sway until perhaps the late 1950s. New, far more violent sounds were then demanded and were supplied; these styles, too, changed constantly, indeed more rapidly than ever before, but over the three decades of such development there has been no general reaction, no hint of a return to a less shallow, a more gentle, quality.

Four things above all have marked the course of this phenomenon, each of them unprecedented. First, the long-playing record and television combined to bring the heroes of the hour (the hour, for most, was brief indeed) to hundreds of millions throughout the western world, and to still-growing numbers elsewhere. Second, and following from this, stupendous fortunes were made and spent, and managers, promoters and producers, many of whom were honest, turned entertainment into a gigantic industry. Third, the world of pop music became ineradicably infested with drugs; despite the appalling number of drug-related deaths among some of the leading figures (and far more among the obscure ones), very substantial numbers of the music's followers, to a large extent in emulation of their heroes, entered the world of drugs, though it must be recognized, of course, that there were many other routes into that world. Fourth, not just the phenomenon of the pop music industry, but the practitioners, and even the music itself, were taken seriously.

My three items fit like the finest dovetail joints into the world I have – in a necessarily much over-simplified form – depicted. First, if even a handful of the Goldman 'revelations' about Lennon are true (and, significantly, Lennon's defenders have concentrated mainly on attacking only one of them), then the world of drugs, squalor and madness which he and many around him inhabited for a substantial part of his life represents a Gehenna that would make the sternest and most puritanical believer in retribution weep tears of blood in pity.

Take next the Capital Radio disc jockey who was condemned, it seems, for not knowing what 'acid house' music was. For all I know, poor Mr Dene will truly suffer if there is a gap in his knowledge, but stop and think what he is being condemned for; it is for not knowing that one form of rubbish has been superseded by another (and one, moreover, that is 'impossible to listen to'). Could even a disc jockey deserve such a fate? And while we're on this bit of the story, what about Mr Berkmann, whose ear is so refined that it can accept acid house and reject hip-hop, and who can gasp in mingled amazement and indignation because Number One in the singles chart is 'The Only Way is Up' and Number Seven is 'I Need You'.

And finally, the Definitive Epstein. Did you know he died at exactly the same age as Schubert? Do you know what was the epitaph that Grillparzer wrote for him (him Schubert, not him Epstein)? 'The art of music has entombed a great possession, but far fairer hopes.' No doubt the definitive biography will make similar claims, and millions will believe them, including some who have heard of Schubert.

I could get all solemn here, and denounce the world that has stolen art from two generations of children, and looks like robbing a good many more. I could lay blame – cynical promoters, indifferent parents, the time that's out of joint.

I could even point out – well, I *will*, because nobody

else ever does – that the acquisition of overnight fortunes by young men and women who have never previously had more than pocket money is, or at any rate has certainly been, a broad highway to disaster. If wishes were horses, beggars could ride, but these days wishes *are* horses, and the beggars ride to hell.

But I am not here to provide moral apophthegms to be woven into samplers or burnt into pokerwork shingles. The great thing about both art and entertainment is that nothing precludes anything else; we can all have what we want. On the other hand, there is an element in this story that has nothing to do with art *or* entertainment, but much to do with wealth, illusion, fantasy, madness, poison and self-destruction.

If you like, the whole of popular music, indeed the whole of the popular scene, is a symptom of something else, though I don't know what. Until modern times nobody would have been in any doubt; it would have been clear that the world was coming to an end. Meanwhile, we are living in a society which makes gods of people like John Lennon, which limits the career of a disc jockey if he doesn't know what acid house music is, and which not only thinks that the definitive Life of Brian Epstein has been written, but that it matters. Perhaps the world *is* coming to an end.

Later. I take it all back. Reported, top of the page, in the *Daily Mail*, is the momentous news that 'One of the last great Elvis Presley mysteries may have been solved by a retired pilot who claims to have the first record he ever made . . . Record dealers believe it will fetch well into five figures . . .'

The Times August 29th, 1988

Death be not proud

PROFESSOR GEORGE STEINER, writing in the *Sunday Times* about Martin Gilbert's book on the Holocaust, said, very pertinently, 'This is not a review – how in God's name do you *review* a book like this?' Similarly, in writing about an astonishing work, *Ghetto*, to be seen at the National Theatre, I am not obliged to observe the requirements of theatre criticism, to dissect it, to analyse the nature and quality of the text and the staging, in a word to treat it as a play; for that would inevitably be to diminish it. Then is it not a play? I think it is not, though it is immensely theatrical, and God knows that the stuff it is made of is as dramatic as anything in all the history of evil, courage, heroism and faith.

Ghetto is set in one. Joshua Sobol's not-play is based on a terrible reality; it portrays the ghetto in Vilna, Lithuania, into which the Jews of the city were herded by the Nazis. The characters are real people; they are given their real names; they did the things we see them do, and more, much more. The musical-theatre troupe which dominates *Ghetto* existed, and did put on such shows; the whole population of the ghetto was, towards the end of the war, exterminated.

The drama itself turns on a crux that will be debated until the end of history; it is the very theme that Jim Allen debauched and defiled in *Perdition*. It is summed up in the character of Jacob Gens, chief of the Jewish police in the ghetto, a man driven by an insoluble yet inescapable dilemma. The Jewish councils, to which the Nazis delegated internal power in the ghettos, did the work the Nazis wanted done; they supplied labour, they kept the

victims docile, they even drew up tidy lists for the transports
bound for the gas-chambers.

Their defence, Jacob Gens's defence, was and is that they
could not resist the Nazis; to attempt to do so would bring
death to all, and by co-operating they could save at least
some. In the end, that hope proved almost entirely vain,
but it was not an entirely ignoble one, and Gens puts the
case for the defence in a speech of fire:

> More than a few of you consider me a traitor. And
> you're wondering how it is that I'm still here among you
> with your innocent, your unsullied souls. I, Jacob Gens,
> who gives orders to blow up the hideouts you prepare.
> The same Jacob Gens who puzzles out way after way to
> save the lives of Jews.
>
> I calculate in Jewish blood, not Jewish dignity. The
> Germans want a thousand Jews. I hand them over. If I
> don't they will come here and take them by force. And
> then they won't take a thousand. They'll take thousands.
> And thousands.
>
> You with your morality! There's dirt, there's filth,
> you look away. If you survive you'll show your hands –
> clean. Whereas I, Jacob Gens, will be, if I am anything,
> drenched in blood, dripping with slime.
>
> I'll submit myself to Jewish justice! I will stand trial!
> I'll tell them: what I did was done to save Jews, as many
> as possible, to lead them to freedom. To do this, I had
> no choice but to lead some to death. With my own
> hands I did it. For the sake of your clean conscience I
> plunged into filth. I couldn't afford a clean conscience.
> *Could I?*

No, he couldn't; and if it had not been for men like him, it
is probable that even fewer would have survived. Some of his
kind, to be sure, were corrupt (Weiskopf in *Ghetto*); would
you guarantee that your integrity would remain unblemished
in a world in which (the phrase is Walter Mehring's) a man

would seize on a corpse if he wanted somewhere dry to lie down?

And yet the corpse had died. Gens had to look impassively at scenes that no Satan could have invented (there is one episode which will make you feel physically sick); you can see the iron entering into his soul, even as he bargains for another few hundred Jewish lives. (The real Gens, incidentally, like the stage one, died, by his own choice, with his people.)

So, then, this is a work that depicts, by focusing on one tiny corner of it, the Holocaust, and adds another portrait to the gallery of ultimate wickedness; yes?

No. The author of *Ghetto* is, of course, concerned to bring the reality of mass murder on to his stage, as well as showing the struggle that the Genses had to fight every minute of their lives. But then, an extraordinary transformation unfolds. This work is not about evil, but about good, and just as we know that the killers we see on the stage really existed, and really killed, and know also that the tormented Gens and his kind really existed, and were really tormented, and know in addition that the real Weiskopfs did truly sell death for a profit, and the real Hermann Kruk did spend much of his time splitting political hairs (though much more of it trying to save the volumes that would preserve the knowledge of Jewish culture) – just as we know all these things, and face them with pity, anger, incredulity, we know one more thing, and that the most remarkable of all.

The Vilna theatrical troupe was as real as anything or anybody else in the real Vilna ghetto. And it is on their shoulders that there rests the burden of *Ghetto*; a considerable burden, too, since it is nothing less than turning a tale of death into a shout of triumph. So help me, the refrain of the final song (the massacred cast rise from the dead to sing it in unison, which would alone make the point) is 'We'll live for ever, year after year, We'll live for ever, for we are here, We'll live for ever beyond the flames, and you will never forget our names.'

That was the spirit which animated the Vilna troupe, and which kept hope alive, though it was dead and buried; instead of reckoning the distance to three score and ten, these people had seized instinctively on a measuring-rod *sub specie aeternitatis*, and managed not only to sing, but to laugh.

And the point is made in one of the most dramatic and memorable scenes of the entire work. The Vilna Jews have staged a black, bitter cabaret, the central figure of which is the Führer himself. As the scene reaches its outrageous and sickening apogee, the tempo changes, and the whole company launches fortissimo, into the 'Ode to Joy' from the Ninth Symphony, *while giving, throughout, the Nazi salute.*

That, I can tell you, made the point: heaped up, pressed down, and running over. 'We'll live for ever . . .'; well, nobody lives for ever. But in the longevity contest between Beethoven and Nazism, it is not difficult to forecast the winner.

I hope I have lived up to my claim that *Ghetto* cannot be classified as a play, at any rate without making it something less than it is. Many plays *include*, but very few *are*, a prolonged hymn to the inextinguishable human spirit, and its eternal striving towards the light. This one is; as one of Hitler's countrymen observed, *Edel sei der Mensch, hilfreich und gut.* The test is obvious and inescapable: do you leave the National Theatre bowed down by the horror, twisted in vicarious agony, burning with rage against man's inhumanity to man? No, you do not; you leave it – though the horror, the agony and the rage are no less present and potent – uplifted and enhanced, admiring even more highly the capacity of the human race to distinguish what does matter from what only seems to matter.

In Vilna, what did matter was the future they would never see, and what only seemed to matter was the present of hunger, humiliation and death. And death shall have no dominion.

The Times August 7th, 1989

The evil that men do lives after them

To HAVE BEEN in the Second World War, on either side, a man would now be in his mid-sixties; to have gained any significant rank, he would now be seventy or so; to have had a post of real responsibility, mid-seventies or more.

Why this arithmetic? Because two men who did have considerable wartime responsibility, in a highly specialized field, are in the news; they are respectively eighty-seven and seventy-nine years old. The elder is Captain Ferdinand aus der Fünten, a most mellifluous name; the younger is more demotically identified, as befits a mere NCO: Franz Fischer. They have both had ample leisure to mark the relentless advance of the grey in their hair since they ceased to wear uniform – or, more precisely, changed its cut – and they have doubtless often thought, as the years went by, about their wartime experiences, as all veterans do. *What* they thought about their role is not known, though it would be particularly interesting to learn whether their view of their wartime service has changed in any significant way with the passage of time.

I hope so; certainly they have had more opportunity than most to weigh such questions, and plenty of unbroken quiet to encourage contemplation. For these two have been in prison for over forty years, and all because of what they did in the war.

What they did in the war was to organize the murder of Dutch Jews, and they did it with such efficiency and assiduity that they achieved the notable feat of putting the

Netherlands first in the table of all the Nazi-occupied lands of western Europe, measured by the proportion of the Jewish communities which perished in the Holocaust.

There must, of course, be more such human relics of that time; the wheels of murder took a lot of manpower to turn. Far more are dead, and most of the survivors are as old as this pair. I don't know if they hold another record – length of time in prison for war crimes – but I imagine they do; only a year or two ago the longest-serving war-criminal prisoner in Italy, another mass-murderer, was released, and an Austrian Cabinet Minister waltzed off to Vienna Airport, to shake his hand and welcome him home. (Nobody knows what remnants remain in the Soviet camps, or whether anybody remembers why they are there.)

The point today, however, is that the two horsemen of the Dutch-Jewish apocalypse have been released, and by now must have reached home in Germany. The decision to let them out was taken by the Netherlands Parliament, and it was bitterly fought. An earlier attempt, in 1972, had failed, though it had been pointed out at the time that Dutch criminals sentenced to life imprisonment normally never served more than twenty years. This time the motion for release was passed.

There were hostile demonstrations against the action; Dutch ex-servicemen and, of course, Jewish organizations of Holocaust survivors (who themselves must all be elderly), protested against the release. The Minister of Justice rather quaintly argued that it was right to let them go because their presence on Dutch soil polluted the country; he did not explain why it took him more than four decades to notice.

I realize that the ice beneath me is thin. No member of my family, as far as I know, died in the gas chambers, and I shall be told that it behoves me to be silent when those less fortunate speak. Nevertheless, I applaud the Dutch decision, as I applauded the earlier Italian one; indeed, mine may have been the first voice in this country to urge the release from Spandau of Rudolf Hess himself.

Why do I take this view? (I assume nobody thinks I am a covert Nazi sympathizer.) First, let me be logical, though I know these questions cannot be answered with logic. What conceivable punishment would be appropriate for those who organized and carried out the Final Solution? Imprisonment for life and for 999 reincarnations? Hanging? Hanging, drawing and quartering? Fifty years of torture? The catalogue becomes repulsive, not because it is barbarous but because if it were a thousandfold more barbarous it would still be inadequate, so stupendous is the gap between what happened and what could possibly be done about it. We did what we could. We hanged some at Nuremberg and elsewhere, imprisoned more. The Nuremberg Trials were themselves the most salutary action; by the time the whole of the evidence had been published to the world (I can remember clearly the wave of horrified incredulity that flooded civilization, leaving, as it receded, only the horrified realization that it was all true), the world had changed for ever.

And then? Most countries which include a sentence of life imprisonment in their penal codes have a limitation, formal or customary, on the number of years the criminal actually serves. Some of the Nazis – Hess the most notable – were sentenced in a jurisdiction that allowed of no such simple release; others were recognized as having committed crimes so abominable as to permit of no commutation, parole or clemency. I would like to think that the Inquisitor's charge to Joan had been in mind when they were sentenced, but I doubt it:

> . . . that thou mayest repent thy errors in solitary contemplation, and be shielded from all temptation to return to them, we, for the good of thy soul, and for a penance that may wipe out thy sins and bring thee finally unspotted to the throne of grace, do condemn thee to eat the bread of sorrow and drink the water of affliction to the end of thy earthly days in perpetual imprisonment.

Anyway, when a generation and a half had been born and grown up, those holding the last scraps of Nazi evil began to wonder what good purpose it was serving, and having concluded that the answer was none, began to let them out. Few of the survivors of 'life' imprisonment were young enough to do anything but go home and eke out the days before death claimed them; I know of none who subsequently took part in any neo-Nazi movement. It all comes down to the ancient question: *cui bono?*

Will the slaughtered dead die again when their murderers are released? Will those survivors whom the murderers bereaved suffer any more? Is justice condemned to perpetual impassivity, do the laws admit of no loophole through which old men, their wickedness expiated, may crawl into the light?

Now ask the most important question of all. If such men, in such circumstances, are released, is it likely that the world will be moved even a hair's breadth towards a repetition of what such men did? Surely no one will say yes to that? Then if clemency is not dangerous on the one hand, and helps neither the dead nor their descendants on the other, must it not be right to exercise humanity even for those who showed none? (And this does not take into account the possibility that true repentance has taken place. Who will dare to say that that is impossible? There is evidence that Walter Funk, one of the leading Nazis at Nuremberg, had realized his wickedness even before the trial ended.)

I don't know how many more such aged villains are still imprisoned for what they did as Nazis or the Nazis' servants; time must have dealt with most of the problem already, and even if nothing is done will deal with the rest of it fairly soon. But it would be an act of decency and compassion to let them all out now, and let them lay their bones, even if they have never repented their crimes, in their native land, amid such family as they have left.

I would, indeed, go further, and cease the hunt for those Nazi criminals who have never been brought to justice; their ranks, too, must have thinned almost to nothing, and the poisoned line will soon die out completely. We must never forget; and forgiveness is no business of us who did not suffer. But clemency is another matter, and I can see no legal or moral impediment to a general amnesty for crimes which will soon be half a century old, and which were committed by men already now on the very edge of the grave.

Let Ferdinand aus der Fünten and Franz Fischer go home and never be heard of again, and let the rest of us remember Dogberry's words: 'Why, then, take no note of him, but let him go; and presently call the rest of the watch together, and thank God you are rid of a knave.'

The Times February 2nd, 1989

The index finger points

I WARN YOU: you may not think this matters. Well, I do. It is about indexes, on which I have written before, in a different context.

One of the delusions which writers entertain is that if you can write a book you can also index it. Delusion indeed; indexing is a highly skilled science, and it would be as foolish for a writer unversed in its mysteries to compile his own Index as it would be for him to attempt, without the requisite knowledge, to cut the type from which his book is to be printed.

There is a highly professional body, the Society of Indexers – of which I am a member *honoris causa*, because although I do not compile indexes (oh, no, you must NOT call them indices), not even my own, I have defended the profession and its integrity for many years now. The Society has a very exacting test for those who wish to be considered as professionally qualified, so if you wish to be sure that your book is in properly expert hands, you must go to the custodian of the Register. (Some indexers specialize in particular subjects; the Society keeps a record of these, too.)

My own indexer, who has indexed my last nine books (and whom I dote upon so that I might not beteem the winds of heaven visit her face too roughly), is a Treasure, despite her odd conviction that the poet Herrick's forename was Kevin; she not only provides perfect Indexes, but does so at astonishing speed. The story I am about to unfold will cause her to emit shrieks of horror, while as for the Society of Indexers, they will probably drape the windows in black, and hang a wreath on the door knob.

For the dreadful story which follows ought to be indexed under some such heading as 'Oxford University Press, appalling scandal of', or 'Arson, no reasonable jury would convict for', or 'Departed, the glory is (*see* Ichabod)'.

For on my recent travels I took the new biography of John Henry Newman, by Ian Ker, as splendid and enthralling a Life as I have had in my hands for many a day. Father Ker has digested an immense quantity of source material, handling and shaping it with wonderful precision and clarity, and his portraits, not only of Newman and the principal figures of his life, but of many wholly subsidiary characters, spring to life on page after page. The complexities of the theology, which inevitably take up a good deal of the book, are unravelled in a way which greatly pleases the layman without, I imagine, irritating the expert, and Newman's greatness is undeniable (for all that there were half a dozen occasions on which I began to dislike him quite a lot); Ker has plainly concealed nothing, and indeed most of the time stands back and lets the reader judge for himself.

And then I turned to the Index.

It is not attributed, but the first glance is enough to demonstrate that it is most certainly not by anyone on the Register of Indexers; its full, almost heroic, awfulness needs proper savouring, since every time the reader thinks that the nadir must now have been reached, whoever is responsible for it shows that there is worse to come.

The sign of an indexer who is wholly unequal to the task is the use of strings of undifferentiated page numbers which, as far as the reader's need of an Index is concerned, is literally useless. Here, for instance, is the Index entry for Manning, someone who must figure largely in a life of Newman:

Manning, Henry Edward 159, 178-9, 280, 350, 397, 486, 489, 498-9, 507, 512, 515, 521, 526, 528, 529-30, 532, 540, 541, 553-4, 563, 565-8, 570-4, 576, 577, 578-9, 581-2, 588-91, 597-600, 602, 604, 605, 606, 607, 608-9, 611-13, 615-16, 618, 626, 627, 634, 635, 651, 658-9, 662, 670, 676, 679, 690-1, 695, 696, 715-18, 722, 732, 733, 744.

And here is the entry for one whose life was even more closely entwined with Newman's:

Wiseman, Nicholas 69, 118-19, 129, 133-4, 135, 158, 182-3, 187, 192, 198, 213, 225, 232, 234, 317-18, 321, 325, 328, 330, 331-2, 339, 341, 342, 345, 352, 360, 372-4, 382, 400, 405, 418, 419, 420, 424-7, 435-6, 437, 446-7, 463, 464, 466-8, 469, 470, 471, 472, 474-5, 476-7, 486-9, 499, 506, 507, 512, 515-17, 521, 526, 535, 540, 565, 567, 568, 569-72, 574, 597, 598, 608, 662, 694, 708.

What is the point of wasting space on idiocy of that order? What conceivable purpose could it serve? How *dare* the publishers print it under the noble and meaningful heading 'Index'?

I warn them, I want an answer to those questions. But I assure you that what I have recorded so far is nothing but the cherry; the cake, in all its monstrous glory, is to come. We turn now to the Index entry of the subject himself: Newman, John Henry.

We start rather well, thus:

Newman, John Henry . . . toughness of viii, 10, 42-3, 86, 346, 373, 426-7, 434, 446, 654, 695, 708, 723, 737, 739-40 . . . and the real and unreal . . . viii, 12, 22, 46, 48-9, 59, 60, 61, 65, 67, 68, 80, 91, 92, 93-100, 106, 113-14, 128, 132, 140-2, 152-3, 161, 168, 173, 175-6, 180, 188, 199, 204, 206, 209, 211, 212, 226, 238, 251-2, 253, 255, 263, 267, 269, 273, 276, 277, 279, 280, 282, 283, 284, 285, 290, 294, 307, 320-1, 324, 333-6, 339, 341, 432, 351-5, 358, 370, 396, 421, 445, 484, 569, 582, 588, 593, 628, 640, 642, 674, 681, 685, 686, 692, 698, 700, 702, 708, 709, 745 . . .

So far, so bad; but wait. Two-thirds of the Index is devoted to Newman, under some 500 sub-headings, many of them as ridiculous as they are otiose (Newman and Sicily, and Irish Church Temporalities Bill, on holiness, on preaching, and Dissenters, on praying for dead, and difficulty of writing . . .), but as I read steadily through them, column after column after column, the hair began to rise on the back of my neck, as the truth, and nothing but the truth, dawned: *the hundreds of references are not in alphabetical order at all, but only in the order in which they appear in the book*; twenty-five columns are broken down higgledy-piggledy into these minutiae, and the entire four yards of Index devoted to Newman is as much waste paper as my numerical examples.

And the publishers are the OUP! Not Messrs Rubbish and Buffoon, but the Oxford University Press! This firm goes back more than four centuries, is widely believed to be of good repute, and lays claim to the highest scholarly standards. Yet somebody in a responsible position there saw that Index before the book was published, and left it as it was. Somebody thought it would do for the OUP. Somebody stamped the publishers' secular equivalent of the *nihil obstat* on it, and sent it to be printed.

Well, I want that somebody's blood – all of it – delivered to me in a clean jug, with a paint brush, thus enabling me to inscribe right across the façade of the OUP's main building: 'This firm was once taken seriously, and deserved to be.' And I also want the sum of £500 to be given by the OUP to the Society of Indexers, to be wholly devoted to the relief of indexers who have fallen on hard times, particularly those whose misfortune was caused by working for the OUP.

The Times November 16th, 1989

Invariably upwards

I HAVE A question for you; it concerns principally those who hold shopping credit-cards issued by Top Man, Burton, Principles for Women, Principles for Men, Champion Sport, Top Shop, Evans, Dorothy Perkins, Debenhams and Harvey Nichols, but at one short remove it concerns everybody, even those who have never set foot in any of these places. The question is: are you very stupid – very stupid indeed?

Please do not take offence; this is *not* a comment disguised as a question, but a genuine inquiry, to which I would genuinely like the answer: are you thick as two planks, dumb as an ox, out to lunch, daft as a brush, a couple of coupons short of a pop-up toaster, bird-brained, not all there, *meshuggah*, weak in the upper storey, gormless, addle-brained, pig-ignorant, gaga, clod-plated, dead from the neck up, feeble-minded, barmy, *or any two or more of these*?

I repeat, don't bridle. I am making no accusations, and assuming nothing; I just want you to tell me whether you fit any or all of those descriptions. In asking you, I am of course putting you on your honour to tell the truth, but I shall not cross-examine you or sneer, much less declare that I do not believe you. With that assurance, will those who *deny* that they are very stupid, etc., kindly raise their *right* hands; those who *accept* the charges should raise their *left* hands.

Thank you. If you couldn't see the outcome from where you are standing, let me give you the result: the overwhelming majority – it must have been at least fifty to one – raised their right hands, thus rejecting the imputations I listed. Ladies and gentlemen, you are *not* very stupid indeed. But the people who own the shops I listed – they all come under the three umbrellas of Debenhams plc, The Burton Group plc, and Harvey Nichols and Company Ltd – are convinced that you are.

The evidence is to be found in advertisements which these groups have been putting in the press. Headed 'Notice to Personal Account Cardholders', they list the higher rates of interest which customers will now have to pay for their credit. For instance, charge-account cardholders paying by direct debit will now be charged at an increased APR of 34.4 per cent for goods and services, and a similarly hiked APR of 35.1 per cent for cash and cash substitutes. Meanwhile, Budget Account shoppers (this applies only to Debenhams and Harvey Nichols) will be up-mulcted to APR 38.4 per cent for goods and services and a vertical take-off APR of 39.2 per cent.

Before I explain, I must get my breath back. The pawn-brokers of my childhood were rapacious enough, but a rate nudging 40 per cent would have made the most brazen of them blush. I have said before that those who fail to pay off their bank credit-cards monthly, and thus incur monstrous interest charges, are – well, they should have raised their left hands. But can there really be shop customers who are willing to be fleeced like that? When they could get an overdraft to pay the shopping bill for a very great deal less?

But I digress; I promised you the evidence which demonstrates the shops' opinion of your intelligence. Nowhere in the advertisements listing the new, higher charges is it admitted that they *are* higher; no, the word throughout is 'varied' or 'new'. The preamble says that the rates 'are to be varied': the detailed listings speak of 'the new rate of interest'. The announcement at the bottom, which incidentally tears up the cardholders' agreements, says those agreements 'are varied'.

You can have a lot of quiet fun with this wheeze. What
about a song beginning 'The varied we are together', or
phrases like 'New's the pity', or – for Arsenal supporters –
'Varied the Gunners!'? Then again, another couple of drinks
and you'll be as new as a kite, fashionable girls in shoe shops
will insist on varied heels, and the next time I am near the
Frick Museum, I must pop in and see the Holbein of St
Thomas New.

I said that although the customers of these shops are
directly involved, ultimately it concerns everybody, and so
it does. For it epitomizes two tendencies in our world, and
both of them are nasty.

The first is the one I have dwelt on; the belief that
people are such fools that when they see that prices are
to be 'varied', they do not realize that what is meant is
that the prices are to be increased.

You may say that everybody does realize what is meant,
so no harm, though a good deal of irritation, arises. True,
but apart from the fact that nobody likes to be thought a
fool, there is also the contempt for their shoppers displayed
by such weasel-wording, and that is part of the distancing
effect of modern shopping – typified, of course, by the
supermarket – which is itself a part of the more general
distancing in our society.

The truth is that cause and effect have veered so far
apart that many people cannot see that they are in any way
connected, and in its trivial way, the inability to understand
that shoppers should not be insulted by shopkeepers is a
further sign of the death of empathy.

Another tendency demonstrated in this absurd business
is the belief that words have no life of their own, and
that they certainly have no feelings, so that they can be
pummelled into different shapes, stood on their heads, cut
in pieces, and above all replaced by others at any time and
for any wish or whim.

It is not so. When you say that your prices are to

be varied, when what you mean is that they are going up, you have done something more than make a silly and self-defeating attempt to deceive your customers. You have debased the language as well as truth.

Vary is a noble old word; Chaucer used it, and so did Shakespeare, who also used 'varied'. I don't think either of them would care for their use by some smart-arse in the PR department of Debenhams (incidentally, what became of Freebody – did Debenham murder him?), but more to the point, the words themselves bleed afresh at such rough handling. Even that wicked, *wicked* Dr Burchfield, who will let almost any word into the language if it knocks on his door and looks wistful, and who thinks it no shame to watch a word undress and kit itself out in drag – even he, surely, would not permit 'varied' to mean 'increased'.

Heavy weather; perhaps, but if you leave a baby Hydra alone, it will not only grow up to be a big Hydra, it will grow nine heads in doing so, and you will have the devil's own job to chop them off. (You need an enormous cautery for a start, and where can you get a well trained charioteer – also essential – these days?)

When and how did we forget to say what we mean? The knell was sounded, as I recall, the first time a ratcatcher became a rodent officer, and I laughed as loudly as anybody. Since then, our world has sunk full fathom five in euphemisms, and soon the only sounds to be heard will be glug-glug-glug. But before we go down, let us write our wills in good, clear, plain English, and if we mean our wife to have our second best bed, let us say so. Oh, and let us add a codicil, to the effect that if the gravedigger has varied his rates, we insist on being cremated.

The Times November 20th, 1989

The song of the shirt

NEVER MIND WHAT I was doing in a garment factory off Fifth Avenue, watching a hundred or so women at sewing machines: what *they* were doing was turning out a prodigious quantity of cheap but pleasant dresses and blouses. But never mind that either; pick up the story as I am talking to the boss. I had already noticed that practically all the women working there were of Hispanic origin, and when the factory owner told me that the place we were in was only one of seventeen such factories he owned, I inquired as to whether the others were also staffed by Hispanics.

'No,' he said, 'this is the only one. Everybody in all the others is Chinese.'

A somewhat surrealist image arose in my mind; of hundreds of Chinese heads bent inscrutably over the whirring needles in sixteen factories scattered through the Garment District. I put it aside, and asked the obvious question: why Chinese? His answer illuminated history as by a flash of lightning: 'Because', he said, 'the Jews and the Italians are all doctors and lawyers.'

It was not only history the words lit up; it was also the story of my life. My maternal grandparents emigrated from Tsarist Russia in the 1880s, and fetched up in London (not that they had any idea of what that was). They had no saleable trade, peasants being very little in demand in Camden Town, but there was already an organization for helping the new arrivals, and in no time my grandfather had mastered the rudiments of tailoring, which served him and his wife for a living (a pretty bare one) all his days.

They had three sons; one was killed in the First World War, and the other two became dance-band musicians, though they subsequently went into small businesses. There were two daughters, one of whom died young; the elder was my mother, who lived to be the owner of the most famous bathroom geyser in the world. She was a milliner.

And here am I. I am not a doctor or a lawyer, though my mother wanted me to be the latter and my father the former, but I have made my way in my profession of letters, and have achieved success in it. But the point of all this climbing about in my family tree is the point the New York garment manufacturer was making. Every wave of immigrants breaks on a shore of inability and ignorance; those who come with nothing must fight their way up the beach to find a living.

It can turn out to be a good living; somebody recently counted the number of millionaires in Britain called Patel, and a startlingly large number it is. But what Mr Patel wants for his sons (and, increasingly, for his daughters, even if the daughters have to make him want it) is what every immigrant group successively wants for its children, or certainly grandchildren, and that is the thing they never had themselves: education.

Education, that is, not as outstanding hewers of wood and leading drawers of water, but in the skills that lead to the professions which bring not just money but respect. Of course, millions fail to clear the hurdles; I am over-simplifying. But the point remains valid; immigrants, without the language of the host country or the skills it demands, will toil from dawn until the sun goes down, and for hours afterwards, to ensure that their now native-born children can make their way, equal to any, into the very heart of the society that took their fathers in.

That all flashed through my mind in an instant, evoked by a single sentence: 'The Jews and the Italians are all doctors and lawyers.' When the instant passed, I asked the next question:

'What are you going to do when the Chinese are all doctors and lawyers?'

The factory owner replied with words that lit up the future as his previous remark had enlightened the past: 'It's happening already,' he said. It was time for a third question, as obvious as the first two. 'Well, when it's happened, who's going to do the rough work?' Again, his answer defined our world: 'There isn't anybody left.'

It is true; but it is true for an extraordinary reason. The refugees who produced the American melting pot came to escape either from the persecution of tyrants or from the persecution of poverty. But why would, say, South Koreans, whose country has one of the fastest-growing economies in the world, and whose government has at last begun to be less authoritarian, want to emigrate to a land whose streets they no longer believe to be paved with gold? The Japanese economic miracle is familiar to us all; the South Korean and Taiwanese miracles have only just begun, but before they are accomplished they will have chilled the blood of the Japanese themselves, let alone the all-powerful Americans and the uncertain Europeans.

Back to the factory owner. 'Well, if there isn't anybody left to come in and sweep up, what's going to happen?' He replied: 'We're going to stop making things altogether – and that's started already, too.'

It has indeed; I sometimes think that by the turn of the century Britain will consist entirely of hairdressers. All over the industrialized world the figures for those employed in manufacturing have consistently fallen, partly because new methods have dispensed with many hands (like the print workers in the Wapping Revolution) and partly because if it is cheaper to buy elsewhere than to make at home, buying elsewhere will become the rule, tariffs or no tariffs. Did you know that South Korea now makes motor cars? No wonder even the Chinese, to say nothing of Mr Gorbachev, are desperate to start making their industries efficient; they can see what is coming to even the fittest economies of the advanced world.

Meanwhile it is coming very fast to the garment district
of New York. The Chinese at their sewing machines will
work for lower wages than the Hispanics, who will work
for less than the blacks, who . . . but it goes on up, all the
way to the Lowells and the Cabots.

The Chinese who will take the lowest pay, however, are
the present generation; their children will not know how a
sewing machine works, or care; but they will have mastered
the arts of computer-programming and, for that matter,
medicine and the law, and one of *their* children will entertain dreams, by no means absurd, of running for president.
Do you suppose people called Dukakis and Brzezinski and
Deukmejian and Cuomo (or Schweizer, my brother-in-law,
for that matter) came over in the Mayflower? Jesse Jackson
certainly didn't.

The world changes slowly, but it changes. There will,
of course, always be refugees, fleeing starvation or tyranny; there will always be parents who slave for pennies so
that their children will be equipped to make their way in a
demanding world. But unless (which is inconceivable) the
Western world is willing to throw open its frontiers to the
peoples of Africa and the Indian sub-continent, there will
be no more huddled masses, yearning to breathe free, to man
the sweatshops and to see that their children are educated.

But the point the garment manufacturer made means that
even if it were to come about it would not solve the problem,
because by the time it had happened the transfer from manufacturing to the service industries would have gone so far that
there would be no sweatshops for the incomers to staff.

If any of my readers are wondering where and when they
should be born, I would advise them to see the light of day
in Seoul about thirty years from now. There will be plenty
of Americans to sew the baby clothes.

The Times May 23rd, 1988

Crack pots, not heads

W HO DIES IF England live? The poet did not stay for an answer, but I shall give it today. Indeed, although my theme is made up of the most appalling mutual accusations of forgery, bankruptcy, frame-ups, resignations and the Kentish Town police station, I shall show that amid the shenanigans and the murk the story demonstrates not only that the mighty heart of England is still beating true, but that what at first blush (and there is a good deal of blushing involved) seems to be a scandal of the kind hitherto confined to other countries, is in fact the proof that England is uniquely splendid, just as we have always thought.

The background, which differs from most backgrounds in that it is in the foreground, was provided in these pages by Paul Vallely. It concerns Cecil Sharp House, a handsome building in London which is the headquarters of the English Folk Dance and Song society. The society is in difficult financial straits, and it was proposed that the building should be sold to raise the wind. Thereupon, all hell broke loose; the executive of the organization were thrown out; when elections were held it transpired bundles of suspiciously superfluous ballot-papers were floating around; new ones were printed, whereupon hundreds of forged ones – some pink, some green – turned up; handwriting experts have been called in; wholesale resignations have taken place; the Charity Commissioners have been asked to investigate (if I were the Charity Commissioners faced with uproar on this scale, I think I would don a false beard and tinted spectacles and leave the country until the whole thing had blown

over); and meanwhile the practice of English Folk Dancing
and Singing fades away, and soon there will be none but
greybeards who know the difference between Sir Roger de
Coverley and Come Ye From Newcastle?

Scapegoats and chemical analysis; innuendo and smear
campaigns; Debenham, Tewson and Chinnocks; where is
Agatha Christie – nay, Freeman Wills Crofts – now that we
really need them? But let us not suppose that we need them
in order to unmask the villains in the last chapter; no, their
role is not investigatory but celebratory. It has rarely been
observed – I may be the first to point it out – that the old
school of detective story writers provided the most intense
form of Englishness imaginable, in their books' settings,
characters, actions and, above all, speech. Some of these
writers, indeed, clearly felt that although a straightforward
murder could reasonably be committed by an Englishman,
anything more dodgy must have been the responsibility of
the nearest foreigner. (True, Hercule Poirot was not English,
and he was a detective; but no one would have been surprised
if he had turned out to be the villain after all.)

Cecil Sharp, who seems to have been forgotten in the
goings-on, did a great service to this country, in patiently
collecting traditional songs (many of which had never been
written down) and dances (which had certainly not been
choreographed); his work immediately brings to mind the
Opies and their splendid work of collecting, often from the
most remote corners of the land, a huge hoard of treasure
in the form of children's rhymes and verses.

It must have been very easy to make fun of Sharp as he went
about his work with notebook and pencil (and, I dare say,
galoshes), but the more thoughtful observers should have
realized that he was doing noble work. For what do dance
and song mean for those to whom they have been handed
down from generation to generation? Surely, it is the essence
– the roots, rather – of the country, and surely the tending of
those roots is more urgently needed today than ever before,

as the inexorable homogenization of our country, nationally
as its regions are blurred and internationally as it is fitted into
a succession of bastard 'communities', shrinks and shrivels
the very notion of England.

Now, where in all that does the skulduggery (if any,
m'lud) at Cecil Sharp House fit in? In two places, I think.
The first is obvious; the factions battling for control are certainly not doing so for money (the whole point of selling the
building was the staving-off of financial ruin); they are acting
only out of concern for the tradition in which they believe
and indeed decorously practise. Of course, what they are
doing in pursuit of their ideals is making certain that the
whole movement and all its activities will come to an end
in recrimination, insolvency and tears, but when tempers are
as high as those of all concerned at present, reason is the
first victim to be trampled in the rush. If you ask me,
the version of the Judgement of Solomon we have is a fake;
the truth is that both women said that they were perfectly
happy to have the child cut in two, and it was Solomon who
vetoed their decision – and he only did so because they were
making such a racket over which of them should have which
half.

But it is the other aspect of the extraordinary battle that
is going on in a quiet thoroughfare near Regent's Park
which fascinates me much more.

We are a peaceful people; that's the clue. We have less
violent crime than most comparable countries, but that is
not the test – my test, anyway. We are also an unwarlike
lot; there can be few democracies with less visible indication
of any kind of martial preparedness. But that is not the right
test, either. For the real nature of our peacefulness we have
to look to our politics, of all things. We take it for granted
that even in the most fiercely fought general elections (let
alone by-elections) the 'fought' is metaphorical only. Yet we
shouldn't; instead, we should be marvelling that it should
be so. I well remember the scenes from France in the late
1940s, when French democracy, so recently revived, tottered

on the edge of communist destruction; it was Jules Moch, the Minister of the Interior, supported all the way by de Gaulle, who saved the day. But he saved it by telling the Garde Republicaine (not that they needed much telling) that when it was felt necessary to hit somebody over the head, they should hit extremely hard.

Whence the scenes; whence also the contrast with Britain. And there is another contrast; extremist parties, of the left or the right, have never made any headway here. That may be because we are more politically sophisticated than other nations; but it is more likely to be yet another safeguard against the danger that our citizens (have you noticed that the very word is unused in Britain, smacking as it does of too-earnest foreigners?) might hit one another in furtherance of political differences.

And the foaming at the mouth in and around Cecil Sharp House is there to demonstrate the glorious truth that there is in our people an instinct, buried far too deep to be seen or even sensed, which ensures that any potential murderousness is averted by engaging in quarrels over matters not so much trivial as invisible. You think I am exaggerating? For shame; unsay the word and listen to me. It is common ground among the warring sects at Cecil Sharp House that the entire enterprise – house, society, elections – is up the spout; the bailiffs may be knocking on the door as you read these words. Yet one of the factions is calling for all the ballot papers to be subject to chemical analysis; there are 4,000 of them, and laboratories' time does not come cheap. Fiddling on the *Titanic*? They are *wrestling* on the *Titanic*.

The foreigners laugh. But the more keen-eyed of them may have noticed, as I have, that no blood has been spilt. Who laughs last?

The Times April 13th, 1989

Death 1:
In a pig's eye

BMA ASKS FOR ETHICAL ADVICE ON PIG TRANS-
PLANTS, cried the headline. They shall have it,
they shall have it. My first feeling on reading about the
latest 'breakthrough' was one of revulsion, indeed of horror.
Beware of first feelings, the doctors involved would say – will
say – *do* say. No, say I; trust those first feelings, for in these
matters they are overwhelmingly likely to be right. And there
is a reason for that likelihood. There are impulses in us which
come direct from a level far deeper than reason, and wise men
and women will pay heed to what leaps across the rational
gulf, because it comes from the ultimate repository of moral
truth.

Why, and how, do we *always* know when we are doing
wrong, even if we continue to do it? Because that inner
voice – call it God, call it soul, call it spirit, call it
the subconscious, call it conscience, call it a packet of
prawn-flavoured potato crisps for all I care; it tells us
the truth. Reason, later, finds arguments to back up that
truth (or, too frequently, to deny it), but that extraordinary and inexplicable moral gyroscope which we all have
in us will bring us back into balance if we will only let
it.

Very well; I recoiled in horror at the news that it will
shortly be possible for a pig's kidney to replace a human
being's. But it behoves me to say why.

First, let us consider the heart-transplant operations that
have become so fashionable – nay, all the rage – since Dr
Christiaan Barnard pioneered the treatment. A few voices

were raised at the time, and some more later, at the prodigious waste of resources involved; has any cost-conscious
hospital registrar worked out how many thousands of hip-
operations, cataracts, hernias, prostates, squints, tendons and
sciaticas could have been dealt with if the circus in the next
operating-theatre had not been assembled?

Of course, we must not ask the doctors to play God
(some of them need no asking), and the dilemma is no
less acute than it used to be – indeed, it is more so, because
an ever-rising demand for treatment cannot, this side of
Heaven, be matched by an ever-rising material capacity to
satisfy it. But for that very reason every hospital, and every
surgeon, does in fact choose priorities, and *must* do so. Do
you remember the uproar, some years ago, about the hospital
in which some patients' charts were endorsed NTBR, and it
was discovered that this meant, in the case of those whose
condition was hopeless and who were not expected to live
much longer, 'Not To Be Resuscitated'? The uproar resulted
in the offending letters being expunged, but it is quite certain
that those in charge continued to act as though they were still
there, and so does every other hospital, because they cannot
do otherwise.

The abrupt resignation of the head of the group which
made the pig-kidney discovery is most welcome; to hear his
excited sales-patter, a universal panacea has been discovered,
capable of curing everything from acne to decapitation and
from baldness to income-tax. Mind you, the trouble in the
group seems to have been provoked only by the thought that
such boasting might prejudice their chances of ample funding
for their experiments, and if the money is not forthcoming at
once, howls of protest will be heard, loud enough to ensure
that the more modest weeping of the medical service that is
to be mulcted for their benefit will not be heard.

I would not want to take the tragic decision: if course A is
followed, patient X will live, but patient Z will die, and if
course B is pursued, patient Z will live but patient X will

die. But that brings me to a different part of the argument altogether, where such considerations do not apply. In the first place, it should be recognized that sooner or later patients X and Z will both die, however many nostrums are tried on them, and however many of their vital organs are replaced by those of a passing pig.

This is not just a quibble; I believe that the 'miracle cures' we are now offered three times a day after meals, which are hailed with more enthusiasm than even the inhabitants of Bethany displayed at the raising of Lazarus, are symptomatic of a deeply neurotic fear of death – far greater than ever before in history – which is in turn attributable to the almost total secularization of the life led in societies such as ours. And of all the aspects of that life, it is the end of it that has been most thoroughly purged of any meaning beyond the terrifying nothingness that so many people equate it with.

I am not the first man to wonder why death has become such a terror despite the fact that it is the only thing of which we are certain from the day we are born. I long ago abandoned the thought that it might be because some kind of punishment beyond death is thought to be in store; people stopped believing in an afterlife even before they stopped believing that they had some kind of purpose in this one.

I have gradually come to the conclusion that there is a widespread *resentment* of death, as bringing to an end the pleasures of the world, which will surely soon turn into a demand that it should be abolished. Meanwhile, fear rules people to the extent of refusing even to contemplate death, so that they will snatch at any quacksalver's elixir; when the salesman is not a charlatan but a respectable doctor, the snatching is all the more violent. Who is now allowed to die at home? Very few; in domestic circumstances death will make those around the deathbed to think upon their end, and that would never do.

And so we come to the Island of Dr Moreau. Does anyone read Wells's novels today? Much of the science-fiction has been long surpassed by reality, let alone by even richer imaginations, but this haunting long-short story is a metaphor for our times, and when I read of pigs' kidneys in human bodies I thought of it at once. The eponymous doctor's work consists of blurring the line between animals and men; in effect, he is seeking to make the former into the latter. He succeeds, too, for a time, but God, or possibly biology, is not mocked; the transformed animals begin to revert to their original status, while intoning their tragic slogan: 'Are we not men?'

No, they aren't; but we are. But how much longer will we be when we are emptied out and filled with the kidneys of pigs and the hearts of chimpanzees and the lungs of wart-hogs and the windpipes of rats and the stomachs of cows, and, while we are about it, eye of newt and toe of frog, wool of bat and tongue of dog, adder's fork and blindworm's sting, lizard's leg and howlet's wing, for a charm of powerful trouble, like a hell-broth boil and bubble?

And all for what? For postponing death by a week or a year or several years? Is no one any longer willing even to entertain the possibility that our span on this earth is not only of finite duration, but in some unknowable dimension bestowed for a purpose that is not our own to choose? Stewart Alsop, the American political writer, died of leukaemia; it was a very prolonged death, largely because the course of the malady did not follow the usual pattern, so he had time to write a book about it, called *Stay of Execution*. Towards the end of the book and of his life, he used a haunting phrase: 'There comes a time', he said, 'when a dying man has to die, as a sleepy man has to sleep.' And, in a very different mode, do you remember how Manny Shinwell concluded his 100 years? Conscious and *compos mentis* to the end, he flung up his hands and said 'I've had enough!'

Wise men, both of them. For my part, I shall die when I am good and ready, with my own innards still inside me. Hear Chesterton:

My friends, we will not go again or ape an ancient rage,
Or stretch the folly of our youth to be the shame of age,
But walk with clearer eyes and ears this path that
    wandereth,
And see undrugged in evening light the decent inn
    of death;
For there is good news yet to hear and fine things
    to be seen,
Before we go to Paradise by way of Kensal Green.

The Times August 4th, 1988

Gay go up and gay go down

SURELY THE UNITED STATES is the only country in the world, and San Francisco the only city in that country, which could think up the idea of a male voice choir consisting entirely of homosexuals, 16 per cent of whom are suffering from Aids. Certainly America is the only country in which, when San Francisco had pioneered this curious artistic phenomenon, it would be copied so enthusiastically that there are now dozens of cities with such unisex musical groups, including New York.

It was a good many years ago now that San Francisco became the homosexual (or at any rate male homosexual) capital of the US; after a time, their number was so substantial that the politicians of the city were obliged to take account of a significant voting bloc. Why San Francisco? I have always believed that its well deserved reputation as the most tolerant city in the country drew to its hilly streets many who had experienced rejection and discrimination because of their sexual orientation, particularly those who had 'come out'.

It is said that God is not mocked; probably not, but the devil certainly isn't, for it was in tolerant San Francisco that the infected scythe mowed down the first substantial numbers, and it is mowing them down still. The work of the Gay Men's Chorus is only one of the ways in which the beleaguered army keep up their spirits; many of the singers had found a sense of unity in the choir long before Aids struck. And their spirits, in some cases, need a great deal of keeping up; one of the group, a tenor, has worked to lower his pitch to baritone level because the Aids cancers in his throat make him unable to sing his usual music. Another member put it succinctly, saying: 'Before I joined the chorus, my whole outlook on being gay was going to bars; now there are people who mean more to me than sexual attraction. We're friends.'

I take that quotation from a remarkable article in the *New York Times* by Jane Gross. And I call it remarkable because I am measuring it against British standards of comment on homosexuals. When Paul Johnson can write of 'screaming perverts', and Chief Constable Anderton speak of homosexuals 'swirling around in a human cesspit of their own making', we are in real danger of altogether dehumanizing the image of homosexuality. In my own lifetime uncountable – literally uncountable – millions have been first dehumanized and then done to death as unpersons, whether classified as enemies of the state in the Soviet Union, or race-polluting Jews in Nazi Germany. (Where, incidentally, homosexuals were savagely persecuted; many of them died in the concentration camps, branded with a grisly parody of the Jewish yellow star in the form of a pink triangle.)

I do not suppose that homosexuals in Britain are in danger of pogroms. But I am not here making a plea for more consideration for homosexuals; I am making comparisons between British and American attitudes, and when I make them I find that the British ones are wanting.

Jane Gross's article does not judge, let alone condemn, nor does it patronize or gush; it *describes*, holding fast as it does so to the belief that charity never faileth. But what is much more extraordinary is the tone adopted by New York's two daily tabloid papers, the *Daily News* and the *New York Post*. The *Post* reported the conclusions of a panel set up by the President to study the question of adoption; the panel declared that although race should not be taken into account in adoption decisions, homosexuals should be barred from adopting.

Meanwhile, there was a move afoot for the establishment of homosexual 'marriages', on which the *Daily News* commented. There are practical reasons, on top of emotional ones, for this idea; in certain circumstances and professions, American spouses can obtain a variety of benefits, such as health insurance, and a group of teachers who argue for homosexual marriage are suing the Board of Education for discriminating against them in denying them the financial advantages that married couples automatically have.

Never mind what you think of such proposals; what I want to draw to your attention is that both the *Post*'s presentation of the report that came down against homosexual couples adopting children ('We feel that the American public is not ready to give, and we are not ready to give, support for homosexual adoption'), and the editorial in the *Daily News* arguing against homosexual marriage ('Unmarried *heterosexual* couples could then claim entitlement . . .'), were couched in generous and decent tones. There was none of the coarse jeering that would accompany such reports in the tabloids of Britain, none of the odious cartoons that decorate such stories, none of the brutal headlines that mingle prurience with contempt.

America is widely thought of as much more straitlaced than Britain, at least by those who do not confine their soundings to the East and West coasts. Certainly, there has been much cruel rejection of American sufferers from Aids. Yet I note here an almost complete absence of the tittering about homosexuality that is so prevalent in Britain. The tittering, I believe, is part of the dreadful infantilism of the British when it comes to anything concerning sexual matters, and represents, as most tittering does, nervousness.

Oddly enough, there is a precedent in Britain for homosexual adoption. Some years ago a lesbian couple were allowed to adopt a child; one of the two women was very well known publicly, but the confidentiality that surrounds the procedure of adoption ensured that the *secret de Polichinelle* never got into the headlines. The relationship between the

two women was stable and serious; even so, the judge who
ruled in their favour must have been an exceptionally wise
and far-seeing man. (But no one who knew anything about
the ménage of Benjamin Britten and Peter Pears doubted that
homosexual relationships could be as close, full and enduring
as any marriage, at any rate a childless one.) I think, though,
that it would be inconceivable today for any homosexual
couple to be allowed to adopt a child, so far has the clock
been turned back.

It is unlikely to go forward again in Britain until a
cure or a vaccine for Aids has been found, and the fire
has burned itself out; that will not be for many years, even
if the magic pill is found tomorrow. But must we really
continue with our refusal to come to terms with the very
fact of homosexuality? After all, the number of Aids cases
in Britain is proportionately almost invisible when compared
to the thousands in America; besides, if Aids had never been
heard of, we would still, as a nation, display all the lack of
comprehension or empathy that has again and again driven
homosexuals to despair and indeed suicide.

For a start, we could be less fond of the word *they*. Literally,
of course, homosexuals are 'they', when heterosexuals are
discussing them. But 'they' has come to mean very much
more than merely classification. 'They', in truth, are fully
as varied, in their habits, nature, behaviour, character and
tastes, as are 'we', but our theying inevitably leads us to
feel not only that they are different from us but that they
are inferior to us.

It ought to be possible for even the dimmest of homo-
phobic Tory MPs (Dame Elaine Kellett-Bowman, I presume)
to notice, even if it takes a supreme and exhausting effort, that
apart from the fact of their sexual nature, there is no reason
to believe that homosexuals have any more in common than
heterosexuals have.

When you come to think of it, it really is very odd
that that one distinction has been turned into a kind of

Morton's Fork, on the prongs of which homosexuals are to writhe for ever, proclaiming in vain that they should not, and in fact cannot, be defined by the only thing they all share. Somebody once said, in a more terrible time than this, that a society can be judged by the way it treats its Jews. It is high time that Britain began to treat its homosexuals at least as well as America does.

The Times June 2nd, 1988

Death 2:
Dying for a drink

MOURNERS AT A cremation, expecting appropriately solemn music, were treated instead to a spirited rendering of that ballad of my youth, 'Champagne Charlie':

> Champagne Charlie is my name,
> Champagne drinking is my game . . .
> All I want is lots of fizz, fizz, fizz,
> I'll drink ev'ry drop there is, is, is,
> All round town it is the same,
> By pop, pop, pop I rose to fame,
> I'm the idol of the barmaids,
> And Champagne Charlie is my name.

It seems that the deceased had not only specified the music which was to accompany his passing from the world, but had also taken the precaution of recording it. Unfortunately, he had put it on a tape with other musical matter, and someone in charge of the proceedings had run the machine to the wrong point.

I have to say that if it had been *my* funeral I would have much preferred the drinking song to the deceased's choice, which was an excerpt from *Götterdämmerung*, presumably Siegfried's Funeral March. For a start, the precedents are not auspicious; Hitler chose that piece for his self-ending, and the German radio, or what was left of it, then played the damned thing for hours on end.

But this unfortunate error has been made before, more than once or twice. The funeral of Tom Mann, that tireless agitator (he was one of the founders of the British Communist Party), was greatly enlivened when the official in charge of the ceremony (strictly secular, of course) accidentally turned the record over. Mann had naturally specified 'The Red Flag', but the flip-side held a medley of satirical left-wing ditties, and it was one of those that floated out, with dreadful appositeness; Mann, at one stage in his career, had run a pub, and to the horror, outrage and hilarity of the comrades, they heard:

> Oh, I am the man, the very fat man,
> Who waters the workers' beer . . .

Or so it is said. (One scandalous version, indeed, has it that Mann had, in his time as a publican, been prosecuted for giving short measure, but this sounds to me like an invention of the capitalist press.)

Another tale of sound and fury is, I believe, less apocryphal; it concerned a most distinguished musicologist and critic. Instructions for the music to be played at his funeral had specified a Bach chorale, but they had been specified over the telephone, and to the amazement of the congregation there was suddenly heard the familiar – all too familiar – plink, plink-plink, plonk-plonk, plink-plink of the *barcarole* from *The Tales of Hoffmann*.

Axel Munthe, in one of *his* tales (tales indeed, for he was no mean weaver of whoppers), goes further, and tells of two bodies being buried in mutually wrong graves, so that the deceased in both cases couldn't understand what the mourners were talking about in their eulogies, besides, presumably, getting cross at hearing the wrong music.

But that brings me to my real purpose today, which is to discuss the extraordinary attitude to death that is now almost ubiquitous in societies like ours.

Not just death, but the very notion of death, particularly our own, almost invariably seems to come as an unpleasant surprise, which really is surprising, in view of the fact that even the vainest of us can hardly believe that it applies only to other people.

We have taken to heart (though in a meaning very different from what the sage intended) the first half of the ancient Chinese rubric – 'Live every day as though you are going to live for ever,' but we steadfastly refuse to accept the second half: 'And live every day as though it is your last.'

Why is it that from the earliest times of which we have any knowledge at all we find that the most solemn and profound ceremonies are those surrounding death? Even the celebrations of harvest or the hunt – which might have been thought to have a higher priority, since on these life rather than death depended – are less impressive and less central. William Golding, in *The Inheritors*, which is set in a time long before history, includes an astonishingly moving scene of a funeral – astonishing because the characters in his book are not even *homo sapiens* but the last pre-men, and moving because Golding's artistry is such as to make us feel both the depth and the almost infinite continuity of the last rites.

Yet a funeral today is likely to be a miserable and uncomfortable affair. A real Christian burial, attended by real Christians, is of course impressive, but however Christian the deceased, if the congregation lack the same faith it will be empty. The Jews' Kaddish is a beautiful prayer, but the Jews have the advantage of their religion's attitude to death, symbolized by the feast of rejoicing, not mourning, which follows a funeral: the Lord giveth, and the Lord taketh away; blessed be the name of the Lord.

St Paul said that we brought nothing into this world and it is certain that we can carry nothing out; an obvious truth, though you would be surprised by the number of people who implicitly deny it, up to the millionaire who, told 'You can't take it with you,' replied 'Then I'm not going to go.' (Incidentally, I have just read First Timothy, which is where St Paul said it, right through, and am appalled at the sexism; any bishop who said a tenth of such things today would be tarred and feathered by the members of the Equal Opportunities Commission.)

I begin to think that all the arguments about what follows death are not only pointless (which they obviously are, since we shan't know the answer until we die, and we *shall* know it then), but are standing in the way of a different realization altogether. Let us stop wondering whether our inability to discuss, let alone face, death is the result of the secularization of our society or a suppressed fear that we have in fact not secularized it at all. Let us instead begin to think that the real terror of death, even if nothing but perpetual oblivion follows it, is rooted in what has gone before, not what goes after. Perhaps what haunts our world is the realization of what we have done with our lives.

I don't mean the wrongs we have done, the sins committed, the harm left in the wound; the parable of the talents governs not our future, but our past; what have we done, what have we failed to do, with what we had and what we gathered as we went along? We cannot step twice into the same river, even if there is no court before which we shall have to justify our lives; we are, if we have any capacity for thought at all, our own prosecutors, witnesses, judges and juries, and there comes a point, not necessarily the point of death, at which we have finally to stop deceiving ourselves and true deliverance make.

Is that, perhaps, the clue – the clue, that is, to our wretched failure to come to terms with anyone's death, not just our own? Have the symbols withered, the ceremonies faded, because we would bring to them only the realization that we have learned nothing from our lives, so that it is not surprising that we are unable to learn anything from our deaths? Have we really been looking in the wrong direction all this time?

I can make no judgement on the man who was buried to the wrong music, and I wouldn't make one even if I could. But if his spirit is still, in some category, susceptible to comfort, let him take it from the fact that his friends, when they had got over the shock, must surely have smiled, if only behind their hands, and to leave your friends a legacy of smiles is at least something accomplished.

Will my executors kindly note that although the order of service at my funeral may specify the *St Matthew Passion*, I want a prankster standing by to substitute for it – going further than the man who started this excursion – the 'Champagne Aria' from *Don Giovanni*, the 'Champagne Chorus' from *Die Fledermaus*, and (even in death I must show off), the 'Champagne Invitation' from *Die Bajadere*.

The Times February 9th, 1989

And all the trumpets sounded

WE LAID TOM WALSH in the earth on Friday, under a glorious Indian-summer sun, in the Barntown cemetery outside the town; that way he can sleep amid the soft green hills of his native County Wexford which he loved so much. After the Requiem Mass in his home church, the cortège formed up; we filled the street from side to side and end to end. Solemn robed figures walked immediately behind the hearse; easily mistaken for members of the Guild of Mastersingers, they turned out to be the entire Borough Council, in full fig.

The town band wasn't there; perhaps it had been wrongly thought insufficiently reverent for such an occasion. The Taoiseach, though, had sent a telegram. The flowers, piled up, made an Everest of beauty and farewell; the church was heady with their scents. We sang 'Abide With Me', and meant it.

Well, your man had done a lot for the place, starting by being born there, in 1911 (he missed his seventy-seventh birthday by a fortnight). He qualified as a doctor at Dublin University in 1944; he practised in the town from 1944 to 1955; from 1955 to 1977 he was the anaesthetist for the Wexford County Hospital. In 1951 he founded the Wexford Opera Festival, and was its Director until 1966.

His worth and achievements were recognized; the University of Dublin made him first an hon. MA, then an hon. Doctor of Philosophy, then an hon. Doctor of Literature. He was an hon. fellow of the Faculty of Anaesthetists of Ireland, a fellow of the Royal Historical Society, a Knight of Malta, a freeman of Wexford (well, I should think so). He wrote a series of scholarly books on the history of opera – another, finished, is in the press; he was twice married and widowed; he is survived by his daughter and sister.

Facts, facts; useful things for charting the stops of life, and seeing who gets off or on; not much good at conjuring the actual man on the actual bus. That shall be my task this morning.

Tom died smiling. At least, I assume he did; he was certainly smiling when I saw him in Wexford Hospital a few days before the end. As a doctor, he could not deceive himself about his condition, and his colleagues did not try to bluff him. But there were no solemn farewells; solemn farewells were not much in his line, except, to be sure, operatic ones.

Wexford knew him as 'Doctor Tom', and would call him nothing else. He had retired from active practice a decade before, but until recently he would keep his hand in by slipping over to England to do an annual locum.

When his health began to fail, some way into 1988, we devised Operation Tomplot – 'we' being the group of friends who go, every autumn, to his festival. We lured him to Sussex, he all unsuspecting while we were hiding out in the hedges and ditches around him, togged up and ready to carry him off to Glyndebourne; the girls had dressed more beautifully than ever, for him. The Plot held: 'Bernard, you swindler!' he cried, as the whole gang crashed through the door. I had wondered mildly, and put the point to his daughter Victoria, what she would say if he asked why the tea-table was set for fifteen. 'We'll keep him out of the room,' she said, 'and anyway, Daddy wouldn't notice.'

It was perfect Glyndebourne weather that day; a cloudless sky, a breeze to cool it, the gardens beginning to recover from the devastation of the hurricane. In the interval, up on the roof-terrace, the Christies poured libations, in which we drank his health. Brian Dickie was of the company; he is now General Manager of Glyndebourne, but in 1967 he had had the alarming task of stepping into Tom's shoes as Director of the Wexford Festival.

The Glyndebourne meeting was a moving moment; George Christie, a man who inherited a festival and thereafter dedicated his life to it, stood beside Tom Walsh, a man who created one out of nothing, and lived to see its fame spread wide. Then we went back into George's Festival Theatre, for the rest of *Die Entführung*; of course it had to be Mozart for Tom, whose love for that composer was passionate and unwavering.

Not many men devote their lives to the selfless service of their fellows. Tom Walsh did it twice over; as doctor and as man of music. 'Doctor' says all that is necessary for the first part, and if you think it doesn't, ask his patients in Wexford. But 'man of music' is a feeble phrase for what it encompassed in his case. He simply decided that the quiet little town of Wexford should have an annual operatic festival to which, in due course, the world would come. And the money? Tut; the ravens fed Elishah.

I often wish I had been living in Wexford at the time; I would have loved to watch the scene as he went about the town telling people of his plan, while the news went much faster about the town that Doctor Tom had gone mad. For consider: Wexford in 1951 was not only a quiet place, hardly heard of even in Ireland; it was also savagely poor. The theatre hadn't been used as such for a century (some say two); moreover it would hold only 400 people, and anyway it was now a furniture repository.

The very Muses wrung their hands and wept at so forlorn a hope, but they didn't know Doctor Tom; the iron-clad principles of rectitude and honour that guarded his life were translated into an irresistible determination to see his dream realized. The Wexford Opera Festival, with the weeping Muses engaged for the chorus as a token of forgiveness, opened its doors on time; that was thirty-seven years ago, and they haven't shut yet. *Si monumentum requiris, circumspice.*

On Sunday morning during the festival, Tom always kept open house for his friends. Now he was adamant that he would be there to preside as usual, even if his hospital bed had to be put on wheels and pushed all the way to Lower George Street; as the week went by, though, even he had to admit defeat. But when he did, he was even more adamant that the ritual would be kept to, even if our host was from home.

Tom's Catholicism was deep, tenacious and complete; he suffered great distress when his beloved daughter married out of the faith. But there was no estrangement, and he died full of joy in the knowledge that a grandchild was soon due.

He sought no fame, no fortune. He had got hold of the notion that he was on earth to tend the sick and spread the love of music, and he pursued both vocations with great diligence and no fuss. It pleased him, as it pleased all of us, that over the years Wexford had become noticeably better off; his festival brought a good deal of money into the town.

We returned, *en masse*, to the hospital, to see him for the last time; the group was almost identical to that of the Great Tomplot. The doctors wouldn't let us in all together, but said we could go in two by two, each pair strictly enjoined to stay only a few minutes. He had been wandering a little, but he was perfectly clear with us.

He fought on for another week; death would not have dared approach his bedside until the 1988 festival was over. Last Tuesday afternoon, he fell asleep, and in sleep he left us. We who knew him will keep his memory bright, forever in his debt for the joy and friendship he and his festival have given us. We are even more blessed by having known and loved a man of such goodness, wisdom, generosity and laughter. Doubt not that he feasts in Heaven this night, with Mozart on one side of him and Hippocrates on the other, and a glass of good red wine in his good right hand.

The Times November 14th, 1988

Faith and fainthearts

I T WAS G.K. CHESTERTON who, faced with the view that any religion is as valid as any other, suggested that those who held it should try thinking of something blasphemous to say about Thor, and that seems an appropriate point to begin consideration of the uproar caused by the new film about Christ. I have not seen it, so I shall not comment on its nature, quality or content (a precaution many people in America and here, as usual, seem to think unnecessary). In any case, it is not the thought of the film that I find fascinating, but the uproar itself.

We have, of course, been here before: the Monty Python team gave us their *Life of Brian* a few years ago, and indeed there have been two more such films, one French and one Italian. The last two were largely ignored here; presumably it was thought that nothing else could be expected from foreigners. But the Monty Python epic aroused much the same kind of reeling, writhing and fainting in coils, the disputants being divided into those who thought that the outrage was at least softened by the fact that the film was meant to be funny, and those who insisted that that made the whole thing worse.

Already voices in Britain have been raised in demands for the new film to be banned here, not only from dial-a-quote MPs. I have seen no statement from Mrs Whitehouse yet, though no doubt she will soon give tongue, and no doubt she will fail to take the precaution mentioned above before doing so.

'O father Abram! What these Christians are.' Well, perhaps

Shylock is not the most tactful source from which I might seek assistance; how about Othello? 'For Christian shame, put by this barbarous brawl.'

Yes, do, dear Christians all, and let me show you why you should. Jesus was put to death under Pontius Pilate, in the most painful and humiliating form of death then known. Dwell on it for a moment, please; I have a reason for asking. Christ was nailed to the Cross through his hands and feet, after being mocked, scourged and crowned with thorns. He was stabbed in the side by a spear, and when, dying, he asked for water, he was given vinegar. Throughout his prolonged ordeal, he was jeered by the spectators.

Meanwhile, how about Pilate? He was eventually recalled to Rome, though not in disgrace, despite the fact that he couldn't stop the Jews talking (who could?). No one knows how he died, or when; there are legends to the effect that he became a Christian, but (if you don't mind me saying so, dear Christians) that is pretty obviously propaganda. Incidentally, the principal legend says he died in Gaul, at Vienne, and indeed the locals show you his tomb, which is well worth a glance before you cross the road for lunch at La Pyramide. If Pilate's last meal (presumably old man Point was still in charge then) included the *paté de foie gras en brioche*, he died well.

And yet I must ask: which of them ended up with more egg on his face – Christ or Pilate? Assuredly Pilate, and not only because many millions now revere Christ and few him. I trust you see what I am getting at; in case not, I shall put it in the most demotic terms. For a man who has been crucified, having a film made about him is a doddle.

The expressions of outrage in the United States ensured that the opening of the film went off in such a blaze of publicity that the queues in Los Angeles were five hours long. But a photograph of one such queue in the *Sunday Times* was extraordinarily instructive and apposite. It showed simultaneously a demonstrator holding a placard saying 'Jesus loves you', and a queuer with a T-shirt inscribed 'Relax, it's only a movie'.

Well, then, if Jesus loves the film-goer, and the film-goer acknowledges that nothing more serious than a film is happening, what means the outrage, the demands for suppression, the screening for weapons and bombs of those who entered the cinemas?

The horrid suspicion will not be denied. Once upon a time, to embrace Christianity was likely to lead to the embracer being burned or boiled or buried alive, to being torn to pieces in the arena, to being beheaded, disembowelled or starved to death, to being thrown over a cliff, shot by a rain of arrows, broken on a wheel, together with many more of what Kai Lung called 'a variety of discomforts less tersely described'.

But now? Even if the National Secular Society staged a successful coup and took over the country, I doubt if the fires of Smithfield would be lit again (apart from anything else, the TGWU would demand double-time payment for tending them), and the Martyrs' Memorial in Oxford would still be adorned, after bump suppers, by no more ghastly a burden than a po. Perhaps the bishops would be thrown out of the House of Lords, and possibly Speaker's Prayers would be abolished, but Cardinal Hume and the Archbishop of Canterbury, to say nothing of the Vicar of St Jack-in-the-Lifeboat, would be free to pursue their calling unmolested.

Let us leave out what might be Christ's view of the matter on the one hand, and the Vicar's on the other, and strike an average. What would be, say, St Lawrence's opinion on the subject of this controversial film? I rather think that he would tell the Christians, after scrupulously attributing the words to my Bessarabian grandmother, that if they never had anything worse than that to worry about, they wouldn't have done too badly.

Why are devout Christians, here and in America, getting into such a tizzy? Of course, they feel that their most sacred beliefs are being mocked, and nobody likes that. Yet do they not also feel, and much more strongly, that Christ and his followers have had to put up with worse than that in their time, and survived? Do they really fear that a Hollywood film, of all insubstantial, meretricious and ephemeral phenomena, will damage Christianity? If so, what can their faith in their religion be like?

It is true that Christianity, like all religions today except Islam, is beleaguered. But the enemy outside the gates is not Genghis Khan or the Emperor Domitian, or even Hitler and Stalin; it is indifference, particularly in the form of much straining after gnats and swallowing of camels. It is not for me to analyse the uncertainties and fears of those who cleave to the Christian religion. But at least I can offer them an exhortation: be of good cheer. If what you believe is true, it will not be the less believed, let alone the less valid, because of this or any other film.

If you doubt it, try an obvious test. Imagine two cinema-goers, one a Christian believer, the other a sympathizer. Then imagine both of them rushing into the street crying 'Faugh! Fie! For shame! Bah! So that's what Christianity is about, eh? We never knew! Down with it!' If you *can* imagine that, you have a nonpareil imagination; and the test works, I may say, for a third cinema-goer, who has no interest at all in religion. Gamaliel knew better:

Refrain from these men, and let them alone: for if this counsel or this work be of men, it will come to nought; but if it be of God, ye cannot overthrow it; lest haply ye be found even to fight against God. And to him they agreed; and when they had called the apostles, and beaten them, they commanded that they should not speak in the name of Jesus, and let them go. And they departed from the presence of the council, rejoicing that they were counted worthy to suffer shame for his name. And daily in the temple, and in every house, they ceased not to teach and preach Jesus Christ.

And another thing; these days, you don't even get beaten.

The Times August 17th, 1988

At full stretch

S O SVIATOSLAV RICHTER has come and gone, for the first time in fifteen years; we can be almost certain that we shall never see him again. He is, after all, seventy-four, and whatever inner or outer trouble dogs him – I shall come to that – is not likely to let go of him now.

Well, it was one hell of a swansong. He gave four recitals – two public and two private – and I went to three of the four. He really is the most amazing pianist I have ever heard, and I make that assertion from the experience of forty years of music-going, during which I must have heard *every* keyboard virtuoso from Schnabel, Gieseking and Backhaus to Brendel, Ashkenazy and Schiff, with Rubinstein spanning the lot (they say he's dead, but I don't believe it), and not forgetting Arrau.

Nor, for that matter, the lost Lipatti; I think I was at every one of his tragically few performances in London, and I can tell you that the legend is no legend at all – his gift was a true miracle, and as I close my eyes to conjure him up, I can hear the storming finish of the Schumann concerto, played as no one else, even in that catalogue above, has ever made it sound.

And then there is Richter. To start with, he looks like no other musician I have ever come across; you could offer a prize of millions for anyone who had never seen him play yet could guess his profession, in the certainty that the money would never be won. His bull neck, the bulk of his torso and his almost bald head, tilted very slightly, make him look ruthless, almost sinister, but the precise, delicate steps with which he crosses the platform could be those of a ballet dancer.

Now look at the face. Look; but be prepared to learn nothing. No trace of any emotion can be discerned; his visage could be carved in granite for all it reveals, and I doubt if there is in existence a picture of him smiling. Yet the granite, for all its silence, speaks with terrible eloquence of a man in some kind of torment unimaginable to the rest of us. With what dark angels he wrestles cannot be guessed at; as well try to understand the dreams of a cat. But if indeed he has problems in his soul or his life it is damnably unfair considering what he has contributed, in the course of his art, to the universe.

Two of the recitals – the one at St James's, Piccadilly (given for Elisabeth Schwarzkopf to commemorate the tenth anniversary of the death of Walter Legge, her husband) and the one in the Festival Hall – had the same programme: Schubert, Schumann and Prokoviev. The Schubert (D.894) was taken more deliberately than usual, but it wasn't that that made me think of a marvellous phrase of Shaw's: 'I did with my ears what I do with my eyes when I stare.'

It was haunting, almost literally so; there were sounds and resonances so mysterious that I began to believe he had discovered a lost work and was giving it its première. (In the Festival Hall, it sounded even odder.) But it was the last performance, the one in the Barbican, which everyone in the packed hall will remember for ever.

We nearly had to remember it for a very different reason; the original programme consisted of Prokoviev, Shostakovich, Stravinsky, Webern, Szymanowski, Bartok and Hindemith. Stap me, I murmured, there'll be many a lilting tune to set my feet a-tapping in that list. Fortunately, wiser counsels prevailed; I assume that Victor Hochhauser, who presented the programmes, threw seven and seventy fits. If so, he writhed to good effect, for in the event the first half was all Mozart and the second half all Chopin. Here, we thought, is an evening to bring out Richter's best, starting with his technique.

We thought rightly. Richter's technique is the most consummate the piano has ever encountered; not even Michelangeli can make it do things as amazing. Sitting directly in front of me was a talented young pianist, not long embarked on his own career, who was literally incapable of keeping still. I don't mean he fidgeted; it was just that he could not control his body's response to the stupefying joy that he was experiencing.

In a pause, he turned round, incoherent with feeling, wanting me to confirm his opinion of Richter's hands; the boy spread his own to make his point, which was that Richter could span a thirteenth without the slightest effort, and a great deal more *with* effort, whereas for normal human beings it would be necessary to sever all the tendons, an operation most inadvisable for a pianist. (As far as *I* could see or hear, Richter could span two and a half octaves just as easily if he felt like it.)

Thus armed, he went forth to meet Mozart and Chopin. O, you who didn't hear it, how shall I convey what you missed? The Mozart consisted of three sonatas – K.282, K.545 (the one everybody knows and most amateurs can even play), and the tumultuous, truly revolutionary K.310. In the first two the place was dripping pearls; the delicacy and tenderness as the notes fell from his hands was enough to bring tears to the eyes every time the music moved into the minor; all around me people had turned to stone, so fearful were they of missing a single semiquaver *ppppp*. As for the third, with its battles and heroics, I felt that if it went on for another bar I would be obliged to rush out and storm Ratisbon single-handed.

After the interval, Chopin; a round dozen of Etudes. Op.10 No.3 (the one that was turned some years ago into a popular song called *So Deep is the Night*) was given such tragic beauty that it seemed to me to sum up its composer's life – indeed, it seemed to have been written for that very purpose.

It is notoriously difficult in Chopin to get the balance of sentimentality right (apart from those who deny – I think I am one of them – that there *is* any sentimentality), but Richter passed the final test; every one of the items sounded entirely definitive, as though they could not be played any other way.

By now, my young friend was delirious; his yells of 'Bravo!' could have been heard in Scotland, and when he could speak, he not only confided that the experience had blown his mind but demanded that I should admit that it had blown mine as well. I cheerfully agreed.

I envy him; not for his talent, but for his lack of experience. I am not so foolish as to become blasé at operas and concerts, even though I have been to thousands, and anyone between the ages of sixteen and twenty-two who hears me pooh-pooh his brand-new enthusiasms from my store of historic ones is at liberty to call me grandpa and ask if I need help in crossing the road. But it is inevitable that we should think that the heroes of our youth, when everything and everyone is new and exciting, will remain for ever on the same plinths in our Pantheon.

Look about; the world is strewn with great conductors, and young music-lovers follow them, quite rightly, as their benighted coevals worship pop singers. But *I* heard Bruno Walter and Wilhelm Furtwängler, Eduard van Beinum and Erich Kleiber, Fritz Busch and Victor de Sabata, Thomas Beecham and Richard Strauss – nay, Toscanini himself – and I could never forget them even if I wanted to, redolent for me as they are of the days when every experience is a first one, and youth will last for ever, and for everything we want to do there is world enough and time.

Richter had been generous with encores at the Festival Hall, but here, after a few returns to the platform for a bow as courteous as it was impassive, he vanished into the wings and was seen no more. The applause went on and on, for five minutes, ten, fifteen; it was as though we knew we were taking our last farewell of him, and could not bear to believe that it was so.

The fainthearts slipped away; the hall began to empty; the stalwarts, including my young musician with the blown mind, stood fast. I dare say he stands there yet, calling his idol back for one more glimpse of a now lifelong memory.

The Times April 3rd, 1989

Monkey business

THE OTHER DAY I received a letter, all the way from Hightstown, New Jersey, which had me beside myself with excitement. In red capitals, the envelope announced that it contained an OFFICIAL PROPOSAL for me; it had my name spelt correctly and my address in full, including the postcode, thus surely guaranteeing its authenticity. And within a box ruled in more red, the following memorable words appeared, neatly typed:

> The recipient whose name appears above has been selected to receive the enclosed Proposal solely because of his or her level of participation and record of achievement in international business. The enclosed Proposal is valid only for the person named above.

Now I bet you didn't know that I have an exceptional level of participation and record of achievement in international business. As a matter of fact, I didn't know either, but I wasn't going to let on, not with an OFFICIAL PROPOSAL waiting for me inside the envelope. True, I had a safeguard: nobody could cash in on my record, because the PROPOSAL was valid only for me. So I poured myself another cup of coffee, took a deep breath and opened the envelope. In it, I found the details of the OFFICIAL PROPOSAL, and amazing details they were too; no wonder they were sent to me solely because of my level of participation and record of achievement in international business.

I don't want to boast, much less make my readers envious,

but it was with a quiet pride that I read this majestic accolade: 'You have been chosen to receive a 25% saving off a 1-year subscription to *Business Week International*.'

Well, now. I have never been able to summon up the indignation that some people feel about the quantity of junk mail that comes through the letter-box daily. I have four wastepaper-baskets, plus a self-sealing plastic rubbish-bag machine, not to mention a sink disposal-unit, and it would take more junk than I dare say even *Business Week International* could generate to fill them all to overflowing. But I do sometimes wonder whether I am the only sane man left alive.

Let us contemplate the facts above. Obviously, when I read that I had been *selected* to receive a proposal *solely* because of my record of achievement in *international business*, I knew that it was a fake, since I have no international business. But suppose I did have such connections – global deals success-fully brought off, world-wide chains of businesses founded, conglomerates and consortiums put together – would I be more gullible, feel more flattered, when I was told in this way that my industry had been noted and was about to be rewarded? And if so, would those feelings survive the opening of the envelope, when I would find that I had been *chosen* to receive a few lousy quid off a subscription to *Business Week International*?

I am decidedly of the opinion that both those questions would be answered with a very firm No; indeed, I think that the sender's manifest contempt for the intelligence of the recipient would be more resented by a genuine international businessman than by me.

Yet some idiot in the management of *Business Week International* clearly thinks otherwise. An arrangement with a list-broker; a computer-generated mail-shot; sufficient gul-libility; and up goes the magazine's circulation, or so the idiot hopes. Never mind the crassness of the message on the envelope, which would surely lead to its being thrown

away unopened by anyone with any sophistication except
those (like me) with even more inquisitiveness; the recipients would have to be very stupid indeed to read all that
guff about being so carefully selected, only to find that the
sender neither knows nor cares who the recipient is, as witness that in the middle of the specification the uniqueness of
the offer is made somewhat less credible by that telltale 'his
or her'.

Presumably there is a formula for such monkeyshines; if x
letters are sent out at random, and y recipients sign up for a
reduced subscription, there will be a profit of z. And after all,
those who are disgruntled by so pathetic a con are not going
to do anything but throw the thing away; they wouldn't
go round to Hightstown and break the windows. I cannot
believe that this is a cost-effective form of advertising, even
without me jeering at it, but presumably there is somebody
in *Business Week International* with enough sense to work out
the arithmetic, even though there seems nobody to improve
the text.

All the same, the most important question is yet to be
asked. There are people who cannot resist January sales,
vouchers worth fourpence off the price of a tin of baked
beans, goods reduced to clear, government surplus stock and
other forms of discount. Some of these people, junk-mailed
by *Business Week International*, will fork out £32 (the reduced
subscription rate) and feel they have made a bargain. But is
there anybody at all who would really swallow the come-on,
anybody naïve enough to believe the rubbish on the envelope
and pay up *because* of it?

It is an alarming thought, is it not? To buy something
that is not needed, merely because it is cheap today, is a
fairly silly thing to do; but to buy it in the genuine belief
that the purchaser has been singled out for commendation
and monetary reward is very considerably sillier. Possibly,
between the genuine international businessman, who would
not base his moves on the junk-mail envelope, and the man
with no such business, who would at once spot the game,

there is room for someone to be deceived. I cannot be quite sure, but I doubt it. For remember, the magazine is not a comic, but a severe study of such subjects as 'Deutsche Bank: Alfred Herrhausen's bid for global power' and 'Dealmaker de Benedetti and the "Battle of Belgium"'. The greater the interest in *Business Week International*, the smaller the effect the scam would have.

It is no use saying that *Business Week International* must know what it is doing: both history and the world of the present are strewn from end to end with falsified assumptions.

I have much sympathy for the businessman who said 'I know that half my advertising is wasted, but I don't know which half,' but I have much less for the outfit which relies on the belief that half the general public is soft in the head. And the general public would have to be very soft-headed indeed to ring up its friends and relations to announce the glad news that it has been made an Official Proposal for its record of achievement in international business, even if it did not add that the proposal in question consists of a cut in the subscription rate of a magazine.

There's one born every minute? Possibly: but surely there aren't ten thousand born every half-hour. I referred earlier to the manifest contempt for the target audience such advertising must imply, but on reflection I am not so sure: the shadowy idiot I postulated may genuinely think that such gushing nonsense will fetch the customers in huge numbers.

One of the most delightful advertising ideas I ever saw was on a packet of American cat food. The brand name, happily enough, was Miaow, and the slogan read: 'So good, cats ask for it by name.' I have always wondered why Miaow did not sweep every other cat food out of existence with such a charming and unforgettable joke, but I was never in any doubt that it *was* a joke. Only think of the horror if the advertising agency which produced it insisted that the claim was nothing but the truth, and that they had an enormous body of research findings to prove it. If so, they must have recently landed the *Business Week International* account.

The Times October 20th, 1988

Just for a handful of silver

I AM BEING haunted by a report, not long ago, of a criminal trial involving bribery. The central figure in the case had been the financial director of a big merchant bank, and he was earning £45,000 a year, which does not exactly involve dining at charitable soup kitchens and sleeping under bridges.

The crime itself was of the greatest and most wretched simplicity. He was in charge of the refurbishment of his firm's offices, made necessary by their decision, in 1984, to go over to complete computerization at the time of Big Bang. This involved contracts worth millions of pounds, and he awarded the work to a firm which paid him bribes amounting to between £60,000 and £103,000.

The two men who gave the bribes, the Managing Director and General Manager of the contracting firm, were also convicted. But for them, or for their firm, millions were at stake; their actions, though crazy as well as criminal (for the first serious audit would blow the enterprise to bits), are understandable. Those of the man who took the *douceurs* are not, at least to me.

Of course, the judge did not fail to say 'It is essential that those in responsible positions in the City and elsewhere should be made to realize that dishonest criminal behaviour cannot be tolerated by the courts . . . it is essential to maintain public confidence in the integrity of those who occupy public commercial positions.' (One of these days I am going to get myself elected to Parliament, solely in order to introduce a Private Member's Bill which would oblige any judge about to succumb to an attack of sanctimoniousness to stuff 400 pages of Law Reports into his mouth until the fit has passed.)

I would very much like to have £60,000 more than I do have, and I would like an extra £103,000 even more. But if I were to be offered such sums, my first question would naturally be (as I dare say it was for the man in the case), 'What do I have to do for it?'

Sing for my supper? Yes, but you will regret it more than I. Allow one of my books to be made into a film starring Robert Redford? I shall agree most graciously. Grow a moustache? Oh, hell, I can always cover the mirrors. Run away with Felicity Kendal? That I would do for nothing – nay, I would be willing to pay a gigantic sum. But commit a crime? Ah, there I jib, and go on jibbing.

Have I ever told the story (skip if I have) about the day my mother took me to Woolworth's? It is one of my earliest memories, and I recall it with such appalling clarity that I have begun to sweat as I write about it.

In those days, the demands of hygiene were not as strict as they are now; Woolworth's set out its sweets unwrapped, shovelled into the divisions of their counters, to be shovelled out again and weighed when a purchaser approached. Along the counter there ran a glass 'wall', some 3 inches high, to prevent the sweets falling out (the counters sloped). My mother was holding my left hand; with my right I was running my fingers along the ledge that projected beyond the glass retainer. I was looking straight ahead, and therefore did not see that one sweet – a particularly large and succulent-looking sugar-coated jelly – had escaped and fallen over the guard on to the ledge.

My infant fingers met an object; instinctively, I picked it up, and went on walking. A few seconds later, my mind went into gear, and I looked at what I was holding. It was a sweet, *and I had stolen it.* Stolen? Yes, for was I not holding it in my hand? And was it not the property of Woolworth's? For a nano-second, which lasted a thousand years, I looked at the hand of a thief – my hand – and I then slammed the sweet down on to the bit of the ledge I was now passing, heedless of the fact that the display had changed, so that the jelly was incongruously sitting in front of the chocolates. My mother had noticed nothing.

I don't know how the abhorrence of any kind of illegality – so strong as to be almost pathological – got into me. There were no dire warnings at home about what happens to those who are insufficiently aware of the distinction between *meum* and *tuum*, no dinning into my young ears the Ten Commandments, let alone the Statute Book. Most people *don't* commit crimes, even trivial ones; most people *wouldn't* do so, even if great riches were promised. But I do believe that if I had been the executive who was approached with the suggestion of a massive bribe for massive gains, I would have been physically sick then and there, on the carpet.

Oh, no, no, no; I am *not* holier than thou, I am not holy at all. Some of the things I have done in my life have been as bad as many a crime. You may think that that convicts me of hypocrisy, and perhaps it does; but what I am saying is not that I am good, only that in no conceivable circumstances would or could I find myself in the position of the poor sod who was sent down for eighteen months.

Poor sod? Yes, emphatically so; if the judge had no pity for him, I have much. The case revealed that he had been working for his firm for ten years, presumably without blot; indeed, it must have been so, for he had risen to a position of great responsibility. And then that gleam of gold, for which men and women through the ages have thrown away honour, position, trust, home, family, country, friendship, 'for a fantasy and trick of fame' – that gleam so blinded him that for the moment he could see nothing, not even the throng of devils around him preparing to rejoice, or – worse – to laugh.

He is fifty-eight; with full remission, which a man of that kind would certainly earn, he will be out in a year. And then? Our laws say that if a man has committed a crime and served the punishment meted out to him, he is entitled to a fresh start. That's what they *say*; but who will give such a man a reference that will enable him to get a job fitting his ability?

Money! It is widely, though erroneously, believed that St Paul said it was the root of all evil. He didn't; he said the *love of it* was. But I now begin to think, with evidence such as this case provides, that the Saint was wrong, and the common man right. We all need money; we all like it, or what we can do with it. Yet we rarely face the fact that it is a deadly poison, and must be handled with very great care if it is not to destroy its owner; the man in the case had failed to see the warning on the bottle.

I have no moral to declare, no new rule to propose, not even a proverb to rely on. There is a man in prison, who walked into it with open eyes, and feet that did not stumble on the threshold. If he lives to be older than Methuselah he will never understand why he did it, and if *he* doesn't know, how can any of the rest of us? As I say, I don't know how the canon against stealing in any form got so deep into me. But I have remembered the episode with the sweet for more than half a century, and the agony of the moment in which I had taken possession of something that did not belong to me is as vivid and piercing as it was when it happened. Well, I did say, when I started, that I was being *haunted* by a court case.

The Times May 8th, 1989

Rude forefathers

SOMEWHERE IN ITALY, probably but not necessarily Rome, an unmarked grave is heaving in a most striking manner. The man in it has been there for well over 2,000 years; he always loved a joke, and made hundreds of his own. But the joke he is laughing at now – laughing so hard that the very trees around him are being uprooted – is one to top his very best.

The London University Schools Examination Board has announced that three of his poems set for A-levels in Latin are being withdrawn, because they are too rude. Mr Alan Stephenson, secretary to the board, was the hapless figure who announced the decision; it seems that in some schools the teachers (I can assure you it wasn't the children), when they came to the set poems, had a fit, and, pausing only to shut the book with a bang and tell the class to turn immediately to Livy, wrote a letter of complaint to those in charge of the syllabus.

Mr Stephenson, growing more hapless every minute, explained that in one of the poems the man it is addressed to is being exhorted to refrain from making homosexual advances to a boy in his charge, in the second the poet indulges in word-play with such expressions as 'bugger you', and in the third he is comparing his victim's general flabbiness to an old man's cobwebbed member.

The first thing that has to be said is that Mr Stephenson was not using a very good translation; I have five on my shelves (he may care to note that in the standard numbering of the poet's works the ones that caused the trouble are Nos. 15, 16 and 25), if you count the Bohn prose version, and they are all much better than anything the Examination Board could manage. But then, the original is a good deal better than any of them.

Catullus (for it is he) is one of the most untranslatable poets in all history; Villon himself hardly poses greater problems. The trouble is that he is so pure and limpid (I am talking about his style, not his subject matter) that if a translator lays a hand on him he bruises at once; it is like playing Mozart – there is nowhere to hide. Take what I suppose are his two most famous lines, and see how they are done by G.P. Goold in the Duckworth classical series:

> You ask, Lesbia, how many kissings
> of you are enough and to spare for me.

As you say, somewhat wooden. Now try Peter Whigham, in the Penguin Classics:

> Curious to learn
> How many kiss-
> es of your lips
> might satisfy
> my lust for you . . .

Even without the idiotic lining, you can tell at once that that is a dud. Well, what of Bohn – the metrical version?

> Thy kisses dost thou bid me count,
> And tell thee, Lesbia, what amount
> My rage for love and thee could tire
> And satisfy and cloy desire?

A touch twee, would you say? (Apart from using twenty-six words where Catullus has nine). Finally (though it can never be final), Frederic Raphael and Kenneth McLeish:

> Your questions, Lesbia, are these:
> (a) How many kisses to sate
> (b) How many to surfeit my passion?

Strictly, it needs a comma after surfeit, but it is the

neatest version, as well as being close in fidelity to the original. But why bother, when the original is to hand?

> Quaeris, quot mihi basiationes
> tua, Lesbia, sint sapis
> superque.

That is all very well, but you are following me, you dirty-minded lot, to get to more of the bits that caused the trouble, and I propose to disappoint you by retreating, like Gibbon, into the decent obscurity of a learned language. Nor shall I give you titillating hints, though I do assure you that *Pedicabo ego vos et irrumabo* does not mean 'I will trim you and trounce you,' as Bohn demurely has it; two entirely different actions – opposite ones, you might say – are here threatened. Yet Catullus's obscenity, which is surely making two dozen doctoral theses at this very moment, is not only exceptionally unrestrained but also light-hearted in the most inoffensive manner. And the strange thing is that when he is left in the Latin it does not bring a blush even to those who understand it, whereas when he is translated, however unlubriciously, even the most broad-minded feel uneasy. Landor, of all unlikely people, got it right:

> Such stains there are – as when a Grace
> Sprinkles another's laughing face
> With nectar, and runs on.

If there are any very wicked schoolboys reading this, they might try asking their Latin teacher what exactly Catullus meant by

> O Memmi, bene me ac diu supinum
> tota ista trabe lentus irrumasti.
> sed, quantum video, pari fuistis
> casu: nam nihilo minore verpa
> farti estis,

though I shall disclaim all responsibility when the uproar

starts. (I take it that the wicked schoolboys aforementioned are not so wicked as to have failed to make sure there are no schoolgirls present before they start.)

Yet we do not elevate Catullus into the highest poetic firmament for the extravagantly uninhibited nature of his language and imagery; he is among the very greatest of the world's lyricists for the story of his life and of the poetry he made of it. It is well enough known, though we have practically no facts at all to go on; all we can do is to assume that his autobiographical poems are his autobiography. (After all, we do that when we read the Sonnets of Shakespeare, of whom we know a good deal; and in the case of both poets we are safe in the knowledge that our view of them from their verses can hardly be disproved now.)

If we are right, then Catullus's life story consists of his love for a woman he called Lesbia, though it was not her name; she was voraciously promiscuous; he was entirely in her thrall; he broke away from her, but returned and fell under her spell again; he broke away again, and resigned himself to the loss of her. There is a legend that he committed suicide; another that she poisoned him; certainly he died young.

But he died one of the world's immortals for the beauty and truth with which he records his love and his feelings. Where in all poetry is there anything to touch the two consecutive poems in which he first celebrates the sparrow that was Lesbia's pet and the light of her eyes, and then records its death (the translation is Goold's):

> o factum male, quod, miselle passer,
> tua nunc opera meae puellae
> flendo turgiduli rubent occelli!

> Ah cruel event, that through your doing,
> hapless sparrow, my sweetheart's eyes
> are red and swollen with weeping!

And now this free spirit, born to sing through the centuries for ever, telling us what we need to know about love and pain and loss, laughter and air and sky, wine and life and death, this Apollonian, immortal youth is condemned, by no less a body than the London University Schools Examination Board, as not fit for our wives and servants and, more dreadful still, our sons and daughters to read. What would he say – apart, that is, from *Pedicabo ego vos et irrumabo?*

He would say that men have become deaf to the cadences of poetry, blind to the glory of mankind, dumb to the call of love, afraid of poetry, mankind and love alike. He would say that it is no great sin to look upon the wine when it is red, nor no great virtue in spurning love because it is not pure. And he would also say, and if he wouldn't I shall say it for him, that every schoolboy taking the exam with the now banned poems in it most certainly already knows every English word corresponding to the rejected Latin ones, and would be delighted to learn the corresponding expressions, if only to abuse, *sotto voce*, teachers unpopular but unLatined. And that the frankest translation of all Catullus's works is the one by Raphael and McLeish, and if the schoolboys move fast they can get it out of their public library before the London University Schools Examination Board has it removed from the shelves.

The Times March 20th, 1989

An even more modest proposal

I HAVE BEEN worrying about an incident that took place in South Africa a few weeks ago. The facts are clear, and are briefly stated. A black labourer named Eric Sambo, driving a car, accidentally hit and killed two dogs belonging to a local Afrikaans farmer, called Jacobus Voster. (Some reports spell it Vorster.) Mr Voster seized the man, dragged him on to his premises and spent the next two days whipping and torturing him to death.

Mr Voster was arrested and charged with murder. He was found not guilty of murder but guilty of culpable homicide. The sentence was five years imprisonment, fully suspended on condition that he paid 130 *rand* (approximately £30) a month for five years to the widow of the dead man, who had four children. Now read on.

Ignoring inflation, that means that Mr Voster must eventually stump up a total of £1,800. I am not an expert on South African taxation law, so I cannot tell you whether all or part of the sum can be set off as a business expense. Nor does my information reveal whether Farmer Voster is successful and wealthy, or whether he is struggling, and thus must skimp and scrape to meet the impost. But it is not Mr Voster's financial problems that make me uneasy; it is the thought of all the *other* South Africans who would love to spend a relaxed weekend murdering a black man, but who cannot afford even the modest going rate.

It may be, of course, that there is a judicial sliding scale for such actions; the judge who sentenced Mr Voster might well have been taking into account the fact that Mr

Sambo had no fewer than four children, in which case those who choose a childless husband to kill would presumably be charged in a lower band, and bachelors could be done in scot-free. Yet it is notoriously difficult to guess merely by looking at a man how many children he has, and mistakes can be made; suppose someone has saved up, possibly from a very slender income, to give himself the pleasure of culpably homiciding a black man quite slowly, under the impression that the subject has only one small boy (and a naughty one at that), and then discovers that he has confused his victim with a lookalike, and faces a monstrous bill for polishing off some excessively philoprogenitive layabout with nine children of various ages and another on the way.

My regular readers will not make the mistake of thinking me an extreme egalitarian; there will always be disparities in income in any society which encourages and rewards thrift, enterprise and hard work. On the other hand, it goes somewhat against the grain to regulate solely by the mechanism of the free market such amusing South African activities as torturing black men to death; whence my unease.

Certainly, I would be implacably opposed to any suggestion that the practice should be nationalized and made free, or even that it should be available on payment of a token sum, with the state making up the shortfall and providing the equipment; that is the highway to waste and inefficiency.

But there is an alternative, which has the virtue of being based entirely on private enterprise, and demonstrates also the important business principle of pooled resources leading to benefits for all those participating. My idea takes something of the form of a tontine, and it would work as follows.

An umbrella organization would be set up to cover the whole country. Anyone would be eligible to join on payment of a *small* (that is the point) entrance fee and annual subscription, and I even have a name for the enterprise: it would be called the Federation of Kill-a-Kaffir Clubs. (I envisage a time, when the idea has been widely taken up and is running successfully, when a white South African, meeting a friend in the street, will say 'Let's stroll down to the Kill-a-Kaffir' – for I would certainly wish the clubs to be convivial places rather than simply the premises where the purpose of them is carried out. But I digress, and must now explain just how my scheme would be operated.)

The initial entry charge would go to the hire or construction of appropriate meeting rooms, together with the equipment; thereafter, the annual subscription would be wholly devoted to the purpose of the club, viz, to kill a Kaffir (or, more precisely, to ensure that the price set by the courts for doing so would be immediately available). Every month, say – perhaps more often if the scheme prospers – the club will stage a draw, and the member whose lucky number comes up can go out and kill a Kaffir (no doubt after standing a round of drinks!), secure in the knowledge that there are the funds to back the action, as well as a quiet pride in the fact that he has regularly paid his whack, and is now justly entitled to his sport. (One rule, I think, should be universally enforced; all members should pay the same subscription, lest the wealthier ones should in time begin to demand, say, two tickets in the draw, thus nullifying the whole purpose of the scheme.)

Obviously, when a member has drawn the winning ticket, he cannot be eligible to enter the draw again until every other member has claimed the prize; how soon his turn will come round again naturally depends on the number of members and their degree of enthusiasm for Kaffir-killing.

In matters of this kind, it rarely pays to look too far ahead; the best-laid schemes of mice and men . . . But one or two consequences, if my idea catches on, can be tentatively predicted. For instance, the reduction in the numbers of the African population would ultimately lead, by the laws of supply and demand, to higher wages for such blacks as survive; put that together with the extra spending power injected into the black economy from the court-imposed 'Dead-Kaffir money' (as I suggest it might be called), and a generally rising level of black prosperity would result, to the good of all.

It must be understood that my proposal is not offered in any spirit of take-it-or-leave-it; I am sure that many improvements can and will be suggested, and I am equally certain that I have failed to take into account this or that difficulty, which others will spot (and I hope resolve). What I have put forward is in the nature of an outline only, not a blueprint with every detail filled in. In any case, I shall not myself be joining a Kill-a-Kaffir Club, partly because I think it would be embarrassing to be constantly lauded by the members for my pioneering efforts, and partly because for some inexplicable reason I have never got much pleasure out of torturing black men to death; I greatly prefer coloureds.

There is one obvious objection to the whole principle of what I have proposed. Why, some will ask, go to all that trouble to murder black men, when by joining the South African Police it can be done with financial and every other kind of impunity, *and* rewarded with an ample stipend? After all, when the current wave of black unrest began a year or two ago, the Botha government gave the police what was rather amusingly called *carte blanche* to kill any number of blacks, and they have ever since been taking the opportunity with a will, not to say gusto. But those who would follow such a course must have forgotten that the whole purpose of my scheme is to make killing black men *fun*, and I have to say that anyone who would confine the practice to those doing it in the course of paid employment is, in the most literal sense of the word, a spoilsport.

The Times November 24th, 1988

Good night, sweet prince

The courtier's, soldier's, scholar's eye, tongue, sword,
The expectancy and rose of the fair state,
The glass of fashion and the mould of form,
The observed of all observers, quite, quite down.

L ET US BE clear about exactly what it is that we have
lost with the death of Laurence Olivier. Theatregoers have
lost the greatest of modern actors, and one of such gifts that
perhaps only three or four in all history could have counted
themselves his peers; but there is another category, and it is
that that is the most impoverished by his passing, for he
takes with him a quality that is now more rare, yet never
more needed, than at any time in our history. What we have
lost with Laurence Olivier is *glory*.

He reflected it in his greatest roles; indeed, he walked
clad in it – you could practically see it glowing around him
like a nimbus. He had a quality that he shared with some
of the greatest men and women in this country's history,
among whom he would have been welcome and at home:
monarchs like Henry V and Elizabeth I, men of action like
Marlborough and Drake, statesmen like Cecil and Disraeli,
adventurer-artists like Raleigh and Sidney, creators like Van
Dyck, Dickens and Elgar, interpreters like Beecham, shapers
of the mind like Newton and Hume, poets like Byron and
Graves, historians like Clarendon and Macaulay, journalists
like Hazlitt and Cobbett, orators like Fox and Churchill.

There is no name on that list that Olivier was unworthy

to stand beside, and he and they have that quality of glory in common. With that list to provide a framework, it is possible to attempt a definition of it.

Part of it is optimism – not the facile optimism that ignores reality but the profound kind that accepts it but believes that the world may yet be saved. 'Clenching his fist at the death-pale stars', such an optimist faces always outwards, and in his heart it is always noon.

If you close your eyes and think of Olivier in any of his most famous roles, you always see him brightly lit, and although such a memory is an illusion, it is an enormously significant one; a Gielgud our mind's eye sees in a chameleon-play of subtle colours, a Scofield in the half-light of intro-spection, but Olivier we think of in the spotlight of the sun, and if we are asked to say without pausing for thought what musical instrument he brings to mind, there are few, I think, who will not compare him to the blazing trumpet.

Such a picture points inevitably to further qualities. Chief among these is courage, and Olivier radiated it. One of the roles with which he will always be associated is Henry V, but the enduring nature of our memory of him in the part is not provided only by the fact that we have it on film to keep the memory green. He did in truth embody and personify the virtues of Shakespeare's Hal, and courage was the foremost of those.

Optimism; courage; the third quality of glory is romanti-cism. Again, not the sentimental or bombastic kind, but the romanticism of those who live always above the clouds. In a sense, all actors are romantics (what would they be doing in so odd a trade, where they are always pretending to be something they are not, if they did not live in an extra-bright, more intense world than the rest of us?), but Olivier, just as he was built on a larger dramatic and emotional scale than his fellow-players, also had in his art this quality of romanticism to a degree exceptional even for an actor. (His marvellous looks helped make this inevitable; our century has known few more handsome men.)

It adds up to glory: Laurence Olivier's work was glorious in the same way as the Fifth Symphony of Beethoven is glorious, and we can say of it what E.M. Forster said of that music, that 'all sorts and conditions are satisfied by it . . . the passion of your life becomes more vivid . . .'

I suppose I saw him on the stage in upwards of two score roles; there was hardly one that did not demonstrate that he was by far the greatest actor of my lifetime, and – more than that – there was hardly one that did not demonstrate that the difference between him and even his nearest peers was one of kind, not just of degree. Nobody before him could have played Coriolanus as he did; perhaps none but Kean could have conveyed what his Richard III made us feel; and it is impossible to believe that there will ever, even in the future, be a Hotspur to touch his.

Well these are all romantic, spotlit roles, and it may be said that they were his natural home. So they were – but what of his Malvolio and his Shylock, which are far removed from the brightness of such parts, yet in which he also triumphed? What of his soft, melancholy, broken Astrov? What of the ten unforgettable minutes he contributed to the famous 1944 *Peer Gynt* as the Button-Moulder? What of his Sir Peter Teazle, whose heart we could see – no, *hear* – breaking as the screen went down? What of his part as Berenger, the last man alive, in Ionesco's *Rhinoceros*?

These were roles which, running against his natural grain, needed genius to play as he played them, and in which he made the coin of glory ring as clear and bright as in a part like Shaw's Sergius, with which he could not have failed if he had tried.

What a titanic figure he was! What a marvellous man! I knew him a little, and some years ago, in a certain matter, he offered to do for me an entirely unsolicited and unexpected service so far beyond the call of anything even remotely implied by our acquaintance, and so generous and true, that the tears stood in my eyes as I read the letter in which he made the suggestion, and they sprang again, as I remembered the incident, when I read of his death.

No one will ever fill the place he leaves in the hearts of those who knew him; no one will ever play the roles he played as he played them; no one will replace the splendour that he gave his native land with his genius.

Line after line he spoke on stage comes to the mind's ear as I think of him: Sergius folding his arms with his 'I never apologize'; Hotspur's 'My liege, I did deny no prisoners'; Shylock's 'I will have my bond'; John Tagg's (the last part he ever played on stage) 'Build the revolutionary party'; Othello's 'Othello's occupation's gone'. Gone indeed, and part of us with him.

We live in a world awash with pygmies, with scurvy knaves picking and stealing their way through life. Wherever we look – in politics, in letters, in religion, in law, in nobility, in art and journalism and sport and commerce – we see a grey desert world, desperately lacking in figures of size and power and appeal. Who inspires us now? Who makes our hearts race? Whom can we admire without reserve? Whom would we gladly follow?

An echoing silence is all I get for answers to those questions. That is what I meant when I said that the world was short of glory, and that is what I meant when I said that Laurence Olivier provided it.

> . . . and we petty men
> Walk under his huge legs and peep about
> To find ourselves dishonourable graves.

This king among men is no more, and there is none to ascend the vacant throne. Roland's horn is silent; the lance of El Cid is couched; Don John of Austria rides home from the Crusade. Laurence Olivier – actor of genius, citizen of the world, hero of our time – home is gone, and ta'en his wages; golden boys and girls all must like chimney-sweepers come to dust. Let us ring down the curtain, switch off the lights, and tiptoe from the empty theatre.

O, wither'd is the garland of the war,
The soldier's pole is fall'n: young boys and girls
Are level now with men: the odds is gone,
And there is nothing left remarkable
Beneath the visiting moon.

The Times July 12th, 1989

Epic proportions

WHEN THE EARLIEST men had finished discovering fire, husbandry, reproduction and hunting, their next task was to wonder what the world was, and how it came into being. Finding no satisfactory answer to those questions (for which it is difficult to blame our ancestors, in view of the fact that nobody has satisfactorily solved the riddle yet) they put them aside until they had leisure enough. And their very next endeavour, probably when they retired into the cave as winter came down, was to make up stories and tell them to one another.

Countless centuries then went by, during which all the tales thus spun were lost forever. But as soon as memory was securely established, and the idea of committing thought to it for future use became common, followed by the invention of means whereby it could be permanently recorded, the human race began to make *and to pass on* tales of rulers and wars, monsters benign and evil, quests and treasure, heroes with magic powers, personified stars, dark regions beneath the earth and bright ones above the firmament, sages and fools, oaths kept and broken, dynasties and traitors, riddles and rituals, impossible tasks triumphantly completed and gnomic utterances successfully interpreted. Epic was born, and there were few cultures without it, from the Assyrians with *Gilgamesh* to the Greeks with the *Iliad* and *Odyssey*, from the northern *Sagas* to the Germanic *Nibelungenlied*, from the English *Beowulf* to the French *Chanson de Roland*:

The wild village folk in earth's earliest prime
Could often sit still for an hour at a time
And hear a blind beggar, nor did the tale pall
Because Hector must fight before Hector could fall . . .

The greatest in scope and size and imagination of all these tales is the Sanskrit epic called *The Mahabharata*. It is immensely long – fifteen times the length of the Bible – and literary archaeologists will be excavating layers till the end of time, but its form settled down, more or less permanently, around the third or fourth century AD.

Some 1,600 years later, Peter Brook was born. Half a century or so after that auspicious event he began work on hewing from the 100,000 stanzas of *The Mahabharata* a coherent dramatized version of the epic, and a decade later it was done, and taken on a world tour.

A week or two ago I went to Glasgow (its last stop but one) to see it; it is in three parts, in all nine hours long, and the three 'acts' are normally played on successive evenings. Every now and again, however, the whole thing is given in a single day, starting at 1 p.m. and finishing at 11 at night.

I took – and triumphantly passed – the endurance test, and can testify that it is an experience from which I shall continue to draw strength, wisdom, understanding and recollected joy until the end of my life; and, if some of the premises on which *The Mahabharata* stands are sound, also afterwards.

As you might expect of an Indian epic, it mingles all the orders of being; gods, men and women, demons, creatures made up from all those categories. As you would also expect from such a source, it is shot through with moral ambiguities, summed up towards the end in the simple statement: 'No good man is entirely good. No bad man is entirely bad.'

Heroes abound, their heroisms subtly differentiated; beauty draws men with a single hair; miraculous births and magic powers abound; great vows are sworn, honour is honoured, noble renunciations are made, identities are uncertain; hate and love, lust and chastity, blood and earth, cruelty and forgiveness, faith and treachery – all these clash and mingle, exchange roles, reveal new meanings. The dead are as real as the living, the gods as capricious as the humans, the destinies as contrary as fate; and the physical spectacle is an epic in itself, composed of fire, water, sand, blood, silk, swords, armour, gold, movement and every colour on earth and in heaven.

Beware the spectacle, though it gives us, a thousand times, the catch in the breath that tells us genius has been at work. Beware it because *The Mahabharata*, prodigiously dramatic and spectacular throughout though it is, is not to be classified under theatrical entertainment. Peter Brook would not spend upwards of a decade on a circus, not even the greatest circus there has ever been. What we have here is a unique lode of meaning, what the narrator (who is also part of the work) calls 'the poetical history of mankind'.

And what *is* the poetical history of mankind? It is a story, like almost all Indian stories, of struggle, inevitably a struggle from the inchoate darkness of ignorance to the light of full realization, beautifully symbolized in *The Mahabharata* by the blind king whose queen binds a veil across her eyes, to be worn for the rest of her life, in order that he shall never have cause to reproach her; in what follows death, he has regained his sight, and she has taken off the blindfold.

But the greatest symbol of the Manichaean struggle is the plot itself. Two families, whose lives and purposes are inextricably entwined, go to war, a war of almost total destruction, in which the conflagration is ignited by a fateful game of dice. Again and again – this is an epic, after all – there is a chance to avoid the catastrophe, but each time the characters are swept along by the river of fate; well, Troy could have given back Helen.

Yet 'fate' is a dangerously solid concept for something as shimmering and elusive as this masterpiece. Nothing is inevitable until it has happened, and a better word than fate is the Indian *dharma*, which runs through the day like a silver thread. To match the universal moral truth that *dharma* implies (though it is much more than that) is the burden laid upon the players in this gigantic and pitiful game, and if you allow yourself to think that the gods who take part in the action are fulfilling the same role as the Homeric deities guarding their favourites, you will make the long day's journey into night no more than a brilliant and gripping theatrical experience.

Is Krishna, for instance, here man or god? For that matter, is he faithful or treacherous? There is no final scene in which the detective reveals that the butler did it; the whole point of this Krishna is that he is part of our own struggle – indeed, part of us – and we are bound to seek the meaning of our struggle as firmly as he is bound by his dual, perhaps triple or quadruple, nature.

True epic died out of the world with sophistication. It is not easy to envisage anyone today taking a couple of centuries over writing a quarter of a million pairs of rhymed hexameters about the battle between Mr Roy Hattersley and Mr John Prescott.

But the great undying stories from the innocent ancient world will live forever, and the reason can be seen in Glasgow at this very moment. It is because, for all the lurid stories, the impossible bargains and inexorable tragedies, the mysterious figures and their mysterious intentions, the unresolved conflicts and the insoluble puzzles, they are as meaningful and important to us today as ever they were to their audiences and readers over the millennia. If you doubt it, consider this passage, with which I close. It is a catechism shared between the voice of an unseen questioner and the leader of one of the two factions, here undergoing an ordeal:

What is quicker than the wind? *Thought*. What can cover the earth? *Darkness*. Who are the more numerous, the living or the dead? *The living, because the dead are no longer*. Give me an example of space. *My two hands as one*. An example of grief. *Ignorance*. Of poison. *Desire*. An example of defeat. *Victory*. What is the cause of the world? *Love*. What is your opposite? *Myself*. What is madness? *A forgotten way*. Why do men revolt? *To find beauty, either in life or in death*. What for each of us is inevitable? *Happiness*. And what is the greatest marvel? *Each day, death strikes and we live as though we were immortal. This is what is the greatest marvel*.

The Times April 25th, 1988

A man for all seasons

The Shifting Point by Peter Brook*
Peter Brook: A Theatrical Casebook
compiled by David Williams*

THE SCENE IS a disused quarry some miles from Adelaide. In a biting wind, Peter Brook's company from Paris has just given the first English-language performance of *The Conference of the Birds*. The quarry has something of the shape of an amphitheatre, which is why it was chosen instead of a conventional playhouse. There are other reasons, though: the bareness of the makeshift auditorium, the group of aboriginals in the audience who would not have gone into the city, even the challenge of the cold itself.

It is safe to say that not three in a hundred of the audience have ever in their lives experienced anything like what they have just seen. From their faces, it is clear that they fully realize as much, including the aboriginals, who speak no English. The present writer, who has flown 12,000 miles to see the performance, is talking to Peter Brook just outside the gates of the quarry, a few yards up the hill. The car park is in the opposite direction, and the river of spectators has been steadily flowing out of the gate and down the hill.

Suddenly, some members of the audience notice, and recognize, Brook. The river acquires a loop; the whole audience is now going uphill before going down. They

*Methuen, 1987

flow past Brook, just looking at him, almost all of them silent; occasionally one mutters a few incoherent words. Many stretch out a hand to touch him, saying nothing. It is noticeable that couples seem reluctant to meet one another's eyes.

Consider those members of the audience who, incapable of speech or thought, wanted to *touch* Peter Brook. Why did they do so strange, so un-Australian, a thing? They did it because, after what they had seen, they could not think of him as a theatre director, or the performance as a play. They had been present at a profound and mysterious ritual, and wanted, instinctively, a physical connection with the priest, or guru, or shaman, because they felt – though they would deny it under torture the following day – that some of the sacral magic would thereby flow into them, and give them, too, magic powers.

Brook, horrified, would declare that he has no such powers. But he would agree – indeed, insist – that experiences such as *The Conference of the Birds*, and *a fortiori*, *The Mahabharata*, are certainly more than even the most serious and meaningful of conventional plays. All theatre directors except the most doltish of them (I am tempted to name him) know that European theatre began as a religious festival. Brook is the only one who *always* keeps that fact in mind, and who considers it profoundly relevant to everything he does.

Everything he does? That is a large claim for so Protean a figure. But these two books make good the assertion. Brook's first book was *The Empty Space*, a most characteristic title, for the empty space stands not only for the theatre which he is about to fill with a new production, it also represents the void, the chaos, from which creation will in due course manifest itself.

The Shifting Point is no less significant as symbolizing his never-ending search for deeper and greater experiences, his willingness to follow any likely path, always carrying with him whatever of value he has found in his previous explorations. Brook's face is almost never fully in repose; the nearest he can get to an expression of settled contentment is one which consists of crinkling his eyes, chin tilted, looking over the heads of those around him, as if seeking new horizons. And that is exactly what he *is* doing.

Many of those horizons, actual and potential, are discussed in *The Shifting Point*, which consists of everything he has felt worth preserving from all his essays, statements, articles and interviews. These range from a set of twenty-five aphorisms, some of them quite daft, to a comprehensive analysis of the role of the mask (not only in the theatre) which from now on must surely be the starting-point for any study of that most complex and fascinating device for revealing what it conceals.

That essay is typical of Brook in more ways than one. First, as you might expect, it is directly related to theatrical experience, but you would hardly expect the massive and meticulous detail that he gives in discussing his and others' work with masks, in itself an exhaustive study of their effect and use. Casually, and without any reference to the travels and research required, he reveals that he has studied the masks of the Yoruba and the Macumba, the masks of voodoo in Haiti and those that come from the 1,000-year tradition of Bali, the masks of Bahia and the masks he found in a little hall in one of the back streets of Rio, masks worn by a group of men and women each of whom was possessed by one of the ancient gods. But Brook is not content to study the masks he finds; his constant refrain, throughout his life, has been 'what if?'

The Shifting Point is not Peter Brook's considered credo, but it amounts to one. The range is remarkable, from a loving but searching examination of the character and artistry of John Gielgud to the illuminating accounts of three of Brook's more controversial opera productions; from his reverent but wholesome consideration of Shakespeare to his brilliant and convincing solution of the mystery of Chekhov; from his remarkable experiments in pure sound, culminating in Orghast, an epic in a language invented solely for it; to the series of wordless playlets he took into the African bush.

Everything he attempts is based on the great principle that has been the lodestar of his life and art: take nothing – *nothing* – for granted, not even Shakespeare's greatness, or the communicative power of language, or meaning itself. (David Williams's compilation reinforces the reader's amazement at the breadth of Brook's achievement and the restlessness that has driven him on to broaden it still further. It contains a detailed chronology of his work, and much useful background material about almost all of it, in the form of reviews, descriptions and commentaries.)

Not everything Brook touches succeeds, but like all wise men he knows that nothing is wasted. He has always returned from even the most barren of blind alleys with something of value. He came down with a frightful attack of Charles Marowitz some years ago, which for a time looked as though it might be fatal, as Peter Hall succumbed to a massive dose of Adrian Mitchell. Brook recovered completely, though Hall still has annual recurrent fevers, like those Sapper heroes with malaria.

'We live', says Brook, 'in an age which is very frightened of value judgements; we even flatter ourselves at being somehow superior if we judge less. Yet no society can exist without ideals.' Or, he might add, enthusiasms. The excitement that possesses him when he spots a new horizon – Grotowski, Jan Kott, work with deaf children, with Amerindians, with asylum inmates, in a zoo, before junkies in the Bronx – is instant, infectious and compelling, yet it is never shallow, never tangential, never quick to pass.

Knight of the Joyful Countenance, he goes his way. He listens to all suggestions, rejects nothing out of hand, even reads the reviews. Expecting surprises, he is rarely disappointed in them. Once, he asked an aged Indian actor for his secret. The answer was a mirror of his own: 'I try to bring together all that I have experienced in my life, so as to make what I am doing a witness of what I have felt and what I have understood.' So does he, this searching, contemplative, inexorable, multifarious, open, unwavering, inexhaustible and love-guided man.

Sunday Times April 17th, 1988

The baby's bottle

I HAVE FROM time to time chronicled here some of the more appalling abuses of the law that have taken place in the United States, such as the story of the man who, intent on suicide, jumped in front of a train. He was not killed – the driver had been exceptionally alert – but he was injured; he sued the railway company, *and won*.

An American husband and wife, Harold and Candace Thorp, are suing a firm of whiskey makers, claiming that their product – the well known brand called Jim Beam – was responsible for the fact that their son was born both physically and mentally malformed.

Anybody's first thought would be that by some terrible accident or negligence a toxic substance had got into a bottle of Jim Beam, that the Thorps had had the misfortune, all unknowingly, to buy the odd man out, that Mrs Thorp had taken a drink from it, and that the poison had thereupon attacked the baby in her womb; in other words, a parallel to the story of thalidomide.

Would that that had been the explanation; the truth is much worse, and much harder to believe. Mr and Mrs Thorp are both alcoholics (they do not deny it), and Mrs Thorp had drunk (again, she admits it) up to half a bottle of Jim Beam *a day* throughout her pregnancy. (I should point out, though it's a trifle in this story, that Jim Beam whiskey is bourbon, which is considerably stronger than Scotch). I therefore calculate that she had poured getting on for *forty gallons* of the stuff into herself while her baby was gestating, and she now wants to be monetarily compensated for the defects, bodily and psychological, she caused; in the report I have read the sum claimed is not specified, but if I know American litigation – and I do – it will be millions of dollars.

How, then, even in an American court, did she suppose she could get so impudent, shaming and meritless a case on its feet? Thus: she claims that there was no label on the bottle to give warning of the dangers of drinking in pregnancy; since there was no such announcement she boozed on undaunted. She now says (a likely story!) that she didn't know that swallowing 40 gallons of fire-water while pregnant might be dangerous for her child, to which the Beam company has tartly replied that 'You could put a skull and crossbones on the bottle and she will continue to consume alcohol.'

But it must be clear by now that this article is not really about the abominations of American courts and law. It is about responsibility, and therefore comes back to the question I have so often asked: are we, or are we not, responsible for our actions and inactions? Or, to put it in terms of this monstrous business, are Mr and Mrs Thorp responsible for poisoning their child, or are they not?

Yes, they are. If they did not know that a woman getting sozzled daily would present a serious risk to any child she was carrying – well, there is a level of indifference and carelessness below which no sane person has any right to fall, and the Thorps should not be allowed to get away with a plea of ignorance. Indeed, some sympathy for them might be in order, were they to be arraigned on criminal charges such as poisoning their baby, if they pleaded that as alcoholics they were so completely in the grip of an addiction that, much as they wished to behave responsibly, they were unable to do so. But that, in the actual civil proceedings, is not in issue.

Why is it not in issue? Because the drunken Mrs Thorp and her drunken husband plainly refuse to accept responsibility. It is true they have a notable precedent in the third chapter of *Genesis*, where Eve blames the serpent, and Adam blames Eve, but their excuses were of no avail before the Lord, who sentenced them both to banishment, and added for the woman a penance grimly apposite in this case: 'In sorrow shalt thou bring forth children.'

I accept that, even through her alcoholic haze, Mrs Thorp does truly sorrow over the condition of her child. But, as the case she has brought demonstrates, she wants someone else to bear the blame. More, she wants someone else *to pay* for the blame. The child will, I imagine, need special treatment or care or nursing, and this will certainly cost money; there was no mention of insurance in the report. But nor was there any plea by the Thorps that that was why they were seeking money from the distillers via the courts; the whole of their case was that the whiskey firm, and only the whiskey firm, was at fault. Yet the only argument to support such a claim was that the whiskey firm had not specifically warned purchasers, by means of a printed label on each bottle, that the product might be harmful to unborn children.

It is widely agreed that any adult is at liberty to do anything at all to himself or herself, provided it does not harm others; the argument is that we have no responsibility, independent of ourselves, to eschew certain paths through life.

By that test, the Thorps were accountable to nobody for their drunkenness, and they could go unrebuked until they died of it. But even the most extreme exponent of that view would not argue that it doesn't matter if they cause harm to someone else, and in particular someone else for whom they are responsible. Nor, I presume, would they deny that last contention. They are not saying that what happened to their child is of no concern to them; they say only that what happened to him is somebody else's responsibility.

So it might have been, if, say, a drunken driver had mounted the pavement and hit the pregnant Mrs Thorp, thus injuring her child; but would they be in court demanding damages if *they* had driven drunkenly, crashed their car and caused the child prenatal injury? Do you say that even the American legal system could not accommodate a damages suit in such circumstances? In a recent case a man was telephoning from a phone box when a car skidded into it and injured him; he sued the makers of the phone box for not making it sturdier, and won.

I dare say the Thorps will win. Well, if they do, at least the deformed child will get the medical attention he needs; if the damages are in line with the ludicrous sums usually awarded in such scandalous cases, not even this pair could put away so much Jim Beam that the money would run out before they did.

Drinka pinta booza day; it would make a striking slogan for any daring enough liquor company. And possibly it would be even more profitable if the advertisement went on 'and then go to court and demand to be paid for the effects'.

The Times September 26th, 1989

To die will be an awfully big adventure

MR NORMAN MAILER has been giving tongue, no more coherently than usual, on the subject of Mr Salman Rushdie's present predicament. At a rally of several hundred writers (the very thought is enough to give you the creeps) in New York, he declared that the Ayatollah had 'awakened us to the great rage we feel when our liberties are threatened'. ('Liberties' may be a misprint for 'royalties'.) He also said, more mysteriously, that 'we are beginning to feel that we are willing to suffer, even die, for our ideals,' and, more mysteriously still, 'It is our duty to state to the world that if he is ever assassinated it will then become our obligation to stand in his place.'

Let us take the last of those gnomic utterances first. Put aside Mr Mailer's sense of duty; it is likely that the world, ungrateful place that it is, would feel that he had no duty to state anything to it. But that still leaves the claim that, should Mr Rushdie be murdered (by the Ayatollah's agents, presumably, not by a bookshop customer disappointed to find that *The Satanic Verses* was not, after all, the long-awaited Variorum Edition of *Eskimo Nell*), 'it will then become our obligation to stand in his place'.

What, if anything, is that supposed to mean? It can hardly mean that if Mr Rushdie is killed, Mr Mailer and his fellow-writers will be willing to be buried along with him like Cetewayo's wives. Nor, surely, that they would at once all start writing books calculated to give mortal affront to Muslims, and thus put themselves into the same danger as Mr Rushdie is now in. Nor, I take it, that they should all disguise themselves as the controversial novelist. And certainly he is not advocating the formation of a task force that would march on Qom and knock off the Ayatollah. We are left with Mr Mailer's assertion that he and his fellow-writers 'are beginning to feel that we are willing to suffer, even die, for our ideals'. And here, at last, there is something that can be discussed.

First, though, we must remember that the only writer in immediate danger of suffering and dying in an unnatural manner is Mr Rushdie, and it would be stretching the language pretty far to say that he would be doing it for his 'ideals'; after all, it is plain that he had no idea when he wrote the offending words that any such consequences might follow. Moreover, Mr Mailer's circumstances are such that so far from being called upon to suffer and die for his ideals, the only danger he runs is that of experiencing cardiac arrest at getting a bad notice in the *New York Review of Books*. There have been, in our time, many writers who have suffered for their ideals – Sinyavsky, Daniel, Pasternak, Solzhenitsyn, for instance – and no doubt Mr Mailer campaigned vigorously on their behalf, while still finding time to denounce his own country as an evil imperialist state.

It seems, however, that the flesh is willing but the opportunity is remote. How do you demonstrate your readiness to suffer or die for your ideals in a society which has no vacancies, in the Help Wanted columns, for martyrs? I am not just jeering at Mr Mailer and his hollow bombast. I suspect that his words were meant to echo Voltaire's celebrated dictum, 'I detest what you say but I will defend to the death your right to say it,' but, if so, there are two serious flaws in his point. The first is that Voltaire never said it; it was invented and attached to him in a modern biography. The second is that although he might well have defended the unfettered expression of a view he abhorred, it is very unlikely indeed that he would have been willing to die for it.

Nor, I am pretty sure, would Mr Mailer. Nor, most

emphatically, would I, though I not only campaign inces-
santly for the right to the exercise of free speech in even the
vilest cause, but in addition am the most obstinate man you
could hope to find banging his head against a brick wall.

As I say, writers have died for what they had written, but
in a majority of such cases the willingness of the writer was
never tested; the forbidden writing was enough to condemn
them without appeal, and no opportunity for recantation was
offered. (Who could have suffered and died more frightfully
than Boethius? But he hadn't put pen to paper until after he
was condemned.)

Why is it that when writers, and they alone, come together
in gaggles, whether for unimaginably boring 'Writers' Sym-
posiums', or even more ghastly 'Writers' Weeks', or – as in
this case, and perhaps worst of all – for collective protests or
demands, they inevitably make fools of themselves?

It is nothing to do with the soundness of the cause.
Anyone not afire with mad bigotry must feel horror at
the present plight of Rushdie, even if it is unaccompanied
by sympathy for him. The horror, I take it, is primarily
grounded in the realization that one wretched corner of
the world has fallen back so far into mad, ancient evil; the
expression of the horror naturally focuses upon the selected
victim, and the triviality of his offence. But what I want to
know, though I run the risk of being condemned *in absentia*
with a price on my head (£4.37) from the Society of Authors,
is: what is so special about writers?

What a terrible world it would be if we sought only to
succour our own kind, if writers helped only writers, painters painters, businessmen businessmen, Jews Jews, Christians
Christians. Nobody knows how many tens of thousands
have been slaughtered in Persia to slake Khomeini's blasphemous bloodthirst, but among them, I am sure, have
been many writers, and little more than an occasional voice
has been raised in their defence. Yet Rushdie, guarded (by
the police he reviles and despises as racist thugs) from the
moment of the Ayatollah's outburst, prompts a meeting of

hundreds of writers thousands of miles away at which Mr Mailer pledges himself and his fellows to 'stand in his place' if the Ayatollah's hitman succeeds in an errand of murder, and implies, if not declares, that the gathering is unanimous in being 'willing to suffer, even die, for our ideals'.

Doesn't it sound absurd? But that is because of two massive misapprehensions about writers, which writers have assiduously fostered; it is, first, that writers *because* they are writers are different from other people, and, second, that – again because they are writers – they all share the same concerns, attitudes and outlooks. That is why there are 'Writers' Conferences', where enough hot air is generated to bring about the dreaded 'greenhouse effect' overnight, though the meetings of fishmongers, cabinet-makers and brewers are confined entirely to practical matters about refrigerators, varnish and the price of hops. But that, you see, is because those sensible men do not suppose that they have anything in common other than the way they earn their living, or that they are set apart from the rest of mankind because of their calling.

I, too, am horrified at the implications of this affair. But I am not willing to suffer very much, let alone die, for any abstract principle connected with it. Nor, of course, is Mr Mailer. Fortunately, neither of us will be called upon to do so. And another thing: if Mr Mailer *were* willing to give his life for fellow-writer Rushdie, would he do so for fellow-writer me? Come to think of it, would Rushdie?

The Times March 3rd, 1989

For love or money

How DID WE come, when the coinage was decimalized, to fall into the horrible usage 'pee'? (Talk about spending a penny . . .) If you remember the previous system (it ended only eighteen years ago, but seems to have vanished utterly from living memory), you will recall that it, too, included 'pence', just as the decimal currency does; it is only the value that has changed.

Thus, the abbreviated written form of, say, four pence was '4d' (the d went back to Roman times – it was short for *denarius*), but we never talked about 'four dee'; we said 'four pence', invariably elided in writing to 'fourpence' or, in speech, to 'fourp'nce', with the stress on the first syllable.

Why and when did we cease to say 'pence'? The p symbol after the figure cannot be to blame; if anything, it should have strengthened the pence form. (For that matter, why did we abandon the well-accustomed d? Presumably, some horrible Nanny in the Treasury, intent like all his kind on destroying the past, insisted.) There is a theory, and a damned silly one if you ask me, that when the number of pence for which we needed names rose to ninety-nine, it made an impossibly awkward mouthful to say, for instance, 'sixtysevenpence'. But we said 'elevenpence' easily enough in the old days – indeed, we said 'elevenpencethreefarthings' (but we frequently abbreviated it to 'eleventhree'). And anyway, 'penny' and 'pence' are old and hallowed words. Literally hallowed:

Show me the tribute money. And they brought unto

him a penny. And he saith unto them, Whose is this image and superscription? They saith unto him, Caesar's. Then saith he unto them, Render therefore unto Caesar the things which are Caesar's; and to God the things that are God's.

But there is something much more profoundly wrong with our currency than the pee usage, which in any case we could give up if we wanted to. When we went over to the decimal system, we abruptly ceased to *love* our currency, a fact much more important and unsettling than may be generally realized.

In the old days, not only did we humanize our coins – we never said 'two-pence', but always 'tuppence', and we never said 'half-penny', only '*haypnee*'; much, much more important, *we gave them nicknames*. The penny didn't need one, so loved was its real name, but the three-penny coin, always pronounced 'throopnee', with the oo as in book, not as in boot, was a 'joey'. The sixpenny piece was a 'tanner', or – somewhat more reconditely – a 'sprasi', pronounced 'sprarzee'.

Best loved of all was the 'bob', which was a shilling, or 12 pence in the Old Style; it lives on, nastily, as the 5p coin. We knew the word 'piece', but never used it; the florin was invariably a 'two-bob bit'. That lives, too, as the 10p. (Am I boring you? We'll get to some sense in a minute, I hope.)

The half-crown, 'two-and-six', was dubbed half-a-dollar, which says something about the decline of our currency's value, because if you translate into the present coinage, it turns out that the mighty dollar was once worth 25p. (Who was it whose aim was to enable 'the pound to look the dollar in the face'? And what did he mean by it?)

Then there was the ten-shilling note, which had one extraordinary property; its colour was not fast. Ingenious villains would pick on some innocent in the pub, talk him into passing over any such notes he had, rub them on a piece of white paper, and shake their heads at their obviously counterfeit status as the colour came off. Then they would propose – mind you, I've said nothing – that they would take the duds off the victim's hands for five shillings a time.

Then there was the pound, the great glory of the series unless you count the majestic white fiver (it vanished many years before decimalization); the pound was a 'oncer', or, for a generation even older than I, a 'Bradbury', so called because the Chief Cashier of the Bank of England, whose name is always signed on our paper currency, was at that time Sir John Bradbury.

Oddly enough, none of his successors achieved such eponymous standing, and today I doubt if one person in a thousand knows that the signature is still there. (I have just looked at our present-day notes; the fiver and tenner are signed by a Mr Gill, the twenty by a Mr Totally-Illegible.)

What does it mean for a society to feel such affection for its currency? I do not know any other country which does what we did; I *think* 'dime' is the official term for the American 10 cent coin. Most other countries couldn't love their money if they wanted to, because they have only one unit, and the different coins and notes are simply multiples thereof; a *lira* is a *lira*, and a million of them are still only *lire*.

But we British make friends of our money; or rather, we used to, till decimalization killed it. We *could*, of course, have devised new nicknames; the 5p could become 'a nothing', the 10p 'a garbage', the 50p 'a dross', the £1 'an ugly', the 20p 'a useless', the £5 'a horrible', and so on. But the heart went out of us when they stole 140 of our pennies and left us only 100, whence that uniquely repellent monosyllable, pee.

Surely there is meaning in the way we personalized the currency. It must have meant that getting and spending did not constitute our entire horizon, so that coins had a meaning apart from their function. (Now I come to think of it, we had something of the same kind of feeling for bus-tickets, when they came in those curious packs held in that even more curious rack; now that they come off an impersonal and uniform roll, all that has been lost.)

It is not too fanciful to say that we took pride in our currency, and you can see that truth clearly if you think of the greatest of all our money tokens: the last gold coin that was current tender. It was, after all, made of solid gold, not a mixture, or cupro-nickel, let alone the mouldy shavings which, suitably compressed, make the £1 coin today. It was a mark of confidence; many men wore one fixed to their watch-chain, and a handful of them was not just a fortune, but a statement that the ordered course of the universe had not changed, and never would. And with what a resounding, uncompromising, splendid name did we christen it: the sovereign!

Now we live in a less romantic time, and making money fills our horizons much more completely than it once did. It is suitable, then, that our coinage should have become nothing but a means of exchange, with no more feeling in it than a throwaway ballpoint pen – which, in its turn, would once have been a fountain-pen, a thing of substance and meaning.

But once upon a time we could play shove-ha'penny, and read a penny dreadful, and sing a song of sixpence, and take the King's shilling; and once upon a time even further in the past, five sparrows could be bought for two farthings, and yet not be forgotten. Somehow, the transaction would not have had the same effect had the sparrows been sold for two pee.

The Times November 27th, 1989

The helping hand

I HAVE, FROM time to time, referred to what I call the Fallacy of the Altered Standpoint. The Fallacy lies in the belief that if the standpoint is altered the view remains the same, whereas – whether subtly or obviously, and in either case often disastrously – it changes. We are having a demonstration of the Fallacy's effect in the parliamentary debates on embryo research; we shall shortly hear in the Lords, and later in the Commons, things which only a few years ago could not have been said without uproar resulting. The facts have not altered; only the standpoint.

On this particular subject I have nothing to say, though I might perhaps offer up a general but heartfelt prayer that once (just once), and only for a moment (a tiny moment), and without fuss (not even the slightest fuss), and privately (guaranteed privately), and calmly (very, very calmly), and on any question at all (truly *any* question), Dame Mary Warnock might think (only think) that it might be possible (only possible) that she could be mistaken.

But the particular event that has brought me back to the Fallacy, though it has affinities with the subject soon to be debated, took place in the Netherlands, a country not often thought of as being far ahead of the rest of the world with actions which might have been designed to cause a shudder in anyone familiar with the Fallacy.

The subject was euthanasia, an ugly word, not least because of what it actually means. Its proponents, of course, argue that what they are doing consists of helping out of life those who do not wish to go on living, particularly those suffering from incurable, painful or debilitating diseases. And so they are; the science-fiction picture of a mad euthanasiast slaughtering everyone over 50 who sneezes is absurd, though it has to be said that the argument of the euthanasia movement is very weak indeed when it comes to safeguards against – and this is far from science-fiction – elderly, inconvenient relatives being persuaded that they might prefer an easy and painless death.

But if ever I saw the Fallacy in action, I have seen it now, in gentle, placid, lifewise Holland. A doctor has been formally reprimanded by the Dutch equivalent of the BMA, not for practising euthanasia, but *for failing to do so*, on a patient who had requested it. Now euthanasia is illegal in the Netherlands, whether a patient wants it or not; a doctor who gives a lethal dose is committing a serious crime, and the fact that doctors in that position are rarely charged does not make the action lawful. (A measure to permit euthanasia without penalty has been blocked in the Dutch Parliament.) A report I have read, in the *Herald Tribune*, says that the 'guilty' doctor, who was unnamed, had given the patient ordinary tranquillizers instead of lethal pills, though he had agreed to give a fatal dose.

Enter Mrs Tromp Meesters, the spokesdutchwoman for the Association for Voluntary Euthanasia, who reveals that the erring doctor had been reported to the Dutch Medical Disciplinary Board by the patient's son, and had been found 'guilty' of 'breach of trust' for not – no euphemisms – unlawfully killing his patient.

Although I am no expert in Dutch law, I should be surprised and alarmed if it countenanced the Disciplinary Board's decision; such organizations have wide powers over their members, but in civilized nations ruled by law (which Holland certainly is) there must be some form of judicial review, and no court could possibly uphold a punishment meted out for a refusal to commit a serious crime. But although that might assuage the feelings of the condemned doctor, it does not meet my test of the Altered Standpoint and its effect. Why else did it not occur to those who denounced the doctor to his professional judges that *they* were doing wrong, not he?

Euthanasia, it seems, is fairly widespread in Holland; a figure of 5,000 a year is given – reached, I take it, not long ago. Come with me to a year or so before that not long ago, in the days when killing people out of kindness was not only a crime, but a crime that was actually treated as one. What would your plain mynheer in the street have said if he was told that in a year or two, no more, a doctor could be reprimanded (presumably a punishment only short of being struck off) for *not* killing his patient, with no better excuse than that the patient had indicated a wish to be killed? I do not know the Dutch for 'You must be joking', or 'Get away!', let alone 'What have you been drinking, my good man?', though I am quite certain that incredulity at the thought would have been universal.

What has changed in that hideously short span of time? Only one relevant thing: the standpoint has altered. As soon as the euthanasia campaign began, or to be precise as soon as the campaign had made its first serious inroads into a society which previously would have rejected any such concept with horror, the pressure from the like of Mrs Tromp Meesters began to eat away at the foundation of what would have been called (and by me is still called) fundamental morality. Mind; she and most of her kind campaigned for their cause in the profoundly held conviction that they were benefactors to the human race in general and the desperately suffering sick in particular. But by the time the Altered Standpoint had arrived and settled in, the thought of punishing a doctor who would not kill his patient had ceased to be grotesque and disgusting; indeed, it became not only reasonable but necessary.

It is argued that if many people who are incurably ill are in a position to take their own lives, in the full possession of their mental faculties and with all the understanding necessary, it is unfair to forbid others, with no access to a painlessly lethal exit, to seek the help they need to carry out the same decision. But surely there is a difference between those who commit suicide and those who ask someone else – ironically, it must almost always be a doctor – to take their lives for them. (I say 'ironically' because everything in a doctor's training and outlook works towards saving life rather than destroying it.)

I had a beloved friend who died of cancer; her doctor had prescribed greater and greater doses of opiates, knowing – as she too knew – that in stifling the pain, the drugs were hastening her towards death. She made a smiling end, and her last words – mouthed, because she had no voice left – were 'I love you', to her daughter.

Who could object to that? Not I. Yet I maintain that there is a difference between that and what the euthanasienthusiasts advocate. Not, perhaps, in intent, but in effect. For the friend who died, helped by a doctor who had treated her all her life and was indeed intimately entwined in the family, met death amid love and happiness, her agony subdued and her feelings untouched by fear.

It is the impersonal demand for a doctor to kill a patient who might have no such tranquil mind, and who indeed might *in articulo mortis* wish to change his decision, which disturbs me, and which should, I think, disturb any other feeling person.

It should perhaps particularly disturb any feeling doctor who, because of the effect of the Altered Standpoint, might not think deeply enough about the awesome responsibility he was taking upon himself. Or, for that matter, who had in mind the possibility of being arraigned before his profession's governing body for refusing to break the Hippocratic Oath.

The Times December 11th, 1989

The rattle of dry bones

I NEVER MET Antonia White, the novelist, nor have I read any of her books. But I know a great deal about her, and practically all of it is pathetic, repulsive, or both. Who has been thus peaching on the dead, whispering nasty gossip into my ears, describing the awfulness of her personal and family life, counting her toyboy lovers, hinting that she was deranged?

Well, actually, the answer is: her daughters. Both of them have written books about their mother, and both paint her, not always accusingly, and sometimes quite unconsciously, as a monster. I do not propose to go into details, because the nature of Antonia White and her relationship with her children are not my theme, and also because anyone who wants the lot can get it from their books, the second of which has just been published.

But hot on its heels comes the news of the last-minute withdrawal from publication of an autobiography. The publishers say the book was withdrawn 'at the family's request', and it seems that there is dissension within the family. Which reminds me – one of the reviewers of the more recent Antonia White biography recalls 'the corrosive rage of Colin MacInnes in writing of his mother Angela Thirkell'.

With all that and much more, here is my question: what has become of reticence? How did it come about, and when, that if you hated, or were hated by, your father or your sister or your spouse or your entire family, it was deemed proper for you to write a book about it the moment your victims or tormentors were dead, and frequently while they were still alive?

Take that programme, *In The Psychiatrist's Chair*, in which Dr Anthony Clare questions and talks with a succession of 'patients'. I find the entire programme, and indeed the very idea of it, quite repellent, but it must be said that there is no deception as to what is to happen, and that Dr Clare, of course, does not hector or bully his subjects, but indeed handles them with tact and sympathy. (I must add that I do not consider those elements enough to justify such penny-in-the-slot psychiatry.) Anyway, not long since, Claire Rayner broke down on the programme, and again the family details poured out into the nation's laps.

Do you suppose there is anywhere in the land a family without even the tiniest skeleton rattling gently away in the cupboard? Has there ever been a home in which there was *no* resentment, *no* hurt, *no* jealousy, *no* darkness? Does *anybody* grow up without some warp, some wound? I, too, come from a 'broken home', which has certainly left me with enduring emotional problems, and if it comes to that, my life-long arachnophobia was not caught from eating a bad oyster. But you will find no details of any of that in even my most personal and autobiographical writings. We all recognize, in one way or another, the truth in Philip Larkin's most famous poem:

> They fuck you up, your mum and dad.
> They may not mean to, but they do.
> They fill you with the faults they had
> And add some extra, just for you.

But why do so many deem it necessary to tell the world, instead of a trusted friend or – *privately* – a psychiatrist, about those faults and what their effect has been? And it is by no means only the family laundry that is washed in public today. The fashion for kiss-and-tell now prevails everywhere. Autobiographers think it no shame to record, with names and details, their past liaisons, though the partners may still be living and long since happily married; some writers no doubt ask permission to reveal the past, and some no doubt fail to, but for me to suggest that they might omit such matter altogether will be accounted very comical.

'Let it all hang out' is the idiot catchword of our day, and if you have the good fortune to come from a family with a drug-addicted mother, a sadistic father, a transvestite brother, an alcoholic sister, a lunatic aunt, a paedophiliac uncle, a venereally diseased dog, and a first cousin who enjoys all these attributes simultaneously, you must be off to a literary agent as soon as you have collected enough family photographs and diaries and interviewed the surviving neighbours.

There is money in it, of course, though presumably those first in the field have done better than the late-comers, and the more jaded appetites among readers are now unlikely to be impressed unless you have a home movie of your great-grandfather having it off with a chimpanzee. But many, perhaps most, of those who bare their secrets, to say nothing of their private parts (as – most amusing! – they used to be called), are not even doing it for something as healthy as cash; the primary impulse, as far as I can see, is revenge, and the secondary self-justification.

I believe it is true, though my claim is hotly contested, that wherever you wish to go, you must start from where you are. Whatever damage was done to us in our childhoods, we cannot demand a fresh hand from the dealer; our lives are lived forward, and it is a waste of time for us to attempt to rewrite the past. In particular, it is a waste of time for us to do so in the second meaning of the phrase – that is, to falsify the record in an attempt to untie the knot that was tangled forever so long ago.

Was Antonia White like that? Obviously, I don't know; less obviously, neither do her daughters. But my ignorance is due to my not being there; theirs is due to the fact that they *were* there.

If they could have an advance peek at the Recording Angel's

embargoed account, they would be astonished, indignant and – above all – incredulous. Even in the simplest and least charged matters, we all have vivid and totally convincing pictures of youthful experiences which we subsequently learn, by irrefutable evidence, never happened; how much more distorted must our memories be when they concern the deepest and most tender parts of the psyche.

The evil that men do, a wise writer once said, lives after them; the good, he added, is oft interred with their bones. He may not have had today's autobiographers in mind, but he got their number very exactly. For what is the new cult of frankness in which if you hated your parents you rush into print to say so, if not a kind of monstrous vanity? 'Look what they did to me,' it says, 'to *me*, to ME, ME, MEEEEEEEEE!'

Of course, it is disguised, and not least self-disguised from the tale-teller, as exorcism; tell the world why you put rat poison in your grandmother's nightly cup of hot milk, only to see the cat lap it up and roll over, and you will feel better. Judging from their books, I must say, Antonia White's daughters seem to feel a hell of a lot worse. The best thing I know about the present Speaker of the House of Commons is that he has given a public and unambiguous promise never to write his memoirs. Let us hope he starts a fashion.

The Times April 24th, 1989

Parting friends

RING IN THE new; but this New Year is the one in which I shall mark two milestones, each of which has a profound meaning, both real and symbolic, for my life. You may think, when I tell you what they concern, that I am being absurd, or at least sentimental. Well, I have never thought ill of sentimentality – it is, after all, one aspect of being human – and for that matter I can't see what is so frightful about absurdity either. Anyway, here are the two markers: I shall say goodbye to my typewriter and to my wristwatch.

Curiously, both of them are closely associated with my father, though I remember nothing of him from my infancy, and met him later only once. But it was he who sent me, as a present for my seventeenth birthday, the watch, and who also gave me the money, somewhat later, to buy the typewriter.

Both lie before me on my desk; indeed, this is being typed on one of my beloved old friends, and I have just been given the time from the other.

The watch is a black-faced Movado, with Arabic numerals (nowadays confined almost entirely to children's watches, and frequently accompanied by Mickey Mouse) in gold; the hands are rather big for the face, but they are not the originals, though it has been to the menders remarkably seldom. It has a tiny second hand, which has become more difficult to read as my eyes have lost their power, which was never very great to start with. (I have told elsewhere the story of the day I discovered I had wretchedly poor sight, and of the unbelievable joy with which I was filled when I first donned my spectacles and saw a new-born world, the very existence of which I had never until then suspected.) I don't know if the firm of Movado still exists, but if it does, it may take this as a heartfelt tribute to the enduring quality of its craftsmanship.

Now it is in my hand; I turn it over. The back has been repaired; over so many years, and the tens of thousands of times I put it on and took it off, the metal wore right through; I had it neatly patched. The inscription is still perfectly legible, though it has collected verdigris. I always smile at it, because the engraver made a mistake; it reads, following the date, From Dad to Bernhard. I used to toy with the notion of using that more exotic form of my name, like Prince Bernhard of the Netherlands (though look what happened to *him*), but I gave up the idea as too posh.

Forty-four years have passed since my seventeenth birthday; an unimaginable span. Can I really have lived so long? I listen to the watch's tiny heart; a watch ticks two and a half times a second – my calculator, please. (Were I to live to be a thousand, I would never feel for that cold creature – aptly named – anything like the affection my watch and my typewriter inspire.) An amazing, unbelievable figure: one and three quarter thousand million times my little friend has said tick, and one and three quarter thousand million times it has said tock. Surely it deserves its retirement? But why is it being retired anyway?

Because, for all its loyalty, the years have made their mark. It began to fail a few years ago, and every watchmaker I took it to shook his head and said words to the effect of 'It can't go on for ever, you know.' Nor can I; I did hope that we could go together, but I have outlasted my friend. It had a reprieve, when the great Mr Rosenberg of Newcastle upon Tyne said he could keep it going (he made clear that he thought little of London watchmakers), and he did; but after a time, even his magic tweezers were not enough. Mr Rosenberg has himself now retired; this is getting mournful.

Here is my other, younger brother, my baby Olivetti; it cost £12 new in 1951. I had already learned to type, at a secretarial college, between school and university: I also learned shorthand, though I had not then begun to think of

a career, let alone the one I finally chose. Or was chosen by; I
became a journalist by accident, and stayed one. Just as well;
I have no other talent whatever, even in the most modest and
rudimentary form. I can't paint or compose or write novels; I
couldn't be a businessman or financier; I would be impossible
as a teacher and a disaster as an actor.

My mother wanted me to be a lawyer; if I had been, would
I now be telling all those pork pies about my noble, selfless,
admirable, wholly perfect profession, so vilely traduced by
that horrible man in *The Times* and facing its imminent
destruction at the hands of the wicked Lord Mackay?

My father, I learned, had wanted me to be either a doctor
or an engineer; never in all history could there have been
two more inapposite vocations. If I had chosen medicine,
there wouldn't be a patient alive for a dozen miles around;
if engineering, not a bridge standing for thrice the radius. So
journalism it was, and is, nor can I complain that I have lacked
success in my trade; Dead Sea Fruit though the plaudits have
been, I have plucked them, and swallowed. Anyhow, my little
typewriter, the only one I have ever owned, has accompanied
me everywhere, a *fidus Achates* as precious as the watch.

The figures cannot be as exact as the watch's tick; suppose
I have typed fifteen million words on my Olivetti (and it
must be something like that), then allowing for punctuation
and similar supernumeraries, I must have struck my friend a
hundred million times. But he has never complained. (Olivetti
may now step forward for its own congratulations, and shake
hands with Movado.)

From time to time, the typewriter, like the watch, has
seized up; at first, there was no problem about overhauls, but
as the years went by, fewer and fewer firms would – or could
– deal with it. I was on the verge of giving in, when, just as I
was being dismissed by a supercilious receptionist, a mechanic
passed through the room and saw my baby on the counter; his
eyes lit up, and he said 'A Lettera 22! I haven't had my hands
on one of those for years. Gimme.' It transpired that he had a

dead one in the basement, and for some time he cannibalized it to supply my own friend's deficiencies.

I had a special holder made for it; it fitted into its own compartment, and the rest of the case made a neat portable office. I have never been a roving correspondent, or wanted to be; still, my friend has been with me at an American presidential convention, a comprehensive tour of the Moscow theatre, a call on the 'Father of the H-Bomb' (Dr Edward Teller), a clandestine meeting in Soweto, a visit to Dachau, an interview with Bobby Kennedy and another with – ahem – Lee Kuan Yew (watch this space), innumerable British party conferences, at least six journeys round the world (it *is* round), dozens of music festivals, and the last transatlantic voyage of the Queen Mary, there and back. All my books have been typed on it; so have infinite quantities of articles, notes, memoranda and correspondence. I have even written love-letters on it, which may be one of the reasons I am still unmarried. (Mind you, my handwriting would itself be grounds for divorce.)

And why, then, is my other hero to be put out to grass? After all, he is still in very reasonable condition, apart from a tendency to jump a space or two and a reluctance to print the bottom half of the lower-case m. No, I am retiring him for a much sadder reason; very soon now, I shall be going over to all-computerized writing. I have resisted it for a long time, not only on my friend's behalf, but from a deep suspicion of the new technology. (I am firmly convinced that the fax machine is black magic, and that those who use it will eventually be burned at the stake.) But I have got used to the green glass screen at *The Times*, and there are real and massive advantages in being thus linked to the system into which, after all, my words go.

Forty-four years of my wristwatch; only six fewer years of my typewriter; sixty-one of my life; I sometimes wonder what I have got to show for it all. Apart, that is, from a new watch with a quartz movement, and a machine that will count my words and tell me how many more I have to do. And will it count my heartbeats, and tell me how many more of *those* I have? And would I want it to?

I don't know. Disillusion is common in men of my age, but let my coevals take heart; the nation's noisiest journalist is no better off than they. Indeed, he is very much worse off, for he has a gigantic dictionary of quotations in his head, and one, from William James, pierces him every time it comes to mind (more and more often, alas): '. . . born of the bitch-goddess success'.

But what would you have had me do? 'I cannot dig; to beg I am ashamed.' My friends the watch and the typewriter were for four decades the props of my life, and I must now steel myself to make friends of cold strangers on my wrist and my desk, though even when I was young I made friends slowly and with great fear. Yet those two instruments may stand as symbols of the richest, most sunlit part of my life, which has been precisely the part played by my friends; indeed, I truly believe that I have been not just exceptionally fortunate to have friends so steadfast and understanding, but blessed, in them, more than among all men upon earth. Let that be my epitaph; the disappointments can be carved, in smaller letters, on the *verso* of my tombstone.

Meanwhile, two of my oldest friends are to retire. But the ceremony must be appropriate. They care nothing for speeches and dinners; they were two honest working-men, and they shall be treated as such. I am having made two glass cases, one large enough to hold the typewriter, the other, small, for the wristwatch. I have found the place where they are to stand, in my hall, and the watch shall rest upon the typewriter – after all, they never quarrelled with one another. And for an inscription they want no flowery words or hollow phrases. On each, there shall be a brass plate, and on each plate the only fitting words: 'Well done, thou good and faithful servant.'

The Times January 1st, 1989

Index